I0057255

Cryptocurrency Trading & Investment Guide for Bulls:

2 in 1 Blockchain & Bitcoin Revolution. How to DeFi and Make Money in Decentralized Finance. Learn Bitcoin and Ethereum and Altcoins.

Cryptocurrency Trading Guide:

To Altcoins & Bitcoin for Beginners

Top 9 Strategies *to Become Expert in Decentralized Investing Blueprint, Cryptography, Blockchain, DeFi, Mining & Ethereum.*

Crypto Mindset!

The contents of this book may not be reproduced, duplicated or transmitted without direct written permission from the author.

Under no circumstances will any legal responsibility or blame be held against the publisher for any reparation, damages, or monetary loss due to the information herein, either directly or indirectly.

Legal Notice:

This book is copyright protected. This is only for personal use. You cannot amend, distribute, sell, use, quote or paraphrase any part or the content within this book without the consent of the author.

Disclaimer Notice:

Please note the information contained within this document is for educational and entertainment purposes only. Every attempt has been made to provide accurate, up to date and reliable complete

information. No warranties of any kind are expressed or implied. Readers acknowledge that the author is not engaging in the rendering of legal, financial, medical or professional advice. The content of this book has been derived from various sources. Please consult a licensed professional before attempting any techniques outlined in this book.

By reading this document, the reader agrees that under no circumstances are is the author responsible for any losses, direct or indirect, which are incurred as a result of the use of information contained within this document, including, but not limited to, —errors, omissions, or inaccuracies.

© Copyright by Vitali Lazar

All rights reserved.

" Bitcoin is a very exciting development; it might lead to a world currency. I think over the next decade it will grow to become one of the most important ways to pay for things and transfer assets."

- Kim Dotcom

Table of Contents

Introduction

Cryptocurrency has gone mainstream and changed the economic system by becoming a global phenomenon. Bitcoin and altcoin have captured the attention of businesses, institutional investors, celebrities, and the public in general.

But amidst the buzzing press releases, promotional campaigns, and testimonials of people about cryptocurrencies, it is crucial to understand how crypto works for you.

Learning the basic concepts is your first step to comprehending the exciting world of cryptocurrency. It is the future of the economy, so you might as well embrace it now and master the art of crypto trading and investing.

To help you understand the crypto basics 101 and beyond, I am sharing this book **Cryptocurrency Trading Guide to Altcoins & Bitcoin for Beginners**: *Learn about Decentralized Investing Blueprint, Cryptography, Blockchain, Mining, Ethereum, Litecoin to Create Wealth. Best Trading Strategies.*

It is your roadmap to ensure success whether you trade or invest in cryptocurrency. Every chapter provides vital information that will help you understand this decentralized virtual cash system. Whether we like it or not, the future involves cryptocurrency.

And while it seems complex and technical, the key to understanding the jargon of terms and concepts related to crypto is by learning them by heart. Let your knowledge empower your decisions in diversifying your investment portfolio and harnessing the power of digital gold or cryptocurrency.

But remember that in nature, the cryptocurrency market is wild, fast, and in constant motion. Once you're into crypto trading or investing, it is up to you to master the winning strategies to keep you going and enjoy the 'windfalls' that might come your way.

Are you ready to become the new millionaire or billionaire? Let my book **Cryptocurrency Trading Guide to Altcoins & Bitcoin for Beginners**: *Learn about Decentralized Investing Blueprint, Cryptography, Blockchain, Mining, Ethereum, Litecoin to Create Wealth. Best Trading Strategies* guide to your success. Read on.

Chapter 1

What's All This Buzz About Cryptocurrency?

Bitcoin started it all. This revolutionary, trendsetting cryptocurrency that was introduced in the digital world over a decade ago continues to dominate the scene. When the interest of investors and traders grew, Altcoins or alternative currencies were launched to satisfy the growing needs in the market.

This group of cryptocurrencies is patterned after Bitcoin with a slight alteration of the basic functions and operational rules. The purpose of alternation is to create new cryptocurrencies that serve general or specific functions.

But before we delve in further, let's take a look at the rationale of cryptocurrency and why it is very popular today. This digital currency exists only electronically, so you do not possess physical coins unless you cash them out for tokens. Cryptocurrencies use electronic wallets for storage, eliminating intermediaries like banks.

All transactions are made online, using your computer, mobile phone, or any electronic gadget that allows the exchange of crypto from your end to another user.

At a glance

- ✓ Why are cryptocurrencies very popular?
- ✓ What is cryptocurrency?
- ✓ How does cryptocurrency work?
- ✓ Blockchain technology
- ✓ Peer-to-Peer (P2P) System
- ✓ How did crypto come into being?
- ✓ The creation of new cryptocurrencies
- ✓ Mining: The method of creating new coins of existing cryptocurrencies
- ✓ Are crypto coins and tokens the same?
- ✓ Is cryptocurrency secure and safe to use?
- ✓ Where to store your crypto coins?
- ✓ Ways to acquire crypto coins
- ✓ Frequently Asked Questions (FAQs)

Why are cryptocurrencies very popular?

- They are the currencies of the future.

- They are independent and free from manipulation and interference of any central authority or government.

- They are not governed by central banks, so you don't pay bank charges for your transactions.

- They are not affected by inflation.

- They are useful for quick payments and sensitive transactions.

- They are secured by cryptography which prevents double-spend or counterfeit activities.

- They are digital gold and grow in value over time.

- They serve as financial instruments of investment or trading.

What is cryptocurrency?

Cryptocurrency is a digital asset that is distributed in a vast network of computers. It has a decentralized structure that exists beyond the control and influence of central banking authorities or governments. Unlike the traditional or 'fiat' currencies like euros and dollars, cryptocurrencies only exist in the virtual domain. You know that you own them but you cannot see or hold them. You only have the numbers or the amounts in your digital account.

The term cryptocurrency comes from the concept of encryption technique that governs its operation. It is a complex system of cryptographic techniques and encryption algorithms that are similar to solving mathematical problems to secure and authenticate every transaction.

This highly sophisticated encryption process is also responsible for the production of new units of existing cryptocurrencies. Cryptocurrencies are developed by miners as codes. These special codes cannot be replicated by ordinary methods, making Bitcoin and Altcoins virtually safe against cyberattacks.

How does cryptocurrency work?

Cryptocurrency has changed people's shop, pay, or transact business. It allows users to send or receive coins as a form of payment for goods and services anywhere in the world.

Consumers, investors, and traders who like the convenience of cashless and hassle-free transactions prefer to use cryptocurrencies.

Blockchain Technology

The key technology behind cryptocurrencies is the blockchain. This distributed ledger technology (DLT) works as a database for all virtual transactions. Every single transaction is verified through 'consensus', a digital process that requires multiple systems to verify the authenticity of the algorithm output and create 'blocks.' All transactions require the unique signature of users.

Miners confirm the transactions. Their tasks involve accepting the transaction, stamping it as legit, and then sharing it in the network nodes. Each node will confirm its validity and add it to the database, becoming a permanent part of the blockchain.

Blockchain stores all the data in blocks after verification and then chained them together in chronological order.

The decentralized nature of this record-keeping technology makes all entries permanent, irreversible, and viewable by users. All the personal details are kept safe and immutable.

This incorruptible database works continuously and chronologically timestamps and records blocks or transactions. It operates using public-private key pairs, hash codes, and elliptical curve encryption.

Hash codes – All blocks in the ledger system have their own hashes. They are created using a math function that converts the digital information or data gathered into a unique string of letters and numbers.

Hashes verify the validity of information but do not necessarily reveal the details of the information.

The hash code changes when someone attempts to change the information. For example, the hash is 68350abcde12345wxyz of a certain transaction and a hacker altered it by changing one character.

The other nodes will find it suspicious after cross-referencing with their own copies and cast away the version as invalid or illegitimate.

For hacking to be successful, the hacker needs to alter 51% of copies on the blockchain.

It would also require a lot of time, resources, and money to redo the hash codes and timestamps.

- *Public-private key pair* – They are digital keys that allow the encryption and decryption of the user's confidential information.

  The keys are secret strings of numbers and letters that you use to confirm your authority to use your bitcoin balance for any kind of crypto transaction.

- *Elliptic-curve cryptography (ECC)* – It is a public-key approach that secures the crypto account, ensuring that funds can be used only by the rightful owners. Bitcoin, Ethereum, and other crypto use the elliptic curve secp256k1 ($y^2 = x^3+7$ equation).

Peer-to-Peer System (P2P)

A peer-to-peer system is the core of Bitcoin and other cryptocurrencies. It uses a distributed network to make the exchange of coins or digital assets convenient, quick, and efficient. A P2P network consists of nodes or participants that perform similar tasks and have equal power. Every node is an individual peer that works by storing and sharing the files with other nodes.

The distributed architecture of the P2P system works independently and is more resistant to cyberattacks. There is no central server or intermediaries. It makes transferring Bitcoin or any other crypto worldwide quick and secure. Each node in the network has its own copy of the blockchain that it uses to compare with other nodes for data accuracy. Any inaccuracy or malicious activity is quickly denied by the system, making the requested transaction invalid.

How did cryptocurrency come into being?

The idea of using electronic money started in the '80s. The two countries that showed early interest to break into this revolutionary concept of using virtual currency were the Netherlands and the United States.

There were several attempts to introduce digital currency in the market but failed to gain traction.

- DigiCash was one of the noted attempts but eventually ceased from existence in the 1990s. It was created by David Chaum, a mathematician and computer scientist. Some people believe that he played a significant role in the later development of cryptocurrency.

- Paypal and other competitors emerged after that but used a hybrid approach by offering digital transactions with traditional currencies.

- Other attempts include Bit Gold, Hashcash, B-Money, and Flooz.

The idea of cryptocurrency was introduced in 1998 by Wei Dai, a computer engineer that developed the b-money cryptocurrency system and the Crypto + + cryptographic library. Dai also co-authored the proposal to use the VMAC message authentication algorithm. To honor his big contribution to cryptocurrencies and cryptography, the smallest sub-unit of Ether is named 'Wei'.

Wei Dai talked about cryptography and how it can be used to create or transact new forms of money, instead of relying on the central authorities.

When he published a paper about 'b-money,' the anonymous and distributed electronic cash system, Dai caught the interest of the public. The core concepts of b-money were later seen in the operations of Bitcoin and eventually in altcoins.

The breakthrough happened when Bitcoin was introduced by the mysterious Satoshi Nakamoto to the world in 2009. He referenced Wei Dai's b-money paper in his Bitcoin whitepaper and adopted most of the core concepts like:

The need for a specific amount of computational work.
The work done is updated and verified using a collective ledger book.
The fund exchange is done by collective bookkeeping and authentication process that uses cryptographic hashes.
The efforts of workers are awarded funds.
The contract is enforced through the broadcast and uses digital signatures for transactions.

During the inception of Bitcoin in 2008, Nakamoto contacted Dai, He also discussed business with another cryptographer Adam Back who is behind Hashcash, the concept that is utilized by miners during Bitcoin mining.

Dai and Back were speculated to be "Satoshi Nakamoto". Both denied the rumors. Other 'suspects' include:

Nick Szabo is a noted computer scientist and cryptographer famous for his digital currency and digital contract research papers.

Hal Finney was the second developer of PGP Corporation and was one of the early contributors to Bitcoin. The 10 bitcoins he received from Yakamoto was recorded

Key Point

Cryptocurrency is an electronic currency that you can exchange for fiat currency like U.S. dollars or buy another cryptocurrency but is not recognize as legal tender.

The creation of new cryptocurrencies

Blockchain plays a central role in the creation of a new type of cryptocurrency. No one owns or controls this powerful technology, allowing anyone to create his own digital currency.

Satoshi Nakamoto has cleared the path by creating Bitcoin and many developers followed to exploit the innovative system. Charlie Lee, a former engineer of Google, helped the creators of Litecoin. All crypto creators aim to produce a better version of Bitcoin to mimic its traction and popularity.

There are 2 ways to create new cryptocurrencies:

1. By building a new blockchain

This option requires the coding skills of professionals and experts. To make new coins, the developer needs to choose a blockchain platform. The 10 popular platforms are Ethereum (with 82.70% market share), Waves, NEMNxt, MultiChain, BitShares 2.0, Hyperledger Fabric, Blockstarter, IBM blockchain, CoinList, and EOS.

The work begins by designing the nodes. The nodes support the blockchain and are responsible for data storage, verification, and processing of transactions. Blockchains need nodes to ensure efficiency and utmost security.

After the nodes are built, the developer will work to establish the internal architecture of the new blockchain. The features include Address Formats, Permissions, Key Formats, Asset Issuance, Asset Reissuance, Key Management, Parameters, Atomic Swaps, Native Assets, MultiSignatures, Block Signatures, and Hand-shaking.

Once done with the architecture, the developer needs to check the Application Programming Interface (API) that is already provided by the blockchain platform. Then, proceed in designing the Admin and User Interface.

2. By modifying the existing process to form a new 'fork' or variant

Most of the Altcoins are forks or variants of the Bitcoin protocol like LitecoinBitcoin, GoldMain, and CashBitcoin. Garlicoin is forked from Litecoin.

Forking an existing blockchain involves taking an open-source code, making some changes, then launching the new blockchain with a brand new name.

This requires skills to know the sections of the codes to modify. Changing the parameters of the blockchain or introducing new features necessitates creating a 'fork.'

A 'fork' is technically an updated software, where all full nodes or participants are running the same software to access the blockchain. This ensures network security and convenience to verify the transactions.

There are two kinds of forks:

- A **hard fork** requires the developer to update the software by 90-95% because the nodes of the non-updated version can no longer access the system.

- A **soft fork** refers to the majority of nodes that need modification to update existing software while allowing the previous version to continue working.

There are two ways to generate a fork. One is using a fork coin generator like ForkGen. It works for people who are not equipped with programming skills.

The other option is to do it yourself by searching in Github, downloading, compiling the code, reconfiguring, implementing customization, and publishing the code back to Github.

The final step is to create a white paper or documentation and share it via a dedicated website.

As of May 2021, there are more than 10,000 kinds of cryptocurrency in existence. Each of them has its own unique properties and functionalities that leverage blockchain technology in the fields of finance, health, energy, supply and logistics, data storage, privacy and security, content ownership, social networks, and more.

Cryptocurrencies function as:

- Currency

  Bitcoin and the majority of the cryptocurrencies have store value and can be used as a retail payment like the traditional fiats.

- Platform or app

  Some cryptocurrencies function as platform or app crypto. Augur, for instance, is used to launch the Ethereum network.

- Utility

  The group of crypto with utility functions is developed as infrastructure, allowing other cryptocurrencies to be built on top of them. Ethereum has the Ethereum Virtual Machine that allows the creation of token coins.

Technically, cryptocurrencies are secured by solid cryptography, not by trust or people.

The consensus-keeping process enhanced their monetary and transactional properties.

Transactional properties

- Anonymity – Crypto accounts and transactions do not impose a connection to the real-world identities of the users. The addresses are created using minimum personal data and the blockchain does not reveal details, only the flow transactions.

- Global and fast – Instant propagation and confirmation of transactions within seconds. The virtual network is indifferent to geographical locations and borders.

- No gatekeeper – As long as you have downloaded the software and a crypto wallet for your coins or tokens, you can start using them to pay for goods and services or trade with other investors.

- Irreversible – Once transactions are confirmed, they cannot be undone or reversed by anyone including the senders. Nobody can help you retrieve your coins if you send them to a fraudulent receiver.

- Secure – The solid cryptography system locks all crypto funds. All users have private keys to access their own assets.

Monetary properties

- Controlled and limited supply – Bitcoin has a cap that is expected to happen around the year 2140. Most altcoins do not have a limit cap but follow the schedule written in their codes to create new coins and tokens.

- Representation of itself- Cryptocurrencies represent themselves, not numbers or debts like the Fiat currencies. Bitcoin and altcoins are bearers of their own values and follow their proprietary systems.

Trivia

Some of the celebrities who invested in crypto are Floyd Mayweather, Gwyneth Paltrow, Elon Musk, Snoop Dogg, Paris Hilton, 50 Cent, and Rapper Logic.

Mining: The method of creating new coins of existing cryptocurrencies

The only way to produce new units or more crypto coins is through mining. This process involves solving cryptographic puzzles or complex mathematical problems.

Mining requires great computing power and is very competitive. In Bitcoin, the SHA 256 Hash algorithm sets the basis of the cryptologic puzzle.

The first miner who solves the puzzle can build and add a block to the blockchain. As an incentive, he will receive a certain number of coins or tokens.

To ensure that no peer can break the stability of the blockchain, the puzzles become more difficult over time and require the miners to invest more computer power to successfully create new cryptocurrencies.

Bitcoin has a maximum cap of coins while alternative coins (altcoins) limit the available coins in circulation each year but do not have a maximum number of target coins.

Anyone with the knowledge and skills can be a crypto miner. But because there is no central authority to delegate the task, Satoshi requires that all interested miners find the 'hash', which is a cryptographic function product that connects the newly mined block with the existing blocks in the network. It is referred to as 'Proof-of-Work.'

The rationale of this rule is to prevent the breakdown of the cryptocurrency network due to forged transactions created by abusive parties.

Are crypto coins and tokens the same?

While coins and tokens are both cryptocurrencies, they are different from each other. Depending on the given crypto codes, miners can generate not just new coins for existing cryptocurrencies but also tokens.

Coins have independent transaction ledgers while tokens are dependent on the underlying network to validate and secure the transactions or ownerships.

Coins need their own blockchains while tokens operate on the existing blockchains.

- Coins can be used anywhere and for any purpose, while tokens are limited to certain projects only.

- Coins can buy tokens while tokens cannot be used to purchase coins.

- Coins are instruments to transfer wealth possession, tokens only represent a 'contract' (loyalty points, event tickets, physical/tangible objects).

Tokens are usually released through ICO or initial coin offering, which is also called a 'token launch' or a 'token sale.'

This crowd selling technique can be used for raising proceeds to create a product or building a consumer base of early birds to get the offered product. Many companies use ICO because it bypasses the banks' or venture capitalists' regulated capital-raising process. And even if a particular ICO ended, interested people can buy the publicly available tokens using the underlying currency.

Is cryptocurrency secure and safe to use?

Technically, the purpose of encryption is to provide ultimate safety and security to all digital transactions. This advanced coding transmits and stores the data between the users' electronic wallets and blockchains. These public ledgers are hard to tamper or hack, making them more secure.

Moreover, all transactions need users to use a 2-factor authentication process like entering a username and a password. You also need to enter the authentication code that you will receive in your mobile phone messaging system.

But remember that just because securities are high doesn't mean that they are unhackable. History shows that Bitcoin and other cryptocurrencies are subject to online thefts and hacking.

In 2018, the crypto world was rocked when Coincheck and BitGrail were hacked to the tune of $534 million and $195 million respectively. While blockchains are very secure, the other aspects of the crypto ecosystem like wallets and exchange platforms are not immune from scammers and hackers.

Where to store your crypto coins?

You need a 'digital wallet' to buy cryptocurrencies. This kind of wallet is an online app that stores your coins. It acts like a digital bank account that you can open using your private key.

The digital wallet you will need also depends on the kind of crypto you like to possess. If you want Litecoin, find one that stores this coin. If you like Bitcoin, choose a wallet that safely stores bitcoins. It is important to find a secure cryptocurrency wallet to prevent possible theft. Once your coins are stolen, there is no way to get them back again.

2 general types of crypto wallets:

Hot wallet (software)

A hot wallet is easy to set up, but the least safe among the three options. It runs on phones, tablets, computers, or any internet-connected device which makes this type of wallet vulnerable to hackers. It generates your private keys so you can access your coins. So, while it is very convenient to use during transactions, storing the private key on the device makes it prone to hacking.

To avoid possible security and privacy threats, it is crucial to use tighter security such as two-factor authentication, strong password, or safe browsing on the internet. Also, use this wallet for small spending or transactions only.

Cold wallet (hardware)

A cold wallet or hardware wallet is a portable device that you can connect to your laptop or computer via USB. It is the safer option because it stores your cryptocurrency in offline mode. This type of wallet is like a treasure vault that keeps your funds secure when you are not doing transactions or trading activities. Some cold wallets require the internet to connect, while others do not need it.

Under these two categories are 4 types of crypto wallets:

- **Web or Online wallet**

  This wallet allows you to access your Bitcoin fund via a web browser. While it is the quickest option to complete your transaction, it is vulnerable to unauthorized attempts and cyber threats. It is best not to store all your bitcoins in this kind of wallet.
- **Desktop wallet**

  A desktop wallet is an example of a cold wallet or cold storage. It allows you to store your bitcoins privately and securely, but make sure to use ultimate security especially if you need to use an internet connection to make transactions.

- **Mobile wallet**

  A mobile wallet is a downloadable app that is installed on your phone or other mobile devices. It is internet-based, which is risky. What is nice about this thing is you can easily scan your mobile wallet's QR code to complete your purchases.

- **Paper wallet**

    It is another offline storage that requires generating private and public keys, then printing them on paper. The generated code or information on that piece of paper lets you access your digital address, so make sure to keep it safe. Paper wallets are best for long-term and high-security kinds of investment, not for traders or constant users.

Did you know that?

Some of the cryptography used today were

originally created for military apps.

Ways to acquire crypto coins

Cryptocurrencies are available in exchange platforms and brokers who facilitate the buying and selling between investors/traders and the market. They can be bought using fiat currencies and cryptocurrencies (whichever is preferred by the sellers).

To start buying cryptocurrencies, you need to download a digital wallet. A lot of exchange platforms have built-in wallets, but it is up to you to have a separate crypto wallet for your coins and tokens.

Exchange versus brokers

Crypto exchange is an online platform where buyers and sellers directly trade coins and tokens. Using an exchange is the traditional way of trading crypto. It allows people to trade crypto for both crypto and fiat currencies.

It is ideal for both beginners and advanced users who like to speculate on the prices.

The most popular and trusted exchanges where you can buy altcoins are Binance, Coinbase, CEX.io, Bitfinex, Gemini, FTX, Changelly, KuCoin, Huobi Global, Bittrex, Coinmama, Bitstamp, and Kraken.

- **Binance** offers the widest variety of alternative coins and supports over 500 trading pairs. It is best for traders who want a diverse altcoin portfolio and trade their crypto against Bitcoin pairs. It accepts fiat currencies as payment for crypto coins and tokens.

- **CEX.io** is a very secure exchange that also works as a trading exchange. If you are planning to buy or sell Bitcoin, DASH, and Ethereum, it is the best place to invest in crypto. It accepts EUR, USD, RUB, and GBP currencies as well as bank transfer and debit/credit cards. Card fees are around 3.5% plus $0.20.

- **Coinmama** is one of the highly trusted and easiest to use crypto exchanges. It offers Ether and Bitcoin to investors and traders from almost all countries in the world. Coinmama accepts local currency and credit cards for payments. However, it charges a 6% fee to cards which is higher than the others.

- **Gemini** has Bitcoin, Ether, Litecoin, Zcash, and other altcoins. This U.S-based exchange charges $0.99 to 1.49% transaction fees and a fee of 0.5%.

- **Bitstamp** has more options to choose from, including Bitcoin, Bitcoin Cash, Litecoin, Ripple, and Ether. You can pay through your credit/debit cards, bank transfer, Euro, or U.S. dollars. It is a bit more complicated to use, so this is best for advanced traders.

  It is recommended to buy big amounts when you use a credit card because it charges exorbitant fees for small purchases. If you use a debit card, you will be charged $10 if your deposit is below $1,000 and 2% for more than $1,000 deposit.

A crypto broker is either a person or a firm that provides financial services for people who buy or sell their cryptocurrencies. Brokers charge users the use of their platforms. Some platforms like Bitpanda can be both an exchange and a broker.

The best crypto brokers include Coinbase, Kriptomart, eToro, Robinhood, and TradeStation,

- **Coinbase** has a variety of altcoin choices, including Ethereum, Litecoin, DAI, DASH, EOS, and Ripples.

  It is the U.S. biggest broker exchange and is available in Europe, North America, and Australia. If you live in South America, Africa, and Asia, you cannot buy crypto from Coinbase. It charges 0.50% when you buy or sell crypto below $10,000 in value and less as the order becomes higher.

- **Kriptomat** was established in 2019 and is considered one of the safest and simplest brokerages to buy cryptocurrencies. It will only take 5 minutes to upload the required documents and start trading Ether or Bitcoin with this platform.

  Kriptomat has great customer support and is available in 21 languages. The buying/selling fees are only 1.45%. It does not charge extra fees whenever you transfer or withdraw cryptocurrencies.

- **Robinhood** is a mainstream investment broker that facilitates buying and selling of crypto. Its user-friendly platform is secure and ideal for new crypto users who want to invest in a variety of strong altcoins.

  It has wider payment methods and allows users to withdraw funds from their external accounts. It has no purchase fee but charges an order flow fee.

Other buying options:

Bitcoin ATMs

These ATMs work like the traditional machines, but the difference is you will be depositing your cash to buy coins rather than withdrawing money. This is the quickest way to own bitcoins, but be ready to pay 5-10% transaction fees.

To use a Bitcoin ATM, find one and verify your identity. It may require your phone number to send the code. Once you receive it, enter the code and your digital wallet address.

Then, deposit your cash into the machine to enable it to send your purchased coins to your crypto wallet. Wait for your receipt and you're done.

Peer-to-Peer (P2P)

Another cool way to buy cryptocurrencies is P2P because it is direct and does not use a middleman. For this method, you need to find a P2P website and create your account. It is free and simple. For Bitcoin, you can go to LocalBitcoins and if you want Ether, look for Localtherum.com.

The next step is to check the listing of cryptocurrencies and their prices. Check the price that sellers set for their cryptocurrencies.

Find the best available payment option for you.

Don't forget to check the customers' reviews about the seller before making a decision. Once you have chosen one, enter your details that are asked for like:

- Amount or how much is your budget

- Currency or the option you want to pay with

- Payment method

Some sellers or buyers would ask for valid identification, so be ready to send a photo of your ID, a scanned image of your driver's license or passport, or a selfie while holding the document.

Once the trader accepts your request, you will receive the amount of coin in the website's escrow. Then the seller will send you a reference number that you will use to send the payment.

The advantages of using P2P are there are no fees and you can use cash to pay for them. But you need to be extremely careful when selecting sellers.

Other ways to earn cryptocurrencies other than buying:

Mining crypto

For this option, you need to use your computer skills to solve mathematical equations to obtain coins. It will also require a high-end computer model with Application-Specific Integrated Circuit because regular computers do not work for mining. So, that means investing thousands of dollars in the equipment.

If you don't want to spend a lot of money, another option is to work with other miners by joining a mining network.

Staking

Stalking or Proof of Stake system where people are chosen for the number of coins they are holding. The more you hold and place into staking, the more opportunity for you to be chosen to confirm new block creation.

Promoting projects through micro tasks

Find companies and startups that offer crypto coins as rewards or bounties for completing tasks like:

- Writing press releases

- Making video reviews

- Distributing promotional videos

- Writing testimonials

Taking advantage of project campaigns through airdrops

Many companies are using airdrop campaigns to build a community or initial traction in exchange for tokens. These tokens can be sold or traded for crypto coins or cash when the project takes off.

The tasks include:

- Sharing posts

- Following the companies' social media platforms

- Downloading the apps

- Completing forms about the project

- Signing up on the platforms

DeFi Yield Farming

Decentralized Finance Yield Farming, also known as liquidity mining, is a reward system that works like a bond market.

To gain interest and rewards, you need to lock in your cryptocurrency. Aside from the yield you harvest, you can also earn additional tokens depending on the projects that you choose. The popular DeFis are Compound (COMP), Ren (REN), Kyber Network (KNC), and Ox (ZRX).

Accepting crypto payments

If you have an e-commerce website in WooCommerce or Shopify, start accepting cryptocurrencies as a payment option.

Get paid in cryptocurrency by freelancing

Look for platforms that offer freelancing jobs and pay cryptocurrency. You can check Cryptocurrenjobs or Ethlance.

Joining publishers' network

Earn crypto coins by joining crypto publishers' networks and get paid for displaying ads of various companies.

Earning coins from crypto faucets

The faucet system works by simply watching ads, playing games, or completing surveys to earn Satoshis (unit of Bitcoin) or Wei (unit of Ethereum).

When your coins reach the minimum amount, you can withdraw your earnings and cash them out.

Earning cashback

Digital banking is becoming more innovative now, offering opportunities for users to earn crypto by depositing funds or spending using cards to earn cashback.

Gambling your crypto bonus

There are crypto gambling platforms that give a login bonus in crypto. Use the bonus to double up or multiple your funds.

However, the platforms require a minimum deposit before you can withdraw the coins

When choosing a cryptocurrency exchange or broker, look for the following:

- **Security**

  You need to check the background and reputation of the company behind the exchange. If the history shows that it has been hacked before, consider it as a red flag and check the others.

- **Quick verification**

Is it easy to create an account and get verified?

- **Transaction fee**

The lower the transaction fees, the better for you.

- **Payment options**

An exchange that accepts more payment options makes trading more convenient.

- **Cryptocurrency listing**

If you like different coins, choose a broker exchange that offers more than one type of cryptocurrency.

- **Users reviews**

The customer reviews help you know the exchange better.

FAQs

What is the difference between cryptocurrencies and digital currencies?

Cryptocurrencies exist across the network of computers and are not issued by the central banks or governments. Digital currencies also exist in the virtual world but are issued by the central authorities and possess the characteristics of fiat or traditional currencies.

Why are the reasons why cryptocurrencies are the subject of criticism?

Some of these reasons are the vulnerability of the underlying infrastructure, volatility of exchange rate, and use for illegal activities like tax evasion or money laundering.

What are the advantages of cryptocurrency?

They are being praised for transparency, inflation resistance, portability, and divisibility.

Their anonymity nature is also beneficial for people and companies that value their privacy and security above all.

How secure are crypto transfers between users?

Cryptocurrency uses keys (public keys and private keys) to secure the fund transfers from one user to another user. The public key is used to transfer funds to the account address or crypto wallet, while the private key is the owner's 'code' or 'pin' to sign transactions.

Do cryptocurrencies represent a currency, cash, or cash equivalent?

They are not legal tender and lack the backup of any government or legal entity, so cryptocurrencies are not foreign currencies, cash equivalent, or cash. Cryptocurrencies are digital alternatives to traditional money that are primarily used by investors and traders for speculating the rise or fall of assets' value.

Is cryptocurrency a good investment?

Investing in cryptocurrency involves risks and is not for the faint-hearted. However, it also offers lots of potential benefits and financial rewards.

What are the Pros and Cons of investing in crypto?

- *Pros*
  High return potential
  Diversification

- *Cons*
  Greater volatility
  Potential for fraud and scams
  No benchmark for valuation

Will I go rich in trading cryptocurrency?

Crypto trading is just one way to maximize the potential of your coins. Trading however is the quickest and the easiest way to multiply your cryptocurrency. But it is also the fastest way to lose all your crypto.

Are cryptocurrencies taxed?

The 2014 IRS ruling in the United States of America defines virtual currencies like crypto as property. It means that whenever you use cryptocurrency to purchase something, it will be subjected to capital gain tax rules. To avoid tax evasion charges, traders should disclose their crypto transactions to the IRS.

It includes:

- Payment for products or services
- Cashing out or exchanging crypto coins for fiat currency
- Receiving forked or mined coins
- Exchanging crypto for another crypto

The non-taxable activities are:

- Purchasing crypto using fiat money
- Transfer cryptocurrency from one wallet to another digital wallet
- Sending crypto as a gift to third parties
- Donating cryptocurrency to charity or any tax-exempt non-profit organization

Is cryptocurrency legal?

Cryptocurrencies are legal in the United States and some other parts of the world. China, on the other hand, bans its usage. Other countries that restrict the use of cryptocurrencies are Saudi Arabia, Mexico, Egypt, and Zambia. It is illegal in Bangladesh, while users can go to jail when crypto is used in Nepal, Vietnam, Algeria, Ecuador, Bolivia, and Morocco. Ultimately, the legality of crypto depends on the country or state.

Chapter 2

Beginners Guide in Cryptocurrency Trading

The most obvious way to make money out of your cryptocurrency is to engage in trading. If you do it right, crypto trading will give you tremendous returns compared to traditional investments. In just a short period, you can be a millionaire or multi-millionaire, or a loser in the trading sphere.

This high volatility and growth potential of crypto makes it very attractive to investors and traders who want to multiply their money. It is common for crypto coin prices to display exponential growth or fluctuate more than 10%. Interest in cryptocurrency has been increasing.

Many traditional investors and millennials are diversifying their investment portfolio, adding bitcoins and altcoins as investment and trading instruments.

At a glance

- ✓ Trading vs. Investing
- ✓ Top benefits of crypto trading
- ✓ How does crypto trading differ from other trading options?
- ✓ Different kinds of trading styles
- ✓ How to pick the right trading style?
- ✓ Elements that affect crypto trading
- ✓ Basic steps in crypto trading
- ✓ Two approaches in crypto trading
- ✓ Things to remember before trading your crypto
- ✓ Frequently Asked Questions (FAQs)

Trading vs. Investing

Trading and investing are two economic concepts that involve buying assets to grow wealth by earning profits. In the financial markets, assets are called instruments. They come in the form of bonds, stocks, cryptocurrency, options, margin products, currency pairs (Forex market), and many others.

Trading

As a newbie who wants to delve into the exciting cryptocurrency sphere, your first step is to understand what crypto trading is all about and how to be a successful trader. You need to create a game plan and follow the clearly defined steps to achieve your trading goals. Basically, trading is the term for short-term trading because it involves active positioning (enter and exit) in short period frames.

But trading is more than that as it uses different types of strategies like trend trading, day trading, swing trading, and more. When you trade your cryptocurrencies, you speculate on the price movements by buying or selling the coins via a broker exchange or contracts for difference (CFDs) trading account.

Investing

Investing refers to allocating resources or money to buy a property, asset, or financial instrument and selling it in the future at a higher amount. The core of investment is the ROI or return on investment. Unlike trading, investing involves waiting for a longer period like years or decades before selling the asset.

The main objective of investing is building wealth over a certain time which usually takes a decade or more. It is more of a passive approach where investors are not concerned about the price fluctuations.

While both seek to gain profits, the traders and investors use different methods to achieve their financial goals.

- Traders are constantly watching the market trends and taking advantage of its volatility. If you are into trading, you need to enter and exit positions to gain returns.

- Investors wait for a time being to get their target ROI for their investments, which typically are double or larger than the amount they spend to buy the asset.

*The business value that is added by blockchain
would surpass $3.1 trillion by 2030.*

Top benefits of cryptocurrency trading

- ## Volatility

  The volatility element of cryptocurrency makes it more exciting to trade and invest. Its rapid price movements in a single day allow traders to go short or long. These two jargons represent the core of trading. Both reflect the possible direction of the cryptocurrency- either to rise in value or fall.

  When you go "long" or buy a cryptocurrency, you are hoping that you will generate a profit from a certain point. In contrast, when you go "short", you sell your cryptocurrency because you are expecting that its price will fall from a certain point.

- ## Ability to go short or long

  When you trade, your primary aim is to see your asset increase in value. So, during trading, you should always take advantage of the rising and falling of crypto prices.

- ## Availability

  Because of the decentralized nature of cryptocurrency, the market is open for trading 24/7. You can trade whenever you want or make direct transactions with other users via crypto exchanges anywhere in the world. However, there are times when the crypto market is unavailable due to 'forks' or infrastructural updates.

• Anonymity and privacy

If you use decentralized crypto exchanges, you can trade without identifying yourself. While in a centralized trading platform, you share some of your particulars but remain anonymous to other traders.

• Quick account opening

Before you can start trading cryptocurrency, you need to open and register your exchange account. For this purpose, you need to find a trusted broker exchange that offers a simple registration form and quick verification. Creating an account is a breeze and you can begin trading right away.

• Multitude of assets

The cryptocurrency market, despite being new, has given traders easy access to CFDs, leveraged tokens, futures, options, swaps, and other stock market products.

• Leveraged exposure

Opting for CFD or contract for difference gives you leveraged exposure. CFD allows you to go short or go long and trade on margin. It is also used by investors to hedge their physical portfolios. This leveraged product lets you buy a small percentage to trade on margin or open a position.

When trading CFDs, you do not buy or sell the entire commodity, physical share, currency pair, stock index, or any underlying asset, just units you believe will give you profits as their prices go up or down. When the price moves upward, you will be gaining a lot based on the units you sold or bought.

The opposite will entail losses. Your profits and losses depend on the size of your position.

Other advantages of buying CFD are:

- It leverages your market position by trading a fraction upfront.

- It lets you speculate and trade without owning the whole range of assets.

- It gives you the option to trade on more than one exchange.

- It does not impose paying fees when depositing or withdrawing crypto.

How does crypto trading differ from other trading options?

Trading involves a risk, but cryptocurrency is often viewed as riskier compared to other types of traditional trading. To know the risks involved, let me make some comparisons and help you weigh the pros and cons.

Crypto trading vs Stock trading

The market in crypto trading is based on supply and demand, making it highly speculative. The value of the digital coin is dependent on what the investors pay to own it.

There is also a finite supply, making it scarce. The scarcity drives the price upward and gives you lucrative gains. In addition, the crypto market is working 24/7 and reacts to outside events that can double your profits.

In contrast, stock trading is more stable, offering returns of investments for a longer period. Most of the companies offering stocks will remain in the future, so stockholders gain passive income. The stock trading market works in a conventional way, with public holidays and weekends.

Similarities:

- Investing and trading tools are almost similar- Traders of stocks and cryptocurrency use charts and perform Technical Analysis (TA).

- Investing and trading strategies are the same – Stock traders and crypto traders use swing, position, or day trading styles. They can also choose to buy and hold financial assets.

- Use similar market products – Innovative products in stock trading like derivatives, options, futures, and leveraged tokens can now be traded in the crypto market. Crypto traders also utilize stock trading techniques like leveraging to inflate gains.

Differences

- Market volatility – The stock market is less volatile and offers better stability. In contrast, the crypto market is characterized by wild price swings.

- Market assets – In the cryptocurrency market, you are investing your wealth in the currency or token, the technology, or the idea. While in the stock market, you buy shares of stocks from publicly listed companies.

- Market maturity – The trade volume and market value of the stock market is larger compared to the cryptocurrency market because it has been existing for a longer period. The crypto market is just over a decade old which contributes to its wild volatility.

- Regulations-The stock market is governed by rules and regulations, while the cryptocurrency market is deregulated and does not conform to any rule or regulations of the central authority or government.

Crypto trading vs Forex trading

Both involve currency trading. Their prices are influenced by supply and demand in the market. Trading requires knowledge and familiarity with how the market operates and behaves.

Crypto traders buy or sell Bitcoin or any kind of Altcoin and use them as instruments to make profits. To maximize the potential of your crypto, you should have a solid trading strategy, a good understanding of the exchange market, and risk management techniques.

Forex or foreign exchange market involves buying and selling of currencies. Traders know that by trading in this world's largest financial market, they will be benefiting a lot. Some of these advantages include:

- 23 hours trading during the week
- wide choices of available currencies
- low transaction costs
- volatility

Forex is time-sensitive and good for short-term profits, while cryptocurrency does not guarantee when and how much is the potential pay-off until the market displays the positive signs.

Generally speaking, cryptocurrency trading has a higher potential for bigger returns while forex is more stable, regulated, and protected.

Key Point

Avoid slippage risk by trading in low volatile markets or when the market activity is at its peak hours.

Different kinds of active trading styles

Trading strategies guide traders when positioning in the crypto market. They depend on the traders' profile, goals, risk tolerances, and preferences.

Technically, they encompass what you are trading, the approach you are going to use to trade it, and the points of entry/exit.

Scalping, swing trading, day trading, and position trading are **active trading strategies**. These styles of trading work by identifying or timing favorable positions to 'beat the market average' for a short-term period.

1 - Day trading

Day trading refers to the strategy that allows traders to enter and exit positions during the same day or 24 hours. It requires quick decisions and execution, which can be stressful but exciting at the same time. It demands an extended period of watching your computer screen to monitor the price movements and take advantage of favorable positions.

Day traders keep their positions open within set periods and not beyond them. In this trading style, you have to rely often on technical analysis and chart patterns to know which kind of crypto to trade. You should also remember that in this type of trading, your profits can be minimal. But if you are very active, day trading is highly profitable.

Generally, it suits the well-experienced crypto traders or market-makers but beginners can learn by trading carefully. Moreover, the introduction of electronic trading makes it easy for novice traders.

The best cryptocurrencies for day trading are Ethereum (ETH), Tether (USDT), Binance Coin (BNB), EOS, and Tron (TRX).

2- Scalping

Scalping has the shortest time frames, requiring traders to enter and exit their positions within seconds or minutes to make the most of small price fluctuations. During these short time frames, traders earn small profits or lower than 1% percentage of profit that adds up over a longer time. But the goal here is to ensure constant profits and cut losses quickly. This type of active trading employs identifying and exploiting small moves frequently.

However, scalping is not recommended for beginners because it requires a lot of practice and understanding of how prices move in the crypto markets. To get the most of scalping, you need to watch out for short-term fluctuations and trade several positions every few minutes. You can also do spot buying and selling cryptocurrency. It necessitates constant focus and risk management by making short or long positions. It is also crucial where to use stops.

3- Swing trading

Swing trading has a longer time horizon which means you can hold your position from days to weeks. This means you can watch your position go up or down or HODL your position until you reach the next resistance level, hit your target, or meet a favorable exit condition.

Traders who use this style of trading typically buy or sell their coins as soon as the volatility occurs. They make trading rules or algorithms of their own based on fundamental analysis or technical analysis.

4- Position trading

Position trading, also called trend trading, works by purchasing assets and holding them for extended periods like months. The goal is to sell the assets in the future at a higher amount. It is ideal for beginners because the long time frames provide ample opportunity to weigh their decisions. For novices, it is regarded as a buy-and-hold trading style.

Position traders are on the lookout for trends to gain profits with the help of fundamental analysis. You need to take or build a short position high or long position low and stay with it for some time.

It looks like investing but the objective is to create a killer trade by acting on trends. By jumping or riding the 'wave', position traders benefit. They would exit quickly once the advantageous trend breaks.

Other styles of crypto trading:

Intraday trading

This is a type of day trading that lets the traders hold their positions multiple times throughout the regular trading hours. Take note that crypto markets do not really close, so the trading continues. You can use software that allows intraday traders to automate positions in the trading market.

Range trading

Range trading aims to trade the range, not to buy assets after a downtrend or buy during an uptrend. Range traders take advantage of the current range of predictable or profitable trades. They set stops to buy the range's bottom and then scale it out to the top and sell.

In this style of trading, the range provides a clear picture of support and resistance and works well when you use candlestick chart analysis.

The assumption is that the support and resistance hold the edges of the trading range until it breaks. In a simple explanation, it means the upper edge can push the current price downward, while the range's lower edge can push the crypto price upward.

When the price of the cryptocurrency ranges between the levels of support and resistance, you buy the support level/ exit at the support level and sell the resistance level/short the resistance level.

This straightforward style of trading is perfect for beginners, but you need to fully understand the concepts of support and resistance levels, candlestick charts, and momentum indicators such as Relative Strength Index Indicator (RSI) and Moving Average Convergence Divergence (MACD). Both are tools for Technical Analysis.

HFT or High-Frequency trading

High-frequency trading uses trading bots and algorithms for quick entry/exit in multiple positions within short time frames. HFT traders are likely to gain a significant advantage over competitors by taking advantage of a few milliseconds. This style is suitable for veteran traders.

It is popular among the 'quant' (or quantitative) traders who develop algorithms to execute complex strategies. While it may look like a day trading method, HFT is more complicated because it involves backtesting, keeping track, and tweaking the algorithms to match the constant changes in the market conditions. So while the trading bots make it easy for traders, traders are strategizing.

Moreover, developing your own HFT bots necessitated advanced knowledge of the market concepts, computer science, and mathematics. The other option is to buy an HFT bot.

*Some trading overlap so you should know what
style works for you in terms of financial and
emotional well-being.
Stick to your game plan to avoid unnecessary
stress and risks.*

How to pick the right trading style?

There is no right or wrong trading style. It all depends on the individual goals and preferences. Here are some general reminders that may help you during the selection.

- Find your trading style and refine it. You can calibrate your style as you practice your trading skills. Your goal here is to master your methodology by sticking to it. Do not change your style when it does not for some trading session or you feel that it is not delivering your targets, instead review and adjust your strategies.

- Expect failures, miscalculations, and mistakes when you are trading assets, especially cryptocurrency because of its volatility. The bull market does not stay easy or favorable to many traders, so always be prepared for some heartbreaks and financial loss. Learn the lessons and review your errors.

- Apply risk management protocols to reduce loss. This includes not switching from one style to another trading style. Adjust your strategy to have greater opportunities to gain profits.

Do not be afraid to engage in the next trading because statistics show that the next trade can be your ticket to success.

- Take care of your crypto portfolio by avoiding buying high and selling low like the day trading at a low or investing at high. Understand how the market conditions move and learn the trading tricks. Take your time and do not attempt to do frenzy trading to prevent killing your portfolio.

Elements that affect cryptocurrency trading

As a newbie in crypto trading, you need to understand the following factors:

- **Market cap**

  Market cap or market capitalization in cryptocurrency refers to the value of all mined coins. The total value is determined by multiplying the number of coins that are circulating in the market by the present market price of the coin.

  Circulating Supply of Coin x Current Price

  = Market Cap

  So, if the circulating supply is 20,000,000 coins and the current price of the coin per unit is $10, the market cap of the particular crypto is $200,000,000.

The market cap also serves as an indicator to measure and monitor the market value of Bitcoin or Altcoins. It provides insight into the level of risk of the digital asset you have chosen and shows its growth potential. However, you need to remember that the market cap does not represent the money inflow or the amount of money in the crypto market. It is common for the cryptocurrency to jump its price and command a higher amount due to liquidity and volume.

Coins with small market caps are vulnerable to big holders' manipulation, causing wild price springs. High market cap coins are less vulnerable to wild volatility and manipulation.

- **Trading volume**

The trading volume shows the amount of traded individual units at a given time. In the cryptocurrency market, it is the quintessential factor and essential technical indicator. By using it when trading crypto, traders easily measure how strong the underlying trend is.

Coins with higher trading volume are easier to buy or sell, while low trading volume indicates a lack of liquidity. Cryptocurrencies that show very low trading volume is a sign of a declining or ailing trading volume.

The presence of high trading volume and high volatility are leading signs that there will be a massive price movement (win or loss). This means that a lot of investors and traders are active in the market during that price level. It is the best time for traders to make an entry or exit move. Volatility without a high volume marker is an indication of a weak trend.

• Stop-loss orders and stop-limit orders

A stop-loss order is the market order or limit that is activated when the asset reaches a certain price point or the stop price. Its main purpose is to limit the trader's loss and avoid wiping out his wealth. It works by setting your stop price that will invalidate your order or loss during the trading.

The stop-limit refers to buying or selling cryptocurrency at a certain amount or better. This limit-buy order is triggered when your order reaches the limit price or lower price. The limit-sell order is executed when the limit price is reached or higher.

You need to understand the stop-loss can be a stop-market order or a stop-limit order. While they vary, you can use them both if you want. However, you need to remember that the stop-limit order is only fulfilled when it reaches the validation point or better, but not when the market crashes down.

If your stop-loss is the same as your stop-loss when the price drops, it will move away from the set price and leave the order unfulfilled. To make sure that you can exit the market when you reach the limit during these extreme conditions, opt for the stop-market order.

• Storage

Knowing where and how to store your cryptocurrency is another important factor when you are into trading, especially when it involves a huge amount. The rule of the thumb is to set aside a trading fund that you will willingly lose when things get worse. Never use your savings or other investments for trading purposes, whether it involves crypto or traditional assets.

Finding a trusted broker exchange is also crucial because your investment will be under their custody, making it risky and less secure against scammers. To ensure total control and security over your digital assets, it is best to store them on hardware wallets.

Another option is choosing a trustworthy software wallet that you can easily access from your smartphone, laptop, iPad, or desktop by using your private key. However, since the transactions involve internet connectivity, you need to have tighter security to prevent online thefts or hacking.

Did you know that?

Satoshi Nakamoto is a HODLer.
According to Sergio Demian Lerner, there was one
wallet with more than one million BTCs.
The coins remained untouched and Lerner
believed that Nakamoto owns it.

Basic steps in cryptocurrency trading

Step 1: Choose a crypto brokerage or exchange

Like fiat trading, you need a place where cryptocurrencies are traded.

Every crypto exchange has its terms of service and way of trading. Among the popular exchanges are Coinbase, Binance, Bitstamp, Bitfinex, CEX.io, Coinmama, eToro, GeminiKriptomat, and KuCoin.

For beginners, it is best to choose an exchange that offers a variety of crypto coins and has a user-friendly interface. Some exchanges do not accept fiat currency as payment, so you have to purchase a crypto coin first to buy coins.

Step 2: Create an account

To register as a user and start trading, you need to make an account. It will require providing personal information like your date of birth, email address, home address, and Social Security number.

Step 3: Select a crypto wallet

You can choose to store your crypto in software or hardware wallets. Between the two, the hardware is more secure because it is a physical device that you can plug into your computer and use offline.

For software wallets, there are several free options on Android, iOS, and Google Chrome. Most cryptocurrencies come with official wallets like Bitcoin Core Wallet, MyEtherWallet or Ethereum Wallet, Dash Core, or Litecoin-QT. Exchanges and brokerages have also built-in wallets like Coinbase and Poloniex.

You can also find multi-currency wallets if you want to invest/trade using various types of crypto coins. Some examples are:

- Coinomi allows you to transact with 64 cryptocurrencies

- Jaxx Wallet supports Bitcoin, Bitcoin Cash Ethereum, Dash, Litecoin, Ethereum Classic, Zcash, and more

- Exodus can be used for sending and storing Bitcoin, Bitcoin Cash, Litecoin, Ethereum Classic, Ethereum, etcetera

Step 4: Fund your crypto account or wallet

Once your account in a crypto brokerage is approved, you can fund it by connecting to your bank account. You have the option to use wire transfer or debit cards.

Step 5: Pick your cryptocurrency

Before buying, compare the different cryptocurrencies. The most popular are Bitcoins and Ethereums because they move predictably and are easy to trade due to their technical indicators.

However, many smaller Altcoins have higher upside potential that make them attractive to investors and traders. Some of these Altcoins have shown more than 1,000% growth.

You can use comparison tools like Coinmarketcap to know the features and benefits of coins and tokens. Cryptocompare is another site to find information like trade volume, supply, market cap, and more.

To be more updated about the current happenings in the crypto sphere, follow blogs and publications like News Bitcoin, Coindesk, and Hackernoon. You can also dig in on various social media, Quora threads, Discord channels, and other crypt0-related fora for more in-depth knowledge.

Step 6: Mitigate risks and enhance gains by using technology

Take advantage of the available tools and apps that help to reduce the risks and volatility of your trading portfolio. Look for an automated index that analyzes the algorithms of cryptocurrencies. One good example is the CIX100 or Cryptoindex 100.

For tracking coins to help you enhance productivity, use Delta, Blockfolio, and other special apps that provide real-time exchange prices and other valuable insights.

Two approaches used in cryptocurrency trading

There are two key techniques in trading, which have been used by traditional and crypto traders for generations. They are the Technical Analysis (TA) and Fundamental Analysis (FA).

- **Technical Analysis**

Technical analysis is a trading technique that predicts the future price movement of the assets.

This methodology uses technical indicators like chart patterns, candlesticks, moving averages, trend lines, and more to get results.

The idea behind this analysis is that all price movements follow their own patterns and by using verifiable data, you can identify trading opportunities as well as potential entry points. This strategy works well with day trading, scalping, and even long-term investments.

- **Fundamental Analysis**

    FA or fundamental analysis is used in cryptocurrency to determine the outside forces that influence the value of the coins. It involves the evaluation of on-chain metrics and off-chain metrics to know if the digital asset is undervalued or overvalued. By analyzing the current valuation, you can decide whether to trade or not.

    On-chain metrics include the following:

    - Coin/token issuance rate (deflation/inflation)
    - Wallet addresses (dormant/active)
    - Network hash rate

    - Network applications
    - Network fees
    - Transactions

    Off-line metrics are:

- o Exchange listings
- o Community engagements
- o Government regulations

Most cryptocurrency networks are public, so it is easy to access the on-chain metrics. Ethereum and Bitcoin's metrics can be tracked down using Bitinfocharts.com. This site provides a lot of useful data and is easy to navigate.

Which is better? I believe that it depends on your profile as a trader and your financial goals. If you are a swing trader or like to research and make an informed bet, fundamental analysis is for you.

If you are a day trader or someone who prefers short-term positioning multiple times in a single day, you need the technical analysis.

And as always, a smart combination of these two trading strategies can give you more positive outcomes.

Did you know that?

The Bitcoin network is very powerful and can surpass the capabilities of 500 super computers.

Important things to remember before stepping into crypto trading

- ## Learn what's growing

  Find out the top coins in terms of ease of use and tradability. The top three are of course Bitcoin, Litecoin, and Ethereum, but always keep your eyes on other growing cryptocurrencies like Zcash, Monero, Ripple, and more.

- ## Understanding order types

  If you will be trading on other exchanges that are not Coinbase.com or Cash App, you need to remember how a market order differs from a limit order and how the concept of stops works to your advantage. Cryptocurrency markets do not have strong liquidity, which is why you should be careful when placing huge market orders.

- ## Understanding blockchain

  At least learn the basics that can help you speculate price movements in the market as a response to the crypto announcements and news.

- ## Minimizing slippage

Slippage refers to the situation where you will receive a different execution price that is different from what is intended. It results in paying an amount that is more than or less than the price you know you will be paying. It happens between the time when the order is requested and the time of exchange or the time when your order is confirmed.

It happens in fast-moving and highly volatile markets when the orders in the market could not match the traders' preferred prices due to unexpected trends and quick turns. To avoid slippage trading, traders should use a limit order rather than a market order. The limit order fulfills your order at the price you set or better.

- **Keeping your crypto account secure**

    In the world of crypto, loss of access to your digital storage (wallet) or when your exchange account is hacked means saying goodbye to your coins forever. Recovering your account is a difficult process and sometimes, impossible after the hacking. I suggest you have a very strong password, 2-factor authentication, and using a hardware wallet. Always have a backup and write your pin/password/seed phrase. It is also best to encrypt them both.

- **Best to avoid margin trading if you are new in crypto trading**

    Margin trading is the practice where traders can borrow funds against their existing funds or leverage their cryptocurrency to enhance their trading power. Newcomers like you should stick first to purchasing major coins that offer good liquidity. Do not be tempted to engage in market trading until you have mastered the tricks of crypto trading.

- **Mitigate risks**

The volatile nature of the cryptocurrency market is part of its attractiveness to investors and traders. This element can make traders win a fortune or lose a lot in an instant. Consider mitigating trading risks by applying technical analysis indicators to analyze market trends and charts. Learn and master trend trading and support and resistance techniques.

One of the secrets of professional traders is trading Bitcoin and Ethereum (in terms of market cap) or Grayscale Bitcoin Trust (GBTC). The risk element of losing is slim or nearly impossible when you use any of these digital instruments. In essence, crypto coins with lower volumes and market caps offer a greater reward but also greater risks that can wipe out your fund.

- **Remember that derivatives have unique rule sets**

Derivatives are financial contracts that get their values from underlying assets. In cryptocurrency, it works as a proxy tool that loves speculating on the coins' future success. Holding them too long can cost you a lot of money in fees, so learn how to maximize gains by finding the best derivative in the market.

- **Don't forget that crypto trading is taxable**

Cryptocurrency is considered a capital asset or property in the U.S. It is subject to capital gains tax (long-term and short-term) when used for buying services/goods and for investment/trading purposes. Know the implications of tax in crypto trading so you will know to make the most of your trading activities.

Crypto trading is exciting and full of promises. In the beginning, it can be a bit confusing with all the technical terms and jargon but eventually, you will learn the ropes.

While the principles of trading are a bit similar to the trading stocks in the market, the execution is different.

To enjoy cryptocurrency trading and maximize its benefits, you need to do a thorough research about the assets and the market, the best crypto exchange, the most secure crypto wallet, and your chosen crypto.

Fun Trivia

Cryptokitties was the first game built with the help of Ethereum technology. The network experienced 10% purchase increase in just one week after its launching.

FAQs

Is crypto trading profitable?

Yes, if you do it right. Like any type of trading, trading cryptocurrency requires a plan, strategies, and risk management measures. You will be in your most advantageous position if you follow your game plan and strategies

How risky is crypto trading?

Because of the high level of volatility, the risks are greater. Before you start your trading journey, assess your risk appetite first. You also need to have a game plan and risk management strategies.

Are there good cryptocurrency pairs for beginners?

No. Each cryptocurrency is different from the other, offering a range of advantages and risks to both beginners and seasoned traders. To understand them better, study each type and match it to your trading goals and strategies.

What is the best crypto trading strategy for newbies?

All strategies are good. But you should choose according to your goals. If you like long-term gains, go for position trading or HODL (holding your coins over a long period). For short-term outcomes, try day trading or scalping.

What is leverage in crypto trading?

Leverage is an approach to gain wider exposure to underlying digital assets by only paying a margin or a minimal deposit. In essence, you only pay a fraction of the entire value of the trade.

Chapter 3

What About the Crypto Market?

The cryptocurrency market is where investors and traders buy or sell Bitcoin and altcoins at current prices. It is a type of financial market where the exchange of assets happens.

The market of crypto is still relatively young but is growing very fast despite a lot of speculations and uncertainties due to the volatility factor of digital currency.

And while there are unique factors that affect the crypto market prices, global and regional economic events like inflation, political unrest, disease outbreaks, and more can influence the price

At a glance

- ✓ Classifications of crypto markets
- ✓ Understanding crypto exchanges: Centralized and Decentralized
- ✓ Key factors that influence the crypto market prices
- ✓ Market trends
- ✓ Bull market versus bear market
- ✓ Ways to take advantage of the crypto bull market
- ✓ Ways to profit in a bear market
- ✓ The psychology of market cycles
- ✓ What is market sentiment analysis?
- ✓ Indicators of market sentiment
- ✓ Frequently Asked Questions (FAQs)

Classification of crypto markets

Crypto markets can be classified into two:

- **Spot market**

  Crypto assets are bought or sold 'on the spot' in this type of market. Traders place an order, wait for the confirmation and delivery of the coins, and settle the payment right away. The context of delivery in the crypto spot market is 'immediate.' The current market price paid by the traders for the asset is called the *spot price*.

  There are two types of traders in the crypto spot market. The first is the markers or trades' initiators. You are considered as a maker if you list your potential trades on your chosen exchange. An example is opening trades at your desired price points, allowing potential buyers to fulfill the orders. The second type is the takers or the traders who fulfill the orders. You are a trader if you fulfill the existing coin orders.

  There is always a maker or a taker on the spot market. There are takers and markers for buy and sell orders. All the orders of traders can be viewed on the ledger or order book of the exchange. The platform has an automatic feature that matches purchase orders with existing sell orders.

- **Derivatives market**

  The derivatives are financial instruments with an underlying value that is based on the cryptocurrency's current value. They include contracts for difference (CFDs), options contracts, futures contracts, token swaps, and leveraged tokens.

  - The option contracts give traders the authority, but not an obligation, to sell or buy assets at a certain price in the future.

  - Future contracts allow crypto traders to speculate on the asset's future price. They are agreements by two parties to sell the assets on the expiry date at the last trading price. Moreover, the contract settlement is predetermined. It's either cash-settled or the underlying asset is physically delivered to the trader.

  - Leveraged tokens are tradable financial instruments. They offer leveraged exposure without the need to secure a leveraged position. Traders who prefer to use them would not be constantly worrying about funding, liquidation, margin, or collateral. These innovative products in the form of tokens derive values from perpetual futures positions.

  - Contract for difference (CFD) is a financial contract that allows traders to get the difference between the entry price and closing price. So, when the exit price is higher than the entry price, the seller of the crypto pays the buyer the difference. If the closing price is lower than the opening price, the seller gains profits.

Understanding cryptocurrency exchanges

Crypto market is commonly referred to as a cryptocurrency exchange or online platform that facilitates the trading of crypto to crypto or crypto to fiat currency/digital asset. Many crypto exchanges are trading globally and offering hundreds of available coins and tokens. They also have electronic wallets for those who engage in active trading.

Some exchanges are owned by brokers who act as an intermediary between the buyers and sellers of the cryptocurrency. Brokers earn through transaction fees and commissions.

Types of crypto exchange:

1.Centralized cryptocurrency exchange

They are operated by companies and are more reliable. Statistics reveal that about 99% of traders choose to transact business through centralized exchanges. The top exchanges based on trading volumes, traffic, and liquidity are Binance, Huobi Global, Coinbase, Kraken, and Bithumb.

Pros:

- Reliability – They have a developed and centralized platform that facilitates trading and transactions, offering more security and reliability.

- User-friendly – They work best for beginners because of their easy to navigate platform interface where traders check their accounts and balances or make transactions whenever they log in.

Cons:

- Transaction fee – Traders pay a certain amount for the services rendered and convenience. The cost of the transaction fee depends on the amounts of crypto being traded.

- Hacking risk – Centralized exchanges usually hold a great number of cryptocurrencies, which makes them a lucrative target for large-scale theft and hacking.

2. Decentralized cryptocurrency exchanges (DEX)

This type of exchange involves peer-to-peer transactions. There is no intermediary or a third party so traders do not pay transaction fees. The top DEXs are Uniswap (V2), Tokenlon, io, Blocknet, and AirSwap.

Pros:

- Anonymity – Traders are not required to provide personal information, which keeps the transactions between the seller and buyer anonymous and private.

- No hacking risk – There is no transfer of assets via a third party, so the risk of being hacked is zero.

- No market manipulation – Due to the nature of transactions, there is no market manipulation. This protects traders from wash trading and fake trading.

Cons:

- No fiat payment – Decentralized exchanges require traders to pay crypto for another crypto. This is inconvenient for beginners who want to pay fiat currency.

- Complexity – Traders who use this kind of exchange should familiarize themselves with the trading process and the platform. It is also important to memorize the password or keys to their digital wallets and have a backup to prevent losing their coins forever.

- Lack of liquidity – Since most crypto transactions are done in centralized exchanges, the decentralized exchanges experience low trading volumes that lead to a lack of liquidity. When trading volume is low, there are not enough buyers or sellers of the cryptocurrency.

Trivia

The global blockchain market would be worth $20 billion by 2024.

Key factors that influence the crypto market prices

There is a market when demand meets supply or vice-versa. The market prices rely heavily on demand and supply. They are also highly sensitive to speculations and potential moves of buyers. In essence, the assets' prices are decided by the sellers and buyers. They hold their value because traders and investors say they do.

- **Supply and demand**

  As a unit of exchange, the bottom line of cryptocurrency is trading. The price soars when more people set their intention to buy a cryptocurrency and more sellers are willing to sell.

  On the other hand, the price goes down when there are more sellers but buyers are not willing to purchase.

- **Market capitalization**
  It is the value of all circulating or existing crypto coins and how traders/investors perceive their growth rate.

- **Integration**
  It displays the easy integration of cryptocurrency into the e-commerce payment system and other existing infrastructure.

- **Endorsements**

  When notable personalities, economic experts, or celebrities positively endorse certain crypto, it can cause a hike in prices as investors and traders begin to accumulate them to ride with the tide. But remember that there is a thing called disguised advertisements.

  They are endorsements used to generate a temporary demand but leave the investors with coins that only promise immediate returns.

- **Press/Media**

  It refers to the way cryptocurrencies are portrayed in media channels and the amount of coverage they get. News stories or rumors about the potential ban of crypto or central bank control can cause price movements.

- **Key events**

  It includes major events like economic setbacks, security breaches, attacks on exchanges that reveal security flaws, and regulatory updates.

- **Disagreements in cryptocurrency communities**

  This pertains to issues over upgrades like when a certain cryptocurrency goes through a hard fork.

Market trends

Market trends refer to the perceived direction of movement of any kind of financial market within a certain period. They are identified in technical analysis with the help of trend lines, price action, or key moving averages. One peculiar characteristic of market trends is that traders believe that they have accurately determined or predicted the future event in hindsight. However, hindsight bias can produce a key impact on identifying market trends as well as making trading decisions.

The primary market trends are the bull and bear markets. The bull market symbolizes the increasing trend in the financial market or sustained uptrend, while the bear market means a declining market or sustained downtrend.

Each market trend can last from 1-3 years. It is important to remember that market trends do not entirely mean that the price is going in the given direction. A prolonged bear market has some smaller bear trends within the period and vice versa.

Both bull market and bear market offer huge opportunities for traders to gain more profits. The key is to use strong strategies to generate earnings under different market conditions. Moreover, you need to be consistent, focused, disciplined, and take advantage of greed and fear emotions.

Bull market

A bull market pertains to financial market conditions where the prices are soaring continuously or have the potential to rise soon. Whenever the demand outweighs the laws of demand and supply over an extended period, bull markets manifest. Investors and traders during bull markets are optimistic and confident as the prices continue to increase faster than the usual average rate.

Most often, bull markets occur during robust economic growth or when people become more interested in the stock markets because of higher returns on investment. Bull markets can also create 'bubbles' or when the price of the underlying asset is greater than its actual value.

Indicators of the bull market include:

- Prices rise at least 80% over an extended period
- Market indexes soar at least 15%
- Stock prices rise by 20% after the two occurrences of declines of 20%

Bull markets show four phases.

1. The first phase begins with low prices, pessimistic views about the prices, and low sentiment.

2. The second phase displays an increasing amount of trading activities and above-average economic indicators. During this period, corporate earnings and stock prices are beginning to increase. Likewise, investors and traders show more optimism.

3. The third phase shows more trading activities. The securities and market indexes reach trading highs while the dividend yields reach their lows.

4. The fourth or final phase is when there are excessive trading activities, IPO activities, and speculations. Investors and traders are raking in profits as the earnings ratios and stock prices reach their historic highs, resulting in unraveling the bull market. During this phase, investors are also busy reacting to various negative indicators.

Did you know that?

*The 3 biggest bull markets in the U.S. happened in
1860-72 during the start of the railroad industry,
1920-28 when the 19th Amendment was ratified
and automobiles were invented, and 1982-99
during the launching of the Internet.*

Bear market

A bear market manifests when there is a 20% or more decrease in the market index for two months. Bear markets' average length is 367 days. Bear markets happen when there is a prolonged decrease in prices. It typically occurs when there are significant factors that change the optimistic cycle of the economy.

When optimism and trust decrease, there is also a decrease in demand for the underlying asset. It creates a tipping point where the cycle hits the bottom before going up again.

The four phases of bear markets:

1. During the first phase, there is a high investor sentiment and high market prices. Eventually, they begin to take in their profits and stop trading.

2. Stock prices, corporate profits, and trading activities start to decline sharply. The economic indicators become below average and the optimistic sentiment of investors turns into panic. It is often referred to as the capitulation stage.

3. The third phase is when speculators are beginning to enter the market again, causing an increase in trading volume and market prices.

4. In this final or fourth phase, the stock prices are beginning to drop gradually. Optimism and low prices start attracting traders and investors again. This last cycle of the bear market leads to a bull market.

Ways to take advantage of crypto bull markets

The best time to buy cryptocurrency in a bull market is during the infancy or first phase period. In this way, you can sell it when the market prices reach their peak position. While there is no accurate way to determine when it will happen, your loss will be minimal.

Here are some strategies that investors and traders use during bull markets:

- **Buy and hold approach**

  It works by buying an asset, holding it for a certain period, and selling it when the market is favorable. The buy and hold approach is fueled by the bull market's optimistic condition.

- **Increase buy and hold approach**

  It is a variation of the buy and hold strategy, but involves continuous buying of assets or security as long as the price is rising favorably.

- **Full swing approach**

  This aggressive approach is meant to capitalize on the favorable conditions of the bull market like using the short-selling method to maximize profits before another shift happens. Short selling means selling borrowed assets and then purchasing them at lower prices.

- **Retracement addition approach**

  It refers to the brief period of price reversal. This is typical in the bull market, even if the market trend is going upward. Many investors and traders use this period within the bull market to buy more assets. The presumption is that the price of the asset will move back fast, albeit retroactively, and give them a discounted buying price.

Ways to profit in crypto bear markets

Despite the sluggishness and pessimism in bear markets, you can still make a profit. As long as there is a movement in the cryptocurrency market, the promise of profits is always possible.

Although nobody can predict when the bear markets will end or hit the bottom, you can always make a position to benefit from any favorable price movement.

Do not let your emotions of fear and doubt get into your rational thinking. Use the bear market trend to study and analyze your preferred trades. It's easy to be crippled by fear when the cryptocurrencies seem to be dipping, but their volatility can cause them to bounce so much stronger. Bitcoin has proven it so many times and other new digital assets are also showing their capability to rebound fast.

- **Buy a dip**

    Be brave and buy the dip. By setting entries beforehand, you are making a shot to lock in your position and sell your cryptocurrencies when their prices regain their strength in the market. To ensure that the opportunity to gain profit during the short period of recovery of the bear market, you should set a Full trade. It is typical for the returns to happen overnight, so by setting your entries, stop-losses, take-profits, and other safety nets, you have your gains while sleeping.

    You can also automate your trades and set take-profit orders in advance so when the market takes a turn positively, you gain the most.

- **Brush up your skills on Technical Analysis**

    Now is the time to have an in-depth understanding of technical analysis and how it can help you during margin or futures trading. Begin with the basics like RSI, moving averages, Fibonacci, and so on. Keep learning the indicators and soon, you will be a pro when it comes to entries and exits.

- **Learn margin trading**

    Margin trading is the practice of trading using borrowed funds from brokers. The collateral of the loan is your financial asset. While it is risky, this type of trading amplifies your purchasing power. It confers tremendous potential of huge profits, but also losses. It is just an option for bold and brave traders with higher risk tolerance.

- **Dig hidden potentials**

While you can buy assets cheaply, their inherent and potential value remains. In the bear market, you don't have to rush into trading your coins because of low prices and low volumes. So, while waiting for positive price movements, research undervalued currencies that have the potential to grow big when the crypto market gets its rebound. A coin that has dropped more than 70% may look less valuable when it lost its all-time high but can rebound with a bang. Sometimes, the reason why assets fall is due to its still developing platform or loss of interest of the crowd.

- **Scalp and earn**

Scalping is an attempt to earn money from small price movements in the market. A scalp trader can position himself many times within short periods to maximize the opportunities of market inefficiency and price movement. This kind of trading strategy necessitates performing a very quick technical analysis.

- **Educate yourself**

In the bear market, there is no rush to keep refreshing your assets portfolio or do frenzy trading to maximize gains. It is time to upgrade your skills and knowledge like researching the next set of phenomenal coins, understanding leverages, or learning how to identify the vital signs of market reversal. All your learnings during the bear market will increase your chances when the bull market starts to manifest.

Trivia

The bull and bear market phenomenon was derived from the 18th-century bearskin trading market.
During that time, bull and bear fighting was considered a sport.

The Psychology of Market Cycles

All financial markets have cyclical nature or have an expansion and contraction cycle. **Market cycles** are trends or patterns that manifest at different periods. They usually emerge when a certain asset class outperforms the other classes. Within the same market cycle, some asset classes underperform because of varying market conditions.

Market cycles happen because of the **market sentiment** or the collective attitude of investors and traders towards the asset. It is true to all financial markets, which include the crypto market. The overall moods, thoughts, and feelings of participants can move the prices of the cryptocurrency, creating a psychological market cycle.

The idea that the price shifts in the market reflect the emotions of the traders is called **market psychology**. It is an important topic in behavioral economics because of its impact on economic decisions. A positive market sentiment creates a bullish trend (bull market) with prices of crypto increasing continuously. The opposite trend results in a bear market, with prices declining continuously.

Uptrend

When there is positive market sentiment, the demand for the assets increases, and the supply decreases. When it happens, there is an overall strong attitude, belief, optimism, and greed in the market climate. These emotions contribute to a very strong buying activity.

And it does not stop there. It is common in the market cycles during an uptrend to see a retroactive effect. It means that as the crypto prices soar, the market sentiment becomes more positive and drives the prices higher.

During this period, there is a prevailing sense of greed that generates a financial bubble. This drives a lot of traders and investors to accumulate more assets, believing that the positive trend will continue. They tend to be irrational and lose sight of the asset's actual value. More assets are sold during this *distribution stage*, creating a sideways market movement.

Downtrend

In contrast, a downtrend brings a negative market sentiment that lessens the demand and increases the supply of assets.

The investors and traders become complacent after losing the euphoric feelings once the market takes a negative turn. And when the prices of cryptocurrencies continue to decline, the sentiment of the participants turns into anxiety, denial, and panic.

As the prices drop, crypto investors and traders start questioning why it is happening. This gives rise to anxiety and unacceptance or denial of the fact that there is a downtrend. Many of them continue to hold on to their positions because they believe that the positive market trend will resume soon. Others feel that it is too late for them to sell their assets.

Panic comes in as the cryptocurrency prices dip down tremendously. At this juncture, the prevailing emotion is fear. Almost everyone wants to sell their digital assets. This is the period of market capitulation or when crypto owners sell their coins at a losing price.

The downtrend period halts when the crypto volatility decreases. This leads to the eventual stabilization of the market. There will be sideways movements that contribute to the renewed feelings of optimism and hope. This period is called the *accumulation stage*.

What is market sentiment analysis?

While market sentiment does not reflect the crypto fundamentals, it can impact its price. This is why traders are constantly reviewing the current sentiment of the majority of participants. A **market sentiment analysis** can be used to predict price movements. It entails tracking the dynamics of the market and the overall attitudes of the participants to fully understand their fear or hype emotion about a certain asset. Aside from providing vital insights on the market demand, analyzing the market sentiment can potentially predict favorable trends that will give you profits.

Like the fundamental analysis or technical analysis, analyzing the market helps traders make sound decisions. Combining the pertinent data from the three methods is a great idea.

- It helps you have a clear concept of short and mid-term price action.

- It helps you discover profitable trading opportunities.

- It helps you get hold of your emotional state.

To perform a market sentiment analysis, you need the opinions, ideas, and views of the participants. You can start by checking the relevant crypto channels and social media platforms. Twitter is one of the most popular social channels among crypto fans.

Joining official crypto forums, Telegram groups, and Discord servers will also help you in analyzing the market sentiment. But be mindful of scammers lurking in these pages or communities. They are always ready to prowl on easy prey, so make sure that you are doing your own analysis and not swayed by some 'sweet talks' of some traders who establish themselves as 'experts'.

You may also consider the following methods:

- Keeping yourself up to date by following crypto blogs and media portals that publish the latest news and trends. Check out Binance News, CoinDesk, Binance Blogs, and Bitcoin Magazine.

- Tracking social mentions with the help of data collection software tools.

- Checking the pricing signals and indicators of market sentiment on CoinMarketCap. They are collated from various reliable sources and the summaries are the current market sentiment.

- Setting alerts or tracking huge transactions by 'whales' or individuals/organizations that are holding a great number of certain cryptocurrencies. They have enough crypto coins or tokens and can create a ripple on the prices by selling or buying large amounts.

- Measuring the hype level that surrounds cryptocurrency with the help of Google Trends.

Indicators of market sentiment

Market sentiment indicators represent the underlying emotions that can change a bull market into a bear market or vice versa. Using a scale or graphic tools, you get to view the current sentiment of the participants.

One of the widely-used tools is the Bitcoin Crypto Fear & Greed Index. It displays the market greed or fear using the scale of 0-100. It uses 5 information sources to get an accurate result.

They are the crypto volatility, dominance, trends, market volume, and social media.

Another useful tool is Augmento's Bull & Bear Index. This market sentiment indicator uses social media impressions through its artificial intelligence (AI) software. It can analyze 93 topics and sentiments by tapping the conversations on Bitcointalk, Twitter, and Reddit.

Did you know that?

China is the biggest crypto miner with around 75%
Control of more than the mining network

<u>FAQs</u>

Why are financial markets important?

Financial markets play a great role in economic activities like growth opportunities, investment, commerce & trade. The fundamental functions of any type of financial market are to provide a free market for an efficient flow of capital and allow investors to earn capital gains.

Who are the key players in financial markets?

Investors who want efficient capital and asset allocation. Speculators who view asset classes like cryptocurrency and make directional bets on their future values.

The brokers are intermediaries that bring sellers and buyers of assets together.

The arbitrageurs who are on the lookout for anomalies or mispricing would always find a way to gain from them.

The hedgers who use the derivative markets in mitigating different types of risks.

Chapter 4

Prepping Up for Trading

Cryptocurrency trading has elements of volatility and unpredictability, hence the importance of making a trading plan that will guide you in making smart decisions. You also need an effective trading strategy or combination of strategies to achieve your goals. Having a smart plan and putting your chosen trading strategies in action helps you when to cut losses, when to take profits, which market to trade, or where to find other growth opportunities.

At a glance

- ✓ **What is a trading plan?**
- ✓ **Do you need a trading plan?**
- ✓ **How to create a solid and winning trading plan?**
- ✓ **Frequently Asked Questions**

What is a trading plan?

A trading plan is your comprehensive trading tool. It is a personal plan that will guide you when, how much, and what to trade. It is your roadmap to successful cryptocurrency trading or any type of trading you want to try.

This plan is a written document that is well-researched and systematic. It can be customized according to your goals, expectations, strategies, and other parameters. It outlines the ways to find opportunities and execute trades, what securities to trade, how large the position you will take, how to manage the positions, and the rules when or when not to trade.

A trading plan may include the following:

- Your motivation or reason for trading cryptocurrency
- Your goals and financial objectives
- Your time commitment
- Your risk tolerance or level of attitude to risks
- Your personal risk management rules
- Your available capital
- Your strategies

- Your chosen trading markets
- Your record-keeping method (trading journal)

Do you need a trading plan?

The answer is a resounding "YES!"

Your trading plan clearly defines your trading parameters, helping you make logical decisions like when to trade or when to stop your losses. During heated moments in the trading market, like when a bullish trend is happening, your trading plan helps you avoid acting irrationally.

Other benefits of having a trading plan are:

- It makes trading easier – You have done all the planning and researching beforehand, so all you need to do is to trade your crypto according to your trading parameters.

- It promotes better discipline – Trading is full of growth opportunities, but not all good prospects can give you the edge you desire and may lead to disastrous events like losing all your crypto in one move. A trading plan helps you stick to your goals and observe your pre-set limitations.

- It helps in making more objective choices and decisions- Because you already know when to cut trading losses or when you should take your profits, you do not let strong emotions obscure your logical reasoning.

- It provides room for improvement – By reviewing your trading journal, you learn the lessons from your previous trading mistakes. It helps you make better judgments and moves.

How to create a solid and winning trading plan?

Remember the famous cliché, 'failing to plan is planning to fail'? It may sound a little glib, but it works excellently in the business sphere, especially in crypto trading. A winning trading plan is what separates successful traders from average traders. They also methodologically follow their sound and strategic plan.

Every trading plan is unique to traders. While you can copy or use the techniques of other traders, you need to consider the factors that reflect your choices and trading styles.

Here are the vital steps you need to do to build your perfect master plan:

Step 1: Outline your trading motivation

Why do you want to join the trading world? Generally, people would say it's all about the lucrative profits. But it is important to write down your reasons why you want to trade.

Step 2: Define your trading goals.

Do not just write a simple statement like "I want to gain profits." You should write SMART (specific, measurable, attainable, relevant, and time-bound) goals. A good example is "This year, I want to add value to my financial portfolio by up to 25%." You can break down your big goal into mini-goals in a week, month, or year. Review your goals and their progress regularly.

Step 3: Know your trading style.

You should know your trading style based on your attitude to risk, your personality, and the amount of time you can commit to trading. Trading requires time if you want to gain a lot of profits.

It is important to set a specific period to do your trading activities. It also depends on the kind of trading style method you will use.

A quick review of the 4 primary trading styles:

- Day trading – It involves opening and closing several trades during the same day. You will be spending hours in front of your computer or mobile screen if it is your choice.

- Position trading – It is about holding your positions for several weeks, months, or years. It does not require too much of your time, knowing it is a long-term trading strategy.

- Scalping – This entails making several trades every day, for a few minutes or seconds, to make small profits that eventually will add up to a huge amount of money.

- Swing trading – It is about holding your trading positions over a few days or weeks and taking advantage of the price movements in the medium-term market.

Step 4: Set your risk-reward ratio.

In trading, you may lose many times, but you can still earn consistent profits. The key is setting your risk-reward ratio. How much are you willing to risk in your every trade? Setting your risk level is important. It should vary from 1% to 5% of your entire portfolio.

Knowing your limit will help you get out of the trade without losing much when the market does not favor your position. A 1:3 risk-reward ratio or higher is ideal.

For example, you risk $100 on a trade with a $300 potential gain. This shows that your target profit is double the rate of your potential loss.

Step 5: Decide the amount of your trading capital.

Your capital should be the amount of money you are willing to lose in the worst trading scenarios. It is extremely important to avoid risking more than you can afford or your egg nest just for the thrill of trading to have more. There are plenty of risks in trading, so you need to do your math before you start your game plan.

Trivia

Backtesting is a practice that allows traders to test an idea with the help of historical data and its viability.

FAQs

What are the crucial questions that my trading plan should answer?

- What are your primary reasons why you want to become a trader?
- What do you want to achieve from crypto trading?
- What are your biggest strengths and weaknesses?
- What are your plans to leverage your strengths and address the weaknesses?
- Do you have plans that will set you apart from the majority of crypto traders who failed in the past?
- What market/markets do you plan to trade your crypto in and why?
- What trading systems are you going to use when entering or exiting trades?
- What are the trading equipment and software you are going to use in trading?
- Do you have a plan to withdraw your profit or reinvest it?

Does a trading plan guarantee my success in altcoin trading?

There is no guarantee of success, but it eliminates major roadblocks and helps you hone your skills. A solid trading plan is about avoiding failure.

Can I change my trading plan?

A trading plan is not static and can evolve based on your skills or changing market conditions.

Chapter 5

The Cryptocurrency that Started It All: Bitcoin

Bitcoin (denoted "฿") is often called the currency of the internet. It is abbreviated as XBT or BTC. It is both a technology and virtual currency that works like digital cash for the exchange of goods or services. Bitcoin is accessible to all, regardless of gender, religion, ethnicity, or political beliefs.

In the context of value, it is the undisputed king of cryptocurrency due to the stability of its network. This electronic cash system has proved its worth amidst the ups and downs of the financial market. Until today, it kept its independent nature without the intervention of any central authority.

The versatile nature of Bitcoin has caught the interest of private corporations and individuals who are on the lookout for lucrative ways to multiply their wealth and passive income.

As a frontrunner, Bitcoin inspired the subsequent explosion of new players in the cryptocurrency, creating a legion of spinoffs and users.

In terms of popularity, user base, and market capitalization, Bitcoin is the leader of the crypto pack. It has become not just the trendsetter but the cryptocurrencies' de-facto standard. It comprises half of the crypto market and sustains its claim as the most-sought instrument in crypto trading. Its history depicts a series of exponential growth and profitability, making a lot of investors and traders multimillionaires in just a few years of owning Bitcoin.

At a glance
- ✓ **A glimpse in Bitcoin's history**
- ✓ **Growing pains**
- ✓ **The value of Bitcoin**
- ✓ **Classification of Bitcoin**
- ✓ **Bitcoin transactions**
- ✓ **Reasons to trade Bitcoin**
- ✓ **Risks that you should be aware of**
- ✓ **Are you ready to trade Bitcoin?**
- ✓ **Best Bitcoin trading strategies**
- ✓ **Popular trading styles for advanced traders**
- ✓ **Frequently Asked Questions (FAQs**

Bitcoin's history

Bitcoin is the first successful feat after so many attempts to create digital currencies using cryptography, which is the science of generating and breaking codes. It was a brainchild of Satoshi Nakamoto, whose real identity until now is still a big mystery. Along with Bitcoin, he also developed the blockchain database.

On January 3, the 'genesis block' or Block O was mined. It is the first-ever mined block of Bitcoin. Nakamoto introduced the first bitcoin software version to the public on January 8, 2009, via the Cryptography Mailing List. And on January 9, 2009, the official mining of Bitcoin commenced with Block 1.

The first-ever Bitcoin transaction in the real world happened on May 22, 2010, when programmer Laszlo Hanyecz bought two Papa John's pizzas worth 10,000 BTC in Jacksonville, Florida. Fast forward today, the said amount is worth over $600 million.

Growing Pains

The journey to the top is not easy for this revolutionary currency. It needed to carve a path on its own.

As expected, many were doubtful about its longevity and success. Not a lot of investors and traders would gamble their money for a new player in the industry, especially because cryptocurrency was still new and has not proven its stability and credibility in the financial market.

Since its inception, Bitcoin has displayed significant ups and downs, violent crashes, and uptrend growth. Its recent all-time high happened in March 2021, when one Bitcoin reached an all-time high of $61,683. Way back then during its creation, 1 BTC was worth $0.008.

What's the difference?

Bitcoin (with capital B) refers to this crypto as an entity, while bitcoin (small letter b) refers to the quantity or the units.

The Value of Bitcoin

Bitcoin is not a coin, but a file with certain values that can be used for initiating payments to goods or services. It is a digital software with a unique set of protocols, rules, and processes that exists in the virtual cloud.

Bitcoin's real value comes from its code, infrastructure, scarcity, and adoption. It has no intrinsic value or is backed by gold and silver. Intrinsic value refers to any kind of currency that has the backing of the government, precious metals, or the people's trust over the government.

Bitcoin and Altcoins do not have these elements, but they have the trust of millions of people. The participants in the crypto network are the miners and traders who trust Bitcoin decides its price based on supply and demand.

In addition, like traditional currencies, Bitcoin has value because it is accepted as a unit of exchange and as a store of value. It also possesses the 6 major attributes of successful currencies:

- Scarcity – Bitcoin's finite availability greatly increases its demand in the market. Currently, more than 18 million bitcoins are in circulation. Mining new bitcoins will stop when it reaches the 21 million limit.

- Utility – Bitcoin's blockchain technology is one of its selling points. The trustless and decentralized nature of this ledger system makes global transactions more convenient and safe.

  Moreover, blockchain technology is also flexible and can be utilized beyond the crypto world.

- Divisibility – The smallest unit of Bitcoin is Satoshi, which is equal to 0.00000001 One Bitcoin is equivalent to 100,000,000 Satoshis. The lowest transaction value in Bitcoin is 546 Satoshis.

- Durability – Cryptocurrencies are not susceptible to deformity or other physical harms that will render them unusable. This characteristic makes Bitcoin tremendously valuable. It will continue its existence in the blockchain as long as there are transactions by the owners and traders.

- Transportability – Bitcoin can be transferred from one user to another in a matter of seconds, regardless of the amount of the transaction via crypto wallets and exchanges.

- Counterfeitability – Attempting to counterfeit bitcoin is incredibly difficult because of the decentralized and complex structure of its blockchain ledger system.

How do you classify Bitcoin?

Is it an asset class, a store of value, a payment system, or a kind of currency? Bitcoin can be all these, making it a versatile virtual phenomenon that is exchanged through blockchain technology or publicly distributed ledger. There is no human-to-human intervention during the transactions.

Technically, Bitcoin is simply a list. For example, Person C transferred X bitcoin to Person D, who sent bitcoin to Person E. All these transactions are processed, tallied, and recorded permanently in the blockchain. Bitcoin's blockchain is open to the public, so anyone can view past and current transactions.

This popular virtual currency is regarded by the Commodity Futures Trading Commission (CFTC) as a commodity while the Internal Revenue Service (IRS) sees it as a property and needs to be taxed.

Bitcoin transactions

The lifecycle of Bitcoin transactions begins when a user creates a request to transfer funds to another user. To authorize the spending of funds, a valid electronic signature is necessary. Then, the transaction is broadcast, confirmed, and shared by the network nodes until it reaches the minding node for full validation and recording. All transactions are irreversible and added to the system's blocks.

It involves three elements to be successful:

- **Transaction input** - It is the bitcoin address from where the fund will come from. Your bitcoin address is a string of randomly generated alphanumeric characters. Along with this address is your private key to help you access it and restrict anyone to view or steal your bitcoins.

- **Transaction output** - It is the public bitcoin address or e-wallet address where the fund goes.

- **Amount** – It is the value (number of Satoshi) of Bitcoin that you want to send to another user for whatever purpose you agreed on.

All these elements are registered in the blockchain and encrypted for security reasons. It allows users to trace all Bitcoin transactions since it was first created, without identifying the user information. People who are viewing the history on the blockchain can only see the public key next to every transaction.

Reasons to trade Bitcoin

Bitcoin is the big brother of all crypto coins that opens the great path of trading and investing in digital currency.

Its popularity is influenced by the following factors:

- 24/7 trading

  Bitcoin trading does not stop, except for regular network maintenance. Traders can open or exit their positions 24/7 in a year. The crypto exchanges are all web-based so you trade around the clock, whenever or wherever you are.

- Global appeal

  Bitcoin operates in more than 90% of countries in the world. This simply means that you can engage in trading or transfer crypto funds even if you are in another part of the continent. Moreover, it is gaining more recognition as a medium of exchange and payment options.

- High volatility

  Traders are fascinated with the uptrends of Bitcoin prices, which means that speculating the movements is exciting and can give you a sudden windfall profit. Of course, the risks are high and could lead to significant losses.

- Deregulated landscape

  The lack of regulations makes it more attractive to people who want to take their trading to the next level. While crypto trading is still not mature, the impressive performance of Bitcoin including its ups and downs gives it clout of influence that appeals to investors and traders.

Risks you should be aware of

For beginners, trading Bitcoin can be riskier. It is necessary to be aware of the obvious and hidden risks before you invest your money in bitcoins. This will help you avoid expensive mistakes that can rob your confidence in trading.

To avoid traps and pitfalls, understand the following factors:

- Dangers of volatility

  Bitcoin is regarded as the most volatile asset in the financial market, much more than gold and stocks. It's true that volatility brings greater profitability in day trading style, it is also surrounded by unpredictability and doubt elements.

- Margin trading

  Margin trading using derivatives multiples profit potential as well as the risk. In worst scenarios, traders who engage in margin trading suffer from a loss that exceeds their deposit.

- Transaction costs

  The cost of transaction fees and charges during the buying and selling of Bitcoin vary. If you are into day trading and doing multiple trades, this can be a significant risk matter. Derivatives including binary options and CFDs can help you mitigate the risk.

- Exchange risks

Always do business with reputable and trusted exchange platforms or brokers with a good reputation in the financial market. It is important that the platform is secure and prevents glitches during transactions.

Also, deal with people you trust to avoid kissing goodbye to your bitcoin because once you transfer it, the only person who can get it is the recipient.

- Regulation

Many governments are looking at Bitcoin and other cryptocurrencies with so much interest, trying to figure out how to impose stringent regulations.

While it is not yet happening, some countries already ban crypto.

Fun Trivia
*Bitcoin is a global phenomenon that is
constantly in trading motion.
It is believed that an average bitcoin
transaction is 350,000 or about
4 transactions every second.*

Are you ready to start trading Bitcoin?

To trade Bitcoin, here's a step by step beginner's guide:

Step 1: Know the price

Head over to an exchange broker or index to find out the current price of Bitcoin. Its price goes up and down because of the impact of supply, integration, bad press, or key events.

Step 2: Select how to get exposure to Bitcoin

There are 3 ways to get exposure:

- Buying through an exchange – traders who like to have direct ownership of their bitcoins and go for a buy-and-hold strategy.

- Trading bitcoin derivatives – traders speculate on the price using CFDs without the need to buy coins. It allows you to take a position by 'going short' or 'going long.'

- Crypto 10 index- a market capitalization-weighted index (B10 index) of top ten performing cryptocurrencies. Market capitalization is the result of multiplying the current market value of the crypto against the US dollar by the number of units of the given coin.

Step 3: Choose a broker

Decide which broker or exchange to use for trading Bitcoin. Some brokers allow trading the Bitcoin's underlying assets via spread bets or CFDs.

Step 4: Set a trading capital

Start small and trade only what you can afford to lose. Again, trading is about speculations so strike while the iron is hot but proceed with caution.

Step 5: Decide on your trading strategy

The trading strategy is your preferred style of trading. It will determine what kind of trader you are. Generally, you will fall into one of these types:

- Day traders – those who take advantage of short term price movements in the crypto market

- Scalpers – active traders who make multiple traders every single day to gain small profits

- Swing traders – those who seek to capture market trends based on the results of their technical analysis

- Passive traders – people who hold their positions to gain long term profits

Step 6: Set stops and limits

They are important tools to manage the risks in trading. A **stop order** allows traders to set the price point where your order will be executed. It works to limit your losses, protect profits, as well as initiate new trading positions.

A **limit order** lets traders set the minimum price that will trigger execution. There is an advanced setting that allows you to choose **Post Only** or **Allow Taker**. Enabling Post Only keeps the limit order on the order book. When it is filled, you will be charged a **Maker Fee**.

Allow Taker allows the market order's fulfillment whenever it crosses the spread, regardless if it is only a portion of the total order. The **Taker Fees** are calculated based on the portion.

Step 7: Open and monitor your trade

Opening a trade means buying when you believe that the price of the Bitcoin will rise or selling your coin when you think that the price will fall. Monitoring the market is necessary to ensure that the Bitcoin price is moving favorably.

Step 8: Close your position

Whenever you feel uncomfortable, cut your loss by closing your position. You can also close it if you like to take your profit. All losses are deducted from your trading account balance and the profits are trading directly to your account.

Do you know that?

*El Salvador was the first country that recognized
Bitcoin as legal tender.
It happened on June 9, 2021.*

What are the best bitcoin trading strategies?

Trading bitcoin for profit is considered the universal strategy in cryptocurrency trading. Bitcoin is accepted as a trading and payment instrument. It is still the hottest trading instrument in the cryptocurrency market, much more than gold trading, oil trading, or stock trading.

Investors and traders believe in bitcoin's ability due to its revolutionary blockchain technology. In essence, the best BTC trading style is the one that aligns with your goals, capital, and risk appetite. Moreover, the strategy should be 85% price action and 15% strategy that utilizes indicators.

Strategies are necessary because they serve as your guide in trading and mitigate huge losses. Without a clear and solid strategy, you will be blindsided by a lot of distracting factors in the trading sphere.

A trading strategy helps you maximize your capital by knowing when to take a position and when to get your profit before the market turns around.

An effective Bitcoin strategy should include the tools and indicators you will use, the setup to take, the factors that will trigger your entries and exits, the elements that can influence the sizing of your positions, and the ways you measure and record the performance of your portfolio.

To find out the right one for you, here's a list of the recommended strategies for beginners:

- Trend trading

    Several times in its decade-long history, Bitcoin has proven itself as a powerful trend driver. Trend traders do not want to experience FOMO (fear of missing out), so they keep themselves updated for any significant events or news that can influence the Bitcoin price.

    Trend trading involves holding your position open in hours, days, or even months. This is because you believe that the ongoing trend will continue moving to its current direction or create another trend. Traders who use this strategy predict the potential direction of the market price's momentum through technical analysis.

    The most effective momentum and trend indicators are the stochastic oscillators, moving averages, and RSI (relative strength index).

- Swing trading

    It is another trading style that suits beginners because of its elements of taking a long time to play out, allowing traders to think about their decisions and choices. It necessitates observing the 'natural swing' of the bitcoin price cycles and positioning until the desired profit is achieved or holding out until the price movement stops. It may involve holding the position open for more than 24 hours but less than a month.

    In essence, swing trading is a crossover of day trading and trend trading.

- HODLing

  HODLing (holding on for dear life) is a popular bitcoin trading strategy that was coined in 2013. It was the year when the price of bitcoins was radically falling and one of the users typed 'hodling' instead of 'holding' to show his intention to sustain his position.

  The term eventually evolved and has become a trading strategy that involves sticking around in a long position in the belief that the price will soon peak. However, this strategy is risky. You need to have a solid risk management plan for this option.

- Hedging

  Hedging bitcoin involves opening several strategic trades to avoid or lessen the risk to current positions. It is a strategy used by bitcoin traders who believe that the price will experience a short-term decline at the soonest time.

  To prevent huge losses, you need to open a short bitcoin position, which means selling your digital assets based on the current price in the market. If the dreaded scenario happens, you can easily buy your bitcoin for a lower cost and earn profit from the price difference. Another way to hedge bitcoins is by using CFDs (contracts for difference).

  This derivative product lets you trade without the need to buy the underlying asset. You just need to buy a portion of the entire asset to leverage your trading exposure.

If you bought $100 worth of Bitcoin on July 10, 2010,
its worth as of today would be almost $20 million.

Popular trading styles for advanced bitcoin traders:

- Day trading

  This is for active and savvy traders who enjoy action every single day. You can day trade from any location 24/7 for 365 days. You can go short or long, be bearish or bullish because every day offers new profit and growth opportunities.

  This volatile market can display price swings in just a matter of hours. Multiple trading opportunities can happen within 24 hours.

  Because of its volatility and liquidity, there will always be a high number of growth potential and profitable windows. Also, bitcoin allows low overhead for big trades. To maximize the benefits of day trading, pay attention to the developing trends in the market and technical indicators which include moving averages, relative strength, volume, and oscillators.

OBV or On Balance Volume is one of the most effective day trading bitcoin indicators. It works by analyzing the total amount of money that flows in and out of the financial instrument. This indicator studies the price activity and volume to predict the direction of the market price.

- Breakout trading

This strategy requires traders to enter the market during the trend and be prepared for the potential 'breakout' of the bitcoin price from its previous range. The rationale of this trading style is based on the belief that when the market breaks due to resistance level or key support, there will be major volatility.

You should watch out for key points and enter the market at once if you want to ride the uptrend until it completes its cycle. In identifying the levels of support and resistance, you need to consider the technical indicators which include the RSI (relative strength index) and the MACD (moving average convergence divergence) as well as the volume level as a confirmation signal.

- Scalping

It is a type of day-trading style that focuses on short-term positioning to earn substantial profits. It requires traders to make consistent attempts repeatedly to take advantage of the small price movements of bitcoin in the market. The rationale behind this strategy is by exploiting small moves with consistency, the risks are reduced and small profits will lead to a big amount.

Did you know that?

It is estimated that more than 4 million Bitcoins are lost forever due to a lot of reasons including inaccessibility to wallets due to key loss.

FAQs

How much capital do I need to start buying Bitcoin?

There is no rule about the minimum purchase but some crypto exchanges have a minimum order size that you should take into consideration. You may also end up paying higher transaction fees if you make small purchases.

What affects the price of Bitcoin?

The price of Bitcoin is generally influenced by the following:

- supply and demand of Bitcoin

- the exchanges it trades on

- the number of competing coins or altcoins

- the cost of Bitcoin mining

- the cost of incentives given to the miners of bitcoin

- the regulations that govern bitcoin's sale

- internal governance of Bitcoin (due to the absence of core authority, it relies on developers and miners to protect the blockchain network)

How can I acquire Bitcoin?

There are several ways to obtain bitcoins – buy at an exchange, receive it as payment for services or goods, exchange bitcoins with other holders, and earn through competitive crypto mining.

Is it easy to make a payment using Bitcoin?

Compared to credit or debit card purchases, using Bitcoin to pay your purchases is easier. You just need to enter the receiver's address, input the amount, and press SEND. You can also scan a QR code to complete the transaction.

What are the advantages I get from Bitcoin?

Bitcoin offers payment freedom – no bureaucracy, no geographical borders, or bank holidays. It has different levels of transfer fees and there are no fees when receiving bitcoins. Transactions are secure, anonymous, and irreversible. All transactions are neutral and transparent in the blockchain (without revealing your identity).

What are the disadvantages of using Bitcoin?

The number of merchants who accept crypto payment is still relatively small and many people are still unaware of cryptocurrency. Bitcoin's volatility is also another factor.

Is Bitcoin a fraud scheme?

No. A Ponzi scheme preys on its investors and when there are no new participants, the network collapses and affects the most recent investors. Bitcoin is a decentralized software project where all transactions utilize blockchain technology and prevent fraudulent representations about the investment.

Is Bitcoin a cult?

No. Bitcoin is a virtual asset that is accepted as a payment option as well as a trading and investment instrument. Whereas, a cult is a group of devout followers who are invested in an idea or mission. The misconception is borne out of the craze that bitcoin has caused, attracting a lot of believers.

Is Bitcoin a bubble?

Some people think that Bitcoin is a bubble because of the phenomenal 10 million % increase of its value since its conception. A bubble is expected to burst after some time. However, Bitcoin proves that while its price goes up and down due to the demand and supply factors, it is still attracting more users across the globe.

Chapter 6

The Moment to Shine for Altcoins

After the success of bitcoin, a lot of digital currencies appear in the market. They are collectively known as Altcoins or alternative coins. The term Altcoin is derived from the combination of the words 'alt' (alternative) and 'coin' (cryptocurrency) to imply that it is a type of crypto other than Bitcoin.

At a glance

- ✓ What are altcoins?
- ✓ How do they differ from Bitcoin?
- ✓ What are the pros and cons when you invest in altcoins?
- ✓ What are the different kinds of altcoins?
- ✓ Tokens: Security versus Utility
- ✓ Meet the most important altcoins
- ✓ Altcoin Watchlist: DeFi coins and tokens
- ✓ Why you should trade altcoins
- ✓ How to trade altcoins?
- ✓ Must-have altcoins to own before the AltSeason
- ✓ Altcoin trading guide for beginners
- ✓ Beginners' trading mistakes to avoid
- ✓ Frequently Asked Questions (FAQs)

What are Altcoins?

Altcoins are patterned after the best features of Bitcoin. They both use the basic framework, blockchain technology, peer-to-peer system, and code sharing functionality.

To distinguish themselves from Bitcoin and create their own market, some Altcoins use a different mechanism to validate their transactions or create blocks. Others offer additional features or breakthrough capabilities to attract users.

Slowly but surely, Altcoins are gaining traction in the financial world. In March 2021, CoinMarketCap reported that alternative coins gained more than 40% share of the crypto market.

And while they tend to follow the trajectory of Bitcoin, a lot of analysts and experts are claiming that in due time, Altcoins will be having their own trading signals.

This is because the ecosystem of crypto investing is already maturing and more markets for Altcoins are emerging.

(Circulating supply and price are subject to changes) Source: Gold Price Org July 20,2021

Cryptocurrency	Market Cap	Circulating Supply	Current Price
Bitcoin	601,438,654,476	18,762,718	$32,038
Ethereum	230,431,849,444	116,784,211	$1,975.81
Tether	62,396,028,960	62,113,782,909	$1

Binance Coin	45,066,256, 841	154,533,652	$292.69
Cardano	38,122,956, 586	32,066,390, 668	$1.19
XRP	26,436,361, 719	46,265,302, 471	$1
USD Coin	26,852,704, 393	26,817,435, 136	$1
Dogecoin	26,245,606, 286	130,521,667, 625	$0.20
Polkadot	12,756,321, 315	1,012,065, 607	$12.63
Binance USD	11,348,554, 555	11,300,776, 231	$1
Bitcoin Cash	8,068,168, 825	18,795,512	$429.66
Litecoin	7,824,010, 397	66,752,415	$117.47
Chainlink	6,792,245, 054	440,009,554	$15.47
Stellar	5,273,932, 865	23,306,946, 972	$0.23
Monero	3,539,110, 083	17,957,194	$197.48

How do they differ from Bitcoin?

Every type of Altcoin has its own set of rules. In terms of mining new coins, Altcoins like Litecoin can produce new coins in a matter of 2.5 minutes. Bitcoin only mines bitcoins every 10 minutes using costly hardware. Litecoin and other alternative cryptocurrencies use new coins using common computer hardware.

Altcoins also work to improve the perceived limitations of Bitcoin, which makes them more interesting in the eyes of traders and investors. They introduced smart contracts where Bitcoin has limited capacity. Instead of using Proof-of-Work (PoW), Bitcoin's consensus mechanism to validate transactions and make blocks in the blockchain, they use the Proof-of-Stake (PoS).

What are the Pros and Cons when you invest in altcoins?

Pros

- The variety of available Altcoins offers the fulfillment of Bitcoin's promise that cryptocurrency can be a medium of everyday transactions.

- They claim to be Bitcoin's 'better versions' because they fill the gap in the crypto market.

- Traders and investors have a wide range of Altcoins that offer different functionalities.

- Low transaction fees

Cons

- Compared to Bitcoin, they have a smaller market in terms of investment

- Difficulty in distinguishing different kinds of Altcoins and their functions, making investors confused and disinterested

- The lack of defined investment criteria and regulations makes them more volatile than Bitcoin

- History of 'dead' Altcoins that left investors with huge losses

- Value volatility

- Higher potential for fraud and scams

Trivia

There are 4 buckets of altcoins – native cryptocurrencies, tokens, stablecoins,
and forks.

What are the different kinds of altcoins?

Altcoins are classified according to their consensus mechanism and functionality. They include the following:

- Stablecoins

  Stablecoins are Altcoins that derive their market values from a basket of underlying assets (precious metals, fiat currencies, other cryptocurrencies). The basket represents the security that traders can redeem during the worst bad market day.

Most Stablecoins use government-backed or fiat security. Tether (USDT) and USDC are examples of fiat-backed crypto coins. DAI is a crypto-backed Stablecoin. Commodity-backed (oil or precious metals) are the Paxos Gold and Tether Gold.

Because of their stability, many investors tend to purchase Stablecoins while waiting for the crypto market to show favorable events. They are also great for payment purposes or money transfers anywhere in the globe.

Stablecoins are highly tradeable and liquid. Their value does not change until you decide to move it into another altcoin or Bitcoin.

- Mining-based

  Mining-based altcoins are created through Proof-of-Work (PoW) method. They are mined through algorithms or solving complex problems. Litecoin, Zcash, and Monero are examples of mining-based altcoins.

  There are also pre-mined coins that are distributed before their listing in the crypto markets. XRP of Ripple is an example of this kind.

- Security tokens

  Security tokens are like the traditional stocks, bonds, equities, or derivatives that hold the tradable value of the external assets. These digital tokens guarantee a dividend payout, equity, or ownership. The price of security tokens appreciates over time. They are often sold to traders and investors through ICOs or initial coin offerings.

In essence, they are investment contracts that represent the users' legal ownership of a particular digital or physical asset.

Ownership rights are verified by the network within the blockchain. Once fully verified, security tokens can be traded away for another type of assets, stored in electronic wallets, or used as loan collateral.

One of the forms of security tokens is the securitized tokens. They are usually set up by startup companies and subject to compliance with the regulations of the Federal Laws. They are offered to the interested investors through Security Token Offering (STO).

Examples of security tokens are Bcap (Blockchain Capital, Sia Funds, and Science Blockchain.

- Utility tokens

Utility tokens are utilized in exchange for services or redeem rewards. They are also called app coins or digital coupons that hold special discounts or access to the product or service.

They are blockchain-based assets that are sold by fundraisers or companies to purchase their soon-to-be-introduced product or service.

Utility tokens do not have intrinsic value or pay dividends. They are not considered an instrument of investment and are not subjected to Federal laws compliance.

But utility tokens can provide holders with the right to use the network, help to build the system's internal economy, and vote for the well-being of the network.

Examples of utility tokens are Filecoin, Civic, and Siacon.

Tokens: Security Vs Utility

Tokens are not cryptocurrency coins, but they play an important role in the success of blockchain. They are a representation of value, asset, voting rights, access rights, stake, or anything issued by companies, in particular startups. They are offered through a crowd or public sale – STO (Security Token Offerings) for security tokens and ICO (Initial Coin Offering) for utility coins.

Crypto tokens gain value through their roles, features, and purpose.

- **Roles** include the rights of the token holder within the ecosystem (rights to vote, etcetera), value exchange (buy or sell tokens), toll (gateway to enable functionalities), function (enrich the experience of users), currency (store of value), and earnings (profits or financial benefits).

For tokens to be considered valuable, they must possess more than one role.

- **Purposes** include bootstrapping engagement (right), economy creation (value exchange), skin in the game (toll), enriching the user's experience (function), seamless transactions (currency), distributing benefits (earnings).

- **Features** include product usage, governance, voting, ownership, contribution, product access (rights), work rewards, product creation, buying, spending (value exchange), running smart contracts, usage fees, security deposit (toll), an incentive for usage, connects with users, joining networks (function), transaction unit or payment unity (currency), benefit-sharing, profit sharing, inflation benefits (earnings).

The Howey Test

For tokens to be recognized as security tokens, they should meet the three criteria of the Howey Test. This test determines if the transaction will qualify as an 'investment contract' under the Securities Exchange Act of 1934 and Securities Act of 1993.

- The token represents an investment of money
- The token's investment is in a common enterprise
- There is an expected profit from the work of the third party or promoters

Meet the most important altcoins

Ether (ETH)

Ether is an Ethereum cryptocurrency and operates on its proprietary blockchain. It is second to Bitcoin in terms of market cap and the largest among all Altcoins. This coin is designed for the Ethereum network, but it is also accepted as payment by several online sites that sell services and merchants.

As a platform, Ethereum went live in July 2015 after programmer Vitalik Buterin talked about the idea in 2013. Together with Buterin who is serving as the public face and CEO is Joe Lubin of ConsenSys. It is responsible for the popularity of ICOs (initial coin offerings). It owns a programming language known as Solidity. Ethereum solidifies its position in the crypto world by introducing a programmable blockchain.

Its network serves as a melting pot for games, apps, and financial services, promising ultimate protection of accounts from theft, fraud, and censorship. It accepts Ether as payment for all transactions. As of January 2021, the market cap of ETH was $1,218.59 and a market cap of $138.3 billion.

By the end of 2030, the fearless forecast
of Coin Price Forecast
for Ethereum market value is $5,000.

Litecoin (LTC)

Litecoin was created by a former engineer of Google, Charlie Lee. It was launched in 2011 or just two years after bitcoin. It has a lot of Bitcoin's features, which is why people called it "a silver to Bitcoin's gold." Its software is faster than Bitcoin but almost the same.

It has a supply limit cap of 84 million. By 2023, it is expected to be 50% at its current 2 ½ minutes to mine a block.

The Litecoin Foundation projected that the last blocks will be mined around 2142. As of January 2021, it ranked as the world's 6th –largest crypto with a per-token value that amounts to $153.88 and a market cap of $10.1 billion.

The market value of Litecoin will hit $2,250
by 2030 according
to the Crypto Research Report Group.

Binance Coin (BNB)

Binance coin is categorized as a utility cryptocurrency. It functions as a payment for trading and paying fees on the Binance Exchange. This altcoin was launched in July 2017, running with ERC-20 token in the Ethereum blockchain. Eventually, it is used as the proprietary currency of the Binance Chain, the decentralized blockchain of Binance. The man behind the creation of the Binance Exchange was Changpeng Zhao.

As of January 2021, one BNB was worth $44.26 with a market cap of $6.8 billion.

Coin Price Forecast believes that
Binance market value
by 2030 would reach $1,191.

Bitcoin Cash (BCH)

Bitcoin Cash is Bitcoin's spin-off during a hard fork in August 2017. This coin has its own unique blockchain and can process an average of 116 transactions every second. The original Bitcoin can only process 7 transactions per second. It was originally created with 8 MB blocks and eventually increased to 32 MB for better scalability.

Its primary function is to serve as a payment method or as a 'digital cash'. When it debuted on major exchanges, the opening market value of Bitcoin Cash was up to $900 and jumped to $4,091 during the end of 2017.

Bitcoin Cash aims to create a 21 million supply, just like Bitcoin. As of January 2021, the value per Bitcoin Cash was $513.45 and a market cap of $8.9 billion.

*According to Digital Coin Price, the
market value of Bitcoin Cash
could reach up to $700 by the end of 2021.*

Tether (USDT)

Tether is a dominant coin in terms of crypto trading. It is categorized as a Stablecoin and one of the most popular. It is actually the US dollar's tokenized version, making it very 'stable' in nature. Many people use Tether to hedge their assets against volatility and for liquidity. Tether coins are issued by Hong Kong-based Tether Limited.

Tether is a most-traded type of altcoin because it is cheaper, easier to use, and has lower transaction fees. About 75% of Bitcoin trading this 2021 is using Tether.

The market cap of Tether as of January 2021 was $24.4 billion and its token value was worth $1.

*While the market price of Tether remains $1,
Trading Beast forecast
it would increase to $1.2817439
by the end of 2022.*

Polkadot (DOT)

Polkadot is a unique cryptocurrency with translation architecture and has a heterogeneous multi-chain interchange. Behind the Polkadot are Peter Czaban, Robert Habermeier, and Gavin Wood. Wood is one of the co-founders of Ethereum. He wrote Polkadot's protocol, which is designed to link the blockchains (permission-less and permissioned) and oracles to form a relay chain that offers interoperability of the different networks.

It also allows the developers to generate their own blockchain using Polkadot's security measures. This concept is referred to as shared security.

As of January 2021, 1 DOT's market value was $12.54 and a market cap of $11.2 billion.

By 2030, Coin Price Forecast predicts that the market price of Polkadot would hit $41.81.

Cardano (ADA)

Cardano is dubbed as the 'killer of Ethereum' because its blockchain technology is more efficient. Behind this cryptocurrency is Charles Hoskinson, who left Ethereum after some disagreements with his other co-founders when he saw the direction it was taking. He co-founded this ouroboros proof-of-stake digital currency based on the research-based methodology.

The various research of the project was done by crypto experts, mathematicians, and engineers. Cardano's digital asset is ADA which is named after the English mathematician and 19th-century Countess Ada Lovelace.

As of January 2021, the trading price of 1 ADA was $0.31 with a market cap of $9.8 billion.

By 2030, Price Coin Forecast prediction
for ADA's market price
is $6.03.

Ripple (XRP)

Ripple is both a digital payment system and a cryptocurrency. The founders Jed McCaleb and Chris Larsen made it public in 2021. Its primary process is a remittance and payment settlement asset exchange. Its crypto token is XRP whose function is to act as an intermediary exchange mechanism between two different networks or currencies.

Rather than utilize the blockchain mining process, it adopts the consensus mechanism to confirm the transactions with the help of bank-owned servers. Transactions in Ripple are cheaper and faster. In the context of market capitalization, it was the 5th-largest altcoin with around $60 billion market capitalization and a market price of $1.60.

Coin Price Forecast for XRP's market price by 2030 would be $5.45.

Dogecoin (DOGE)

Dogecoin is the result of the collaboration of two software engineers Jackson Palmer and Billy Markus. They were joking about the cryptocurrencies' wild speculation and decided to make a payment system. That was a joke also, but some individuals saw it as a legitimate investment instrument.

On December 6, 2013, Dogecoin was launched to the public with Shiba Inu dog face as its logo. On May 5, 2021, the market cap of Dogecoin reached $85,314,347,523. It is the latest altcoin that achieved social media hype, thanks to Elon Musk, Gene Simmons, Snoop Dogg, and other known personalities.

In 2030, Dogecoin's market price would reach $17.50 according to the Cryptocurrency Price Prediction.

Stellar (XLM)

Stellar Lumen is a cryptocurrency that was developed by Jed McCaleb and Joyce Kim in the early part of 2014. McCaleb was one of the founders of Ripple Labs and the developer of Ripple protocol. When he left Ripple, he collaborated with Kim and established the Stellar Development Foundation.

Lumens are traded using the blockchain-based Stellar network. The platform's distributed ledger system connects payment systems, banks, and users in low-cost, efficient cross-border transfers of values and payment purposes. Its shining moment happened in 2017 when lumens price soared more than 300 times.

As of January 2021, the market cap of Stellar was $6.1 billion and 1 Lumen is valued at $0.27

According to Coin Price Forecast, the market value of Lumen would be $1.39 by the year 2030.

Monero (XMR)

Monero is a private, secure, and untraceable cryptocurrency that was introduced to the market in April 2014. The open-source blockchain of Monero is opaque, disguising the users' addresses and making the transaction details including the amount anonymous. This total privacy is due to ring signatures.

As of January 2021, the market cap of Monero was $2.8 billion and the amount per 1 XMR amounted to $158.37.

Coin Price Forecast has predicted that by 2030, the market price of Monero would reach $1,006.

Tron (TRX)

Founded by Tron Foundation headed by its CEO Justin Sun, Tron uses the peer-to-peer (P2P) and blockchain components. To process transactions, it utilizes the proof-of-stake algorithms. It is also becoming a huge competition to Paypal and other payment processors because of its popularity among content consumers and content creators.

Its cryptocurrency is Tronix (TRX), which is worth $0.05 can be used to pay content producers and access what they are offering.In terms of market capitalization, TRX ranked 22nd in the March 2021 list of cryptocurrencies.

In 2030, TRX market price would hit $0.3048 according to the Coin Price Forecast.

ZCash (ZEC)

ZCash is a crypto coin that provides what Bitcoin cannot- the option for the transactions to be viewed if the users allow it.

It means that they can protect their privacy by being un-trackable in the blockchain. The enhanced privacy features of this altcoin are due to the zk-SNARKs (Zero-Knowledge Proofs), which validate transactions without compromising the private details of the users.

It was introduced to the crypto market in October 2016 by its founder Zooko Wilcox-O'Hearn. The currency symbol of ZCash is ZEC. Its market capitalization is $1,145,782,989 with over $11 million in circulation.

Coin Price Forecast predicts
that in 2030, ZCash market price
would jump to $449.

NEO

NEO was founded in 2014 by Erik Zhan and Da Hongfei as AntShares but later rebranded into NEO. Its Onchain technology offers a centralized approach that enables 'dapps' or decentralized applications that generate smart contracts.

This is in line with their goal of creating a digital smart economy that delivers fast, secure, and seamless transactions.

And while the Chinese government still imposes restrictions on crypto transactions in the nation, NEO seems to be thriving well in the virtual ecosystem. It has a 3rd key feature that separates it from other blockchain-based cryptos – the digital identity.

NEO's base asset is the NEO token that creates GAS tokens. NEO has a market cap of over $2 billion. It has more than $70 million coins in circulation.

Lite Forex forecasts that
NEO would be hitting more than
$7,000 in 2030 based

Watchlist: DeFi coins and tokens that are taking markets by storm

Decentralized finance or **DeFi** is an innovative method to execute various financial transactions with the help of apps. It is done over the blockchain, eliminating the traditional intermediaries (banks, exchanges, brokerages). DeFi uses smart contracts or code bits that process the transactions once the required conditions are met. Smart contracts self-execute once the expectations occurred.

In essence, DeFi is the concept that defines any transaction or application that uses cryptocurrency or blockchain technology in creating an alternative financial product. It offers a cheaper, faster option of digital peer-to-peer transactions with no minimum transaction amount. In 2020, DeFi tokens outperformed BTC. As of April 22, 2021, it has reached its TLV (total value locked) at $59.07 billion.

Here's a list of the top DeFi tokens that are showing incredible growth:

- **Uniswap (UNI)**

  The governance token and native currency of Uniswap is UNI. The crypto coins were first distributed to the users of the decentralized finance protocol. Each user that has utilized it before September 1, 2020, was given 400 UNI tokens ($1,400 worth during that time).

Uniswap was a brainchild of the former Siemen's mechanical engineer Hayden Adams on November 2, 2018. It was popular among investors and traders because the protocol provides automated transactions using smart contracts mostly on the Ethereum blockchain.

In terms of daily trading volume, Uniswap was the 4th overall 4th largest crypto exchange in October 2020. It generated $2-3 million in fees every day in March 2021. UNI's market cap is over $10 billion.

- **Chainlink (LINK)**

  Chainlink's token is Ethereum (ERC-677) based. As of January 2021, 1 LINK is worth $21.53 and has an $8.6 billion market cap. Chainlink is the industry's standard decentralized oracle network. It empowers smart contracts to access off-chain computation and real-world data in a secure manner. With the backing up of blockchain technology, Chainlink offers the utmost security and reliability.

  It was established by Sergey Nazarov in 2017 and has garnered $32 million during its ICO (initial coin offering).

- **Maker**

  Maker's TLV (total value locked) is $10 billion and has a market capitalization of 4.5 billion. It experienced its all-time high on April 22, 2021, with a $4,943.66 market price. It experienced its all-time low on January 30, 2017 with $21.06.

  Maker is the MakerDao's governance token that holds the record of being the first blockchain-based protocol that started DeFi's booming market as well as the automated crypto-lending platforms. This token allows users to vote using the borrowing and lending system that creates the Stablecoin DAI, which is a community-managed cryptocurrency.

- **Compound (COMP)**

  After using the Ethereum network for 3 years, Compound finally launched COMP as its native token in June 2020. Its total value locked (TLV) is $9.5 billion with a market cap of $2.8 billion. It reached its all-time high of $612 on April 16, 2021.

  Its popularity in the crypto market is anchored on its borrowing and lending decentralized blockchain technology. Users earn interests or cTokens when they deposit their cryptocurrency in any of the Compound pools. The cTokens represent your C pool stake, so when you deposit Ether, you will be getting ETH. Moreover, for as low as 1% total COMP supply, you can vote for the proposals regarding the protocol change or submit your proposal.

- **Ankr (ANKR)**

  As of April 22, 2021, the market cap of Ankr was $1.05 billion with a limited supply that totals 10 billion. As of today, there are over 7 billion ANKR coins circulating in the market.

  This Ethereum token powers up the Web3 infrastructure of Ankr. It is a cross-chain staking platform that builds dApps and hosting nodes that enhance the blockchain ecosystem's efficiency. ANKR is used as payment for API services and node deployment.

- **Aave (AAVE)**

Aave's protocol allows the users to act as a depositor or a borrower. It has interesting features that offer loans without collateral and flash loans. The protocol also stores digital funds on non-custodial smart contracts of the Ethereum blockchain. AAVE token comes with a voting right to improve the protocols and participate in governance. It reached a $668 all-time high price on May 18.

- **Mantra Dao (OM)**

  The native token of Mantra Dao is OM, which provides full voting rights for the users. This community-based DeFi platform focuses on governance, lending, and staking. The token holders govern the ecosystem and are given rewards for their positive contributions. This is through Karma, which is the system's reputation mechanism (works the same as credit scores). Mantra Dao is utilizing the public blockchain Riochain, which is both secure and scalable.

- **Coti Network (COTI)**

  COTI's reputation has been moving upward consistently since May 24, 2021, when it sparked a bullish engulfing candlestick. This DeFi platform helps various organizations build their own payment systems and digitize their own cryptocurrencies.

  Its crypto is categorized as DAG or directed acyclic graph. It does not need miners and blocks to use blockchain. It uses the consensus algorithm Trustchain which allows one-click requests for payment purposes, uses trust scores when confirming transactions, and utilizes smart contracts.

  Other interesting developments include the integration of margin trading in the platform, the release of credit card processing solution Paywize, and the long-overdue integration with partner Celsius.

- **Serum (SRM)**

  The native token of Serum is SRM, which has a 10 billion maximum supply. Ten percent of the total supply was already unlocked during its first year, while the remaining ninety percent will be unlocked within the 7-year period. About 50 million tokens are already circulating in the crypto sphere.

  The decentralized ecosystem and exchange offer a very fast and low fee in processing transactions. Working on the SOL or Solana network, it can make 50,000 transactions every second.

- **Beam (BEAM)**

  BEAM tokens have a total value of $21.9 million as of December 2020. Currently, its trading price is between $0525 and $0.96. The Beam is a private DeFi platform that guarantees safe, quick, and anonymous transactions.

  It is utilizing two protocols- LelantusMW and Mimblewimble. They work together in creating smart contracts between crypto users without a third party. All transactions do not show private information on the blockchain, making them private by default.

  ### Key Point

  *When trading crypto, always treat it
  as a part-time or full-time business
  and not a job or a hobby.*

Why you should trade altcoins

The breakthrough success and its decade-old staying power in the crypto market make alternative coins more attractive to people who want to start small and test the trading game.

History showed that during the Bitcoin bull cycle in 2014, its previous $250 all-time high reached $1,200. During that time, the market value of Litecoin hit $50. Bitcoin soared again when Elon Musk invested $1.5 billion, creating a new all-time high. Again, the price surge benefitted the altcoins.

Many crypto experts are predicting that 2021 can be an altseason or year of altcoins. Altcoin season is an exciting period for altcoin holders because of the lucrative opportunities to gain substantial profits. The most notable Altseason happened in December 2017.

Other reasons:

- You can start small or just with $100 and gain a 100% to 1,000% return.

- Crypto is the future. It literally alters the future of the payment system, trading, investing, and more. And technology keeps innovating and transforming every single moment.

- As Bitcoin grows stronger, altcoins follow.

- There is thrill and fun in riding the crypto waves- the phenomenal gains and the dramatic lows. While there are risks, the promise of profiting from altcoin trading is exciting.

- Getting started in altcoin trading is easy. Once your account is verified and activated, you are in. Trading does not need huge capital, qualifications, or experience.

How to trade altcoins?

To begin trading altcoins, you first need to register an account. Registration is open and free to any interested trader. Study the different available exchanges and select the one that matches your goals and expectations.

- Accomplish the online form with the necessary information which typically requires name, contact number, email address, and password.

- The system will send a verification message to your email address and you need to press the link to activate your trading account.

- Invest an initial amount as your trading fund.

- Buy your altcoins and start trading.

- Monitor your profits/losses.

- Know when to sell your altcoins.

- Cash out.

If you are still testing the waters, you can try these investment strategies:

1. Buy & HODL
Holding out on your altcoin longer is always a safe and effective way. All you need is a reliable exchange and a crypto wallet to generate passive income. You can also buy just small fractions of coins or tokens to increase your crypto holdings.

2. Compound interests
Focus on creating a small percentage gain a day through compound interests. You can earn 10% every day for 30 days and double your initial investment

3. Follow the hype.

Remember that in altcoin trading exchanges, you are not competing with the hardcore Bitcoin traders, but more of the average traders.

4. **Stake and save**

Staking is a great way to support the ecosystem of the crypto network. It involves holding the tokens in a staking pool or a network to earn interest. The network will use the staked tokens for transaction verification and then paying a return.

Must-have altcoins to own before the altseason:

The Top Three

Ethereum (Ether)

This popular crypto coin was the first altcoin that drove the previous altseason. In 2018, it set a phenomenally high price for altcoins when it jumped to $1,500. At present, Ethereum is the world's second-largest cryptocurrency that gained over 450% growth in 2020.

Many are speculating that Ethereum can break the all-time high and hit $2,000 or more because of the following factors:

- o strong fundamentals

- o growing interest of the institutional investors

- o increased developer activities

- o infinite innovation potential of its ecosystem

- o store value as a payment unit

- o rise of DeFi

- o the launch of the Ethereum 2.0

Binance Coin (BNB)

In terms of market cap and market value, this coin is gaining significant growth since 2017, the year when it launched its own decentralized exchange BNB's success can be attributed to its cheaper fees and faster transaction process.

Litecoin (LTC)

Its parabolic cycle gives Litecoin momentum to rank 8th in the total market cap of the largest crypto. It has gained more than 250% growth in 2020 and is regarded as one of the must-have altcoins. Litecoin is known for its affordable and lightning-fast transaction speed.

The Runner-Ups

Bitcoin Cash (BCH)

This P2P altcoin offers relatively quick, low-cost cross-border transactions. It was created to become a good alternative for a more expensive Bitcoin transaction. This alternative coin is on the list of the top 10 cryptocurrencies in terms of market cap.

Tron (TRX)

Tron is continuing its journey to the top, becoming one of the most exciting altcoins to trade these forthcoming years. Its network shields user's data and privacy.

Moreover, it gained huge traction among content creators because they can easily monetize their digital works using TRX.

Fun Trivia

History shows that the largest ICO happened in 2017 when Filecoin collected its first $200 million in about 30 minutes and $257 million in total.

Altcoin trading guide for beginners

Are you excited to join the millionaires' club by trading Altcoins? Crypto trading is one of the easiest, but also the riskiest undertaking to earn your millions. So, how to profit from Altcoin trading? Preparation and understanding how it works are the keys to success.

1. Understand the dynamics of the cryptocurrency market.

While you are seeing people who are generating huge profits, many are losing significant amounts, too. Just like forex markets, the crypto markets operate in buying and selling assets. What makes altcoin trading highly volatile is the lack of regulatory rules because of its free operation model. But this volatility is viewed by traders as a profitable opportunity while mastering the strategies of winning.

2. Get yourself familiar with the 2 main trading strategies.

- Short-term strategy

  It refers to trading where traders hold the altcoins for weeks, days, hours, or even minutes. Holding the cryptocurrencies for several months can also be classified as short-term trading. Day trading is an example of a short-term strategy.

  Pros

- High-return opportunity – Prices of altcoins can swing overnight or double in a few hours.

- 24/7 trading – This strategy does not conform to the U.S. Pattern Day Trading Rule that prohibits traders with below $25,000 balance in their accounts to trade more than three days a week.

Cons

- Higher volatility – The market prices of Altcoins change swiftly due to their volatile nature.

- Requires big investment to gain huge returns – Beginners who lack the financial muscle to trade consistently despite some losses along the way will lose the shining opportunities. Another factor is the lack of confidence or fear of losing lots of money.

- Long-term strategy

Traders who use this technique buy altcoins and hold them for a certain period like 1 year or until the price has grown considerably.

Pros

- Easy trading – All you need to do is to buy and hold your cryptocurrency as long as you want. You don't need to stress yourself by monitoring the price movement constantly and looking for windows of opportunity to sell your altcoins.

- Does not require a lot of money to start trading- This strategy lets you buy altcoins progressively to expand your investment portfolio.

Cons

- Missing quick gain opportunities – Price rises and falls within short periods regularly, so you miss the golden chances to earn profits when you opt for a long-term strategy.

3. Anticipate the Altseason

During this season, traders do not preserve or hold altcoins. Instead, they seize the opportunities to reap large rewards. There is a buzz of positive anticipation in the air as the value of altcoins starts to rise.

Investors and traders become more active in the virtual sphere, accumulating more crypto or fiat to maximize their chosen trading or investing strategies.

Here are some tips to optimize the benefits of the next altseason:

- Learn the meaning of Bitcoin dominance

  Bitcoin dominance simply means that Bitcoin has a larger market share percentage. It is characterized by the number of traders holding or selling their BTC. As the number spikes, the bitcoin's market cap also surges and negatively impacts the altcoin's market value.

  But when this dominance of bitcoin drops and holders begin to sell their BTC, the value of altcoins will soar. This is the onset of the much-anticipated altseason. It is typical during this period for bitcoin owners to exchange their assets for alternative coins or fiat currency.

This is an excellent time to dispose of your long-term altcoin holdings because many investors would prefer to buy altcoins instead of BTC.

- Make sure that you are using the right tools

  The right investment or trading tools will make your journey in the crypto market much easier and provide better outcomes. It is necessary to invest in the most efficient and effective tools to help you as a beginner.

  And because the altseason does not stay for long, it is crucial to use a trading app or crypto exchange that will give your profits every time there is a price fluctuation.

  What are these tools? They refer to portfolio balancers, portfolio managers, crypto news aggregators, market watchers, charts, electronic wallets, trading apps, and trading exchanges.

- Do not FOMO

  FOMO or fear of missing out always brings a snowball effect, spiking the prices of altcoins. When people sense that the altseason is on the horizon, the majority is afraid to be left out so they invest more, resulting in the spiraling of altcoins' market value to the top.

  As a beginner, do not live in FOMO to avoid costly mistakes. While losing is part of the trading journey, it's best to delve deeper and learn how the crypto market can work to your advantage. Do not just rely on your instincts. Learn and master the best techniques that can help you gain more.

- Always take your profits

Be smart and sell your altcoins when the bitcoin dominance is declining.

During this period, the prices of altcoins are at their peak. Do not miss the chance of profiting significant gains by holding on to them longer. Some traders hold on longer thinking that the momentum will continue, then get surprised when the market displays a sudden retracement.

- Diversify your portfolio

As the cliché goes, "Never place all your golden eggs in a single basket." This means diversifying your portfolio with altcoins that are showing great potential as winners. To know which are the best ones to trade, always conduct technical and fundamental analyses. Altcoin diversification helps you avoid many losses when one or two of your crypto coins/tokens do not perform well. You can still break even or gain profits from other performing altcoins in your portfolio.

Beginners' trading mistakes that you should avoid

- Never trade what you cannot afford to lose.

- Do not take unnecessary risks, trade wisely.

- Do not be greedy when you start making money in trading. Take out your profits whenever possible.

- Don't chase 1,000% and live in FOMO.

- Make your own decisions based on technical and fundamental analysis, not because of others' opinions. Stop living in fear, uncertainty, and doubt (FUD).

- Don't fall in pump and dump or when the altcoin prices are inflated by trader's groups.

- Avoid making an emotional decision or panic buying and selling altcoins.

- Set stop loss to protect your gains.

- Higher potential for fraud and scams

TRIVIA

Namecoin (NMC) was launched on
April 18, 2011, considered the first altcoin.
It is now a dead coin after a 7-year history.
NMC has been credited for showing that there
is space in the crypto world other than Bitcoin.

FAQs

Can I cancel my altcoin trade that has not been fulfilled yet?

Yes. To cancel your trade order, simply press the system's "CANCEL" button. Once the cancellation is processed, your payment will be credited back to your trading account.

Is there a fee for canceling a trader order?

You don't need to pay fees for canceling trade orders.

What if I make a trading error, is it possible to reverse it?

No. All trades are final and irreversible.

Chapter 7

Best Exchanges for Bitcoins and Altcoins

In the general context, exchange refers to the marketplace where financial instruments, commodities, derivatives, and securities are traded for profits. Its core function is to provide a venue for orderly and fair trading transactions. It disseminates updated price information and other details of the trading assets.

An exchange is a platform where individuals, companies, groups, or government entities sell securities or stocks to interested investors to raise capital.

At a glance

- ✓ **What is a crypto exchange?**
- ✓ **How does it work?**
- ✓ **Top exchanges to check out**
- ✓ **Other trading exchanges to consider**
- ✓ **Frequently Asked Questions (FAQs**

What exactly is a crypto exchange?

To jumpstart your trading journey, you need a place to buy altcoins. The kind of altcoin you wish to access is determined by the trading platform you select. With hundreds of choices, you need to be smart in the selection. The best exchange for you has the features and the crypto coins or tokens you want to invest in.

A crypto exchange or DCE (digital currency exchange) allows people to trade cryptocurrencies to own other digital currencies or fiat money. It can be a matching platform or a market maker. The first type matches the needs of buyers and sellers and charges transaction fees. A market maker exchange provides bid-ask spreads and gets commission for rendering its service.

How does it work?

In the crypto business, exchanges are essential.

- They send coins to the digital wallets of users.
- They facilitate trading transactions.
- They transfer profits to the accounts.
- They offer conversion of cryptocurrency balances into fiat currency using anonymous prepaid cards, allowing users to withdraw funds using ATMs anywhere in the world.

Some crypto exchanges allow altcoin-bitcoin pairs or buy/sell altcoins using BTC. It works well for traders who like tracking the performance of their investment portfolio against Bitcoin-the king of cryptocurrency.

Other exchanges offer interest-bearing accounts, financial derivatives, or pre-approved lending.

Satoshi Nakamoto Quote

"Lost coins make everyone else coins worth slightly more."

Top crypto exchanges to check out

Crypto exchanges support different kinds of altcoins. This is why you need to weigh the pros and cons of every option.

It is also important to review the transaction fees, coin availability, trading volume, security measures, and ease of use of the platform.

Let's take a look.

Binance: The best exchange for traders

Binance offers the widest range of altcoins. It supports 184 cryptocurrencies and tokens, 591 trading pairs, and more than 150 payment methods.

Binance also offers financial derivatives and allows margin trading for those who want to leverage their cryptocurrency positions.

It is the leading exchange that allows a variety of trading choices: altcoins against Bitcoin, altcoins against the U.S. dollar or other fiat currency, and USDT trading pairs.

Features and benefits:

- Has various tools for efficient trading
- Peer-to-peer crypto trading with zero fees

- 24/7 customer service
- Compatibility with Web, PC, and iOS or Android devices
- Delivers an average daily trading volume of 1.2 bn or over 1,400,000 transactions in every second
- Offers both advanced or basic trading exchange interfaces

- Has supporting services that allow users to transact using digital currency
- Provides an electronic wallet to store the virtual funds
- Offers programs to traders to make intelligent investment decisions and program for miners
- VIP program that frequently offers discounts and rewards

Binance is also known for offering the lowest fees for transactions. You can use their native token Binance coin (BNB) to pay transaction fees and get a discount. Binance does not charge fees for fund deposits, only when you withdraw your balances.

TRADING ON BINANCE

Before you trade your altcoins on Binance, you need to be aware of minor details that can impact your trading success. This includes fees, security measures, and possible taxes. In terms of fee, the exchange charges a flat fee of 0.1% to execute both buying or selling cryptocurrency. You get to pay the transaction fee once your order is fulfilled.

- If you are using another wallet, you need to transfer your altcoin to the Binance wallet.
- Once you have the fund, you can sell your altcoin for Bitcoin or Ethereum.
- If you're buying, set a market order (instant purchase or sell at current price) or a limit order (lets you enter/exit at a certain price point).
- Choose your base currency (the mainstream crypto that you wish to trade) for BTC or ETH.

- Pick the altcoin you want to sell (for example Stellar, EOS, or BNB) by tapping the ticker that opens up to the market page of the coin.

- Add your chosen altcoins to Favorites by tapping the star that is located in the upper right corner of the page for easy tracking.
- If you use a limit order, you need to tap the 'Order Book' on altcoin's market page. Input the price you wish to offload your crypto coin for and the quantity, then execute trading by tapping the red button 'Sell'.
- If you are utilizing the market order strategy, simply tap the 'Market Trades' in your altcoin and press the green button 'Sell'. After entering the quantity, tap the red button 'Sell' to execute your trading transaction. Binance will automatically convert the altcoin to ETH or BTC.

Coinbase: The best exchange for beginners and earning rewards

Coinbase is a friendly exchange for newbies who want to explore the potentials of cryptocurrencies. It was initially created for Bitcoin trading but eventually evolved to include altcoins and tokens to suit its decentralized nature. Now, it has more than 50 altcoins you can choose from. This online platform can be used for transferring, storing, buying, and selling digital currency. It supports over 100 countries that allow crypto transactions.

Features and benefits:

- provides an advanced trading platform to track your digital currency
- offers staking rewards

- provides an app that is compatible with Android and iOS mobile
- offers a digital wallet for retail investors and traders
- allows users to schedule their trading (daily, weekly, monthly)
- provides a custodial account for institutions
- has own stable coin that is backed-up by the U.S. dollars
- allows automatic conversion of one type of altcoin into another altcoin
- offers multiple investment options for institutional and individual clients
- has a Coinbase Earn account option where you receive crypto assets after watching educational videos
- allows fund deposits using a bank account, debit card, or credit card
- offers phone support and great customer service
- allows setting up of two-factor authentication for tighter security
- stores 98% of customers' money in cold storage
- low withdrawal and trading fees

Coinbase offers two other options:

- Coinbase Prime – It is designed for high-net-worth individuals and institutions. Individual accounts should have at least a $1 million deposit. Institutionalized clients gain access to the Asset Hub (where issuers can list and grow assets), cold or offline storage, and commerce services.

- Coinbase Pro – It is specially created for advanced traders. It allows users to access features like real-time order books, charting tools, and secure trading bots.

TRADING ON COINBASE

Log in to your account to check your portfolio balance and the performance of your crypto in time frames.

- To purchase altcoin, tap the 'Buy crypto' button above the portfolio balance. Enter a market order and a dollar value for the coin you want to buy. The button also gives you an option to set up a recurring order, convert crypto, or sell it.

- Check the page's top-right section to see the Send and Receive options. The action lets you transfer crypto by withdrawing funds from your Coinbase wallet or receive crypto via the virtual wallet.

Coinbase trading rules

- Every Trader's Account has a list of available Order Books. It settles trades in Fiat Currency and Digital Asset Trading Pairs.
- Users can place a Market Order, Stop order, or Limit Order. You can still cancel your order before it is fulfilled. Coinbase does not charge a fee for canceling orders.
- Traders who will try placing an Order to partially or completely fill more than 2% of the last trading price would receive a slippage warning.
- All types of Orders are subject to minimum and maximum size requirements.
- Traders are subject to Price-Time Priority or the time when the Taker Orders are posted.

- Both Coinbase Prime and Coinbase Pro charge a Taker Fee and a Maker Fee. Fees are calculated based on the quantity of the Order and charge in the Quote Asset.
- All Coinbase Trades are final and irreversible.
- Traders are not allowed to act as both takers and makers. Any attempt results in the cancelation of both Orders or self-execution.

Gemini: The best exchange for mobile users

Gemini has versatile features that work excellently for mobile users. It has a reliable mobile app for Android and iOS, letting you manage or monitor your crypto wherever you are. It is a fully regulated cryptocurrency exchange, offering bitcoin and other cryptocurrencies. This privately-owned exchange was introduced by Cameron and Tyler Winklevoss in 2015.

Features and benefits:

- has its own currency- the Gemini stablecoin
- allows users of the exchange to sell, buy, store, and trade crypto
- has a user-friendly mobile app and platform
- has an interest-paying savings account that gives users up to 7.4% balance interest
- has a payment app
- will have a Gemini credit card sometime in 2021
- offers up to 0% discount for volume traders
- operates 24/7, except during occasional maintenance window
- offers various options of limit orders like the IOC (immediate or-cancel), MOC (maker or-cancel), and AO (auction-only)

- is duly licensed by the NYDFS (NY State Department of Financial Services) to provide custodial services
- offers options for big institutional clients to have a segregated custody account that uses the Cold Storage system
- offers fee-free for extremely high-dollar transactions and separate fee structures for its mobile app, Active Trader, and Gemini Exchange offerings
- allows users to use a bank account to deposit and withdraw their funds

TRADING ON GEMINI

The interface of Gemini has a simple design that makes placing an order and trading convenient, even for beginners.

- To accumulate coins, find Buy on the Gemini's menu bar and select the crypto you wish to have.
- Check your remaining fund near the top of your computer or mobile screen. It shows both in bitcoin value and US dollar value.
- Review the total amount of your purchase together with the transaction fee before confirming your purchase. To complete the process, click Buy.
- To sell your altcoin, the process is the same. Select Sell and then input the quantity of coin you like to sell.

For more advanced traders, Gemini has the ActiveTrader. It features a block trading technique, multiple order types, advanced charting, and auctions. It can process and execute crypto trades in microseconds, with no security or reliability compromises.

ActiveTrader also provides order book visibility and has trading pair selectors that let you maximize the trading opportunities. It is optimized for smartphones and other mobile browsers.

eToro: The best exchange for active cryptocurrency traders

eToro is a social media trading platform for beginners. It was initially created as a forex platform that later on adapted the necessary tools for trading cryptocurrencies. This makes it excellent for active traders in both fields.

It eliminated the withdrawal for all U.S. clients, but still imposed a $5 fee for customers from other countries. Moreover, all U.S. traders can trade crypto in registered states.

Features and benefits:

- allows 24/7 trading of 15 cryptocurrencies
- has a unique feature CopyTrader, which allows the users to imitate the popular portfolio of traders by allocating a part of their funds and copy the way they trade
- comes with an easy-to-navigate, graphical interface and advantageous features
- allows traders to communicate ideas to help each other

TRADING ON eTORO

eToro's trading system requires manual input. Its capability to do social copy trading in real-time makes it a popular trading platform.

- To make money in eToro, you need to make the right choices such as keeping average loss smaller against average profit or taking risk-management decisions.
- When copy-trading, analyze the database of traders and decide what to copy, set maximum draw-down threshold, and how much funds to budget for each provider.
- Open leveraged or short positions with the help of CFDs.
- Opt for eToro long-term investment option which is CopyPortfolio. This concept bundles different financial assets or top traders into one investment instrument.

It has 3 types – Market Portfolio (finance, tech, gaming), Partner Portfolio (created by financial institution partners), and Top Trader Portfolio (traders with best practices).

CEX.IO: The exchange that offers the best cryptocurrency selection

CEX.IO is a crypto exchange that supports global traders in 48 US states and about 99% of countries in the world. It has over 80 crypto coins and tokens. It supports frequency trading and scalping to get data and assets.

Features and benefits:

- traders to use PayPal Debit MasterCard, MasterCard, and Visa card
- has 'instant buy' feature (exclusive for debit and credit cardholders)
- offers crypto-backed loans and staking rewards

- has a mobile app for traders on-the-go
- provides spot trading and margin trading accounts for more advanced traders
- uses taker/maker schedule that is based on a 30-day trading volume
- allows users to trade on the margin platform with over 100 times leverage without securing another account
- provides downloadable reports that show transaction history and real-time account balances
- is registered in different locations across the world as a money transmitter business
- PCI DSS (Payment Card Industry Data Security Standard) compliant
- stores the users' funds on digital wallets that are locked in secure vaults

TRADING ON CEX.IO

There are 4 levels of trading accounts in CEX.IO. The account you get depends on the verification requirements you presented. The basic account can buy up to $2,000 worth of bitcoin and altcoins per month.

Verified accounts require an ID, driver's license, passport, proof of residency, and a selfie holding your valid identification card. You get the chance to purchase up to $100,000 worth of coins every month.

The last two accounts which are Corporate and Individual Business allow holders to buy unlimited amounts of coins.

Using a mobile app:

- To buy altcoins, go to the Trade page.
- Use the Limit Order or Market Order to place your order.
- Go to the screen top to change the currency and click your preferred pair button,
- Click 'Buy' to view the amount of the crypto coin you will get based on the present exchange rate. After agreeing to the conditions, click 'Buy' again to complete your transaction.
- If you are using Market Order, your purchased coin will instantly be added to your account balance. If you are selling your altcoin using this order, enter the amount, tap the 'Sell' button, and confirm your action.
- To track your CEX.IO, open the Trade Pro History page.

Crypto.com: The best exchange for DeFi Exchanges

Crypto.com is one of the most secure and fastest exchanges that allow users to trade, transfer, or store more than 90 types of cryptocurrency. It has its own coin- the CRO or Crypto.com coin that offers more benefits as users stake more. It is both a crypto trading and payment platform.

It has a DeFi wallet, which is a non-custodial e-wallet that allows access to DeFi services, gives you total control of your keys, lets you farm and swap DeFi token, stake CRO to boost up to 20x yield, earn interests without lock-up terms, and send cryptocurrency at your chosen network fee and confirmation speed. It supports over 30 cryptocurrencies and stable coins.

Features and benefits:

- offers lower trading fees
- provides more rewards and interests on crypto deposits
- has a maker-taker pricing structure that rewards clients with greater trading volumes
- offers multiple ways to users who want to earn digital coins/tokens
- has a Crypto.com Visa Card that lets you spend your coins anywhere in the world where Visa is acceptable and earn an 8% interest
- offers 24/7 customer support
- has high liquidity
- offers 3x leverage in margin trading
- offers up to 50x leverage and ultra-low latency in derivatives trading

TRADING ON CRYPTO.COM

Once your account is up, you can transfer funds and begin trading.

- Check Balances using the top right button on the navigation menu to view the list of coins and tokens you can choose to deposit.
- Simply tap the 'Deposit' button to the address where you need to deposit the crypto.
- To withdraw funds, click the 'Withdraw' button. You have the option to transfer fiat currency to the app or withdraw funds from your external wallet.

- The simple interface of the platform is easy to use. On the left side, you can view the trading chart. On the right side, the types of orders and order books can be seen. To monitor the performance, check the chart below.
- To open a trade position, go to the Markets on the top left section of the navigation bar. Choose the market you wish to trade in and the pair you want to trade. Select Trade and input the necessary information on the fields.
- Crypto.com exchange uses a market order and a limit order. Market order simply involves specifying the amount of crypto you wish to purchase and it will be executed at the order's book best possible rate. On the other hand, when you use a limit order, the transaction will be filled once it reaches the lower price.

- There are no deposit and withdrawal fees in Crypto.com, only the on-chain transaction cost. Moreover, the more trades you do, the fewer transaction fees you will pay.

BitSquare: The best decentralized exchange

BISQ or BitSquare is a decentralized exchange, which means that the exchange does not hold your funds and there is no authority controlling the network. It uses a Multisignature wallet that asks for the seller, buyer, and independent arbitrator signatures.

Features and benefits:

- allows anonymous trading
- good list of altcoins and fiat currencies, including the rare ones
- has over 20 payment options like cash deposit, SEPA, bank transfer
- no deposit and withdrawal fees
- offers peer-to-peer trading, so you just need to pay the blockchain transaction fee
  depending on the amount you wish to trade
- buyers and sellers also need to pay arbitrator and holding fees
- excellent security
- easy-to-use interface and charts with trading information

TRADING ON BITSQUARE

The main characteristic of BISQ is decentralization, so each transaction is completely unique.

- To prevent cheating, it requires traders to deposit a security amount of 0.1 Bitcoin and 2 Bitcoins from the arbitrator. In return, the arbitrator earns a fee for successful transactions.
- An arbitrator will be selected randomly to be the third signature holder, adding security to every trading transaction.
- The system will place the coins to be sold and holding fees in the MultiSig wallet and lock them up until the deal is successfully confirmed.
- You can trade any of the altcoins available on the platform.

Kraken: The best exchange for margin and futures traders

Kraken supports more than 50 cryptocurrencies and traders in approximately 200 countries. It is one of the great exchanges for futures and margin trading as well as OTC trading. Its basic and user-friendly platform interface is perfect for beginners. It is a top choice of European traders for altcoin trading. Users who live in most parts of the European Union, U.S., Canada, and Japan can use their bank account for fund deposits and withdrawals.

Features and benefits:

- offers wider options for institutional and retail investors
- global trading and investing support
- has margin accounts that allow users to borrow up to 5x the crypto balance
- allows futures trading for Bitcoin, Litecoin, Ripple, Ethereum, and Bitcoin Cash
- offers staking rewards
- has a mobile app that is compatible with iOS and Android devices
- provides educational resources
- high-net-worth and institutional clients have access to Kraken's account management and consultation services
- trading fees can be as high as 0.26% or low as 0.02%
- offers live chat support

TRADING ON KRAKEN

Once your account is up, you can transfer funds and begin trading.

- The fastest way to sell, buy, or convert crypto in Kraken is using the 'Buy Crypto' button.
- Choose your preferred currency pair (ETH for US dollar or BTC to Euro) from the quote/ticker bar on the Trade page.
- Next, fill out the New Order form and choose whether to use a Limit Order or a Market Order.

- Submit your order and click the large Sell/Buy button. You can double-check the order in the confirmation screen (or skip it by checking a box).

- If you select the Market Order, the trade is instantly executed. Limit Order requires a short waiting period.

Bittrex: The best exchange for account security

Nothing beats Bittrex in the context of security. Along with its two-factor authentication, it keeps funds in cold storage using a multi-stage wallet method. Moreover, the transaction fees are lower than other exchanges. Its trading engine is designed for speed and scalability, providing real-time order execution.

Features and benefits:

- withdrawals and deposits of US dollars are free of charge
- imposes small network fee for crypto withdrawals
- uses maker/taker fee based on the unit of assets you trade in a month or trading volume
- has Instant Buy/Sell feature

- compatibility with Android or iOS mobile devices

TRADING ON BITTREX

Once your trading account is activated, you can begin trading. Check the Bittrex markets to find your base currency- Bitcoin Market, Ethereum Market, and USDT Market.

- Deposit the cryptocurrency you purchased into your Bittrex account. It will serve as your base currency to purchase the altcoins you want.
- Set up your Buy Order by adding the quantity of altcoin you desire to buy and the amount or price you want to spend.
- If you are off-loading your altcoins, set up a Sell order. Select the amount of crypto you wish to sell and the price you want for them.
- Confirm your transaction.

Poloniex: The exchange with a huge list of altcoins

This U.S.-based crypto exchange was established by Tristan D'Agosta in 2014 and has a high trading volume and liquidity. One downside of Poloniex is not supporting fiat currencies. It requires you to buy cryptocurrency to fund your trading account.

Features and benefits:

- deposits and withdrawal of funds are both free, only blockchain fee
- trading fees depend on the amount you spend – 0.25% to 0%
- good customer service, which includes live chat
- 24/7 support team to answer your concerns and resolve issues
- various trading tools like graphs and charts
- excellent security system
- big selection of altcoins
- user-friendly platform that works well for beginners and experienced traders
- allows users to access airdrops or distribution of crypto coins or tokens
- the app lets you connect with banks and cards
- lets you run bot trading strategies and smart algorithms
- allows you to do margin trading using a wide range of crypto pairs for bigger profits
- helps you earn without active trading through soft staking or P2P lending
- easy-to-use interface and charts with trading information

TRADING ON POLONIEX

Poloniex has everything you need to begin trading.

- Use your bank account, debit card, or credit card to purchase or sell your cryptocurrency.

- Trade your crypto assets with about 25 margin trading pairs and more than 200 spot trading pairs.

- Trade Poloniex Futures and leverage your crypto assets with up to 100x
- Earn rewards by joining trading campaigns

To trade either on a mobile device or desktop computer:

- Deposit funds on your trading accounts.
- Pick your preferred coins from the market tabs. Each tab offers a variety of coins and tokens with their current prices.
- Buy or sell your altcoin based on your selected trading pair. Input the number of coins and your desired price. You can do it in 3 ways – manual entry, select from the Order book, or select the lowest ask price.
- Complete your transaction by hitting the 'Buy' button.
- Once the order is filled, it will be part of the Trade History.

Other trading exchanges to consider:

- **Coinmama**

  With over a 2 million customer base, Coinmama is a solid cryptocurrency exchange. It accepts all types of currency for payment and caters to high-end investors. It supports SEPA transfers for European users, SWIFT transfers for customers anywhere in the world, and Faster payment transfers for its UK clients

  Coinmama is not for casual investors or hobbyists. It requires $100 and $200 buy and sell limits. It has a good crypto selection that is available for direct purchase only and a small rotating number of altcoins that can only be exchanged with one another. In terms of transaction fees, Coinmama follows a loyalty system to determine the amount to pay. It does not impose fees for withdrawals and deposits.

- ## Bitstamp

Bitstamp was established in 2011 with features that work best for more experienced traders. It has the highest trading volumes with really good liquidity. This exchange allows users to use bank accounts, crypto, and credit/debit cards for trading and offers a low withdrawal fee for the Single Euro Payments Area (SEPA).

Trading fees for every transaction is 0.25% but go down when you spend over $20,000 in a single month. While it has Ethereum, Litecoin, Ripple, and Bitcoin Cash, Bitstamp does not offer a lot of altcoins. The verification process can take up to 2 weeks and the customer service is low. But it boasts of a range of trading tools for professional traders.

- ## PrimeXBT

This exchange lets traders use a single account to access multiple markets like cryptocurrencies, Forex, Commodities, and Stock Indices. PrimeXBT app supports iOS and Android platforms. It allows users to leverage their accounts to improve results and to respond quickly to changing market trends. Moreover, it allows users to copy the trading activity to get similar profits.

- ## Overbit

This exchange allows cryptocurrency and Forex trading. It allows users to leverage up to 100x on crypto and up to 500x on Forex. Other features that make Overbit attractive to traders include providing protection to your account against negative balance and limiting exposure with the help of advanced risk management.

The platform comes with a streamlined, minimalist design and keeps your fund in a MultiSig cold wallet. It allows opening and closing the trade position with ease and choosing margin allocation to prevent risks.

Did you know that?

Binance was first located in China and moved to Japan in 2018 when China blocked foreign trading platforms' operations. Eventually, it left Japan due to legal problems. Binance finally settled in Malta.

FAQs

How to select the best exchange?

The following factors can help you find the perfect crypto exchange for your trading style:

- platform's reputation
- security
- trading volume and liquidity
- ease of use and navigation
- transaction fees that it imposes on users
- delivery time
- customer support

- geographical location
- accessibility and restrictions
- transparency

What is the best and easiest way to buy coins and tokens?

The only way to do it is by choosing a secure, mature, and solid exchange that offers speedy trading.

Can I use more than one crypto exchange?

Absolutely yes. Having more than one exchange helps you diversify your assets. Each exchange has its own strengths and features that will help you trade more successfully.

Is it okay to transfer my crypto from one exchange to another?

Yes. To send you coins, simply go to your desired crypto exchange and find the deposit address. Now, go back to your source exchange and withdraw the number of coins you want to transfer to your target exchange address.

Are my cryptocurrencies safe on exchange?

As a rule, do not keep your crypto holdings on the exchange. While exchanges have security measures, there is always a possibility that your assets can be hacked. If you are an active trader, just leave the coins that you can afford to lose when the worst happens.

Take note that in 2020 alone, there were about 28 attacks on several exchanges. The largest of these cyber hacks happened in KuCoin, the Singapore-based exchange that lost over $200 million cryptocurrencies.

Do exchanges have insurance?

Some crypto exchanges offer insurance coverage to their customers to protect their digital assets against fraud or hacking. One example is Coinbase with a $255 million insurance policy that secures its reserves.

Why do crypto exchanges have different fee structures?

Exchange fees are typically charged for every crypto transaction. It differs when you are a buyer or a seller. Popular and bigger exchanges have higher fees due to the insurance coverage and added security measures. Other exchanges based the fees on trade percentage and price volatility. Also, different currencies charge different fees.

Why should I choose a popular exchange?

While there are exceptions to the rule, popular crypto exchanges have the highest trade volumes. Trading volume equates to great liquidity, which is an important factor when you want to trade, sell, or buy cryptocurrencies. When there are lots of trades, you can easily buy or sell altcoins at their best prices. An exchange with a low trade volume can cost you more. In terms of volume worldwide, the top 3 exchanges according to CoinMarketCap are Binance, Coinbase, and Huobi.

Why is user experience important when selecting an exchange?

An intuitive user interface provides a great user experience. This often leads to the quick growth of transaction volume. The value of exchanges is significantly tied to the number of users and transactions.

Chapter 8

The Quest for the Best Wallet

Altcoin wallets work like Bitcoin wallets. These digital wallets play a crucial role in the functions and growth of crypto coins and tokens. They serve as storage of holdings and make it convenient for users to transfer funds to each other.

While some altcoins have their own wallets, it becomes difficult in the long run to keep track of all your crypto assets. This is where you would be needing a single wallet that supports a variety of altcoins.

Technically, all wallets can hold more than one cryptocurrency. What makes them different from each other is the number of coins that they can store. Some of these multi-coin wallets can be selective, while other wallets serve as universal wallets.

At a glance

- ✓ **Why is it crucial to choose the best wallet?**
- ✓ **What are the fundamentals of the best altcoin wallets?**
- ✓ **Different types of cryptocurrency wallets**
- ✓ **Guide questions to ask yourself when choosing a wallet**
- ✓ **What I recommend: 5 best software wallets**
- ✓ **What I recommend: 5 best hardware wallets**
- ✓ **Exchanges with secure wallets**
- ✓ **Special mentions: Wallets with special features**
- ✓ **Custodial storage for High Net Worth Individuals (HNWI) and Institutions**
- ✓ **Frequently Asked Questions (FAQs)**

Why is it crucial to choose the best wallet?

The most important factor to consider when selecting a cryptocurrency wallet is security. It must have adaptive features that secure your funds and enable convenient transaction services. As more and more altcoins appear on the market, the number of altcoin wallets become also available.

While many of these digital wallets are designed specifically to provide security, there are others that are created as fronts for scams and fraud transactions.

This is why using the most trusted and the best altcoin wallet is important to avoid the trap of criminal activities and enjoy their perks.

Another factor is your purpose. If you are planning to buy and hold your altcoins for a certain period or long term, your best choice is a hardware wallet. In contrast, if you want to trade actively, a software wallet is the best option.

To limit the risk if you are using less secure platforms like exchanges, it is necessary to have a solid strategy. It means keeping most of your crypto assets in a hardware wallet or employing several wallets.

The safest way to store your funds is to keep them in a wallet that is not managed or owned by a third party (or exchange). It is important that only you know your private key to access your cryptocurrencies.

What are the fundamentals of the best wallets?

Choosing the best altcoin wallet requires careful review of their key features such as:

- Security - It is the most important characteristic of an altcoin wallet. Offline wallets or hardware wallets are more secure compared to online or web wallets. Wallets that use 2FA or 2-factor authentication are much more secure.

  If someone is trying to access your wallet, he still needs to go through the next level of verification which is entering the code that the system sends to your mobile phone. It prevents any unauthorized access to your funds.

- Control over your funds – Having full control and access to your coins offers peace of mind.

- Multi-currency – If you're planning or already have an array of crypto coins and tokens, a multi-currency wallet helps you store and manage them in a single storage.

- Multisignature – There are crypto wallets that act like joint bank accounts, requiring more than one signature to authorize transactions.

- Anonymity – If you value your privacy so much and want to trade without divulging personal information, consider a crypto wallet that offers this feature.

Cryptocurrency Wallets

A crypto wallet is a web-based application that stores the coins and tokens of users. Technically, your crypto does not leave the blockchain but is transferred to an 'address' that represents the wallet. The address is the 'specific location' of your account on the blockchain's network. Your wallet's public address is used by other crypto holders to send coins to your account. The crypto wallet stores your private keys so you can access your funds and send coins to others.

Crypto wallets are separate 'non-custodial' storage that gives you an option not to store your funds in the exchange's built-in wallets. They are also the necessary tool to interact with the blockchain of your preferred exchange or platform.

In essence, the function of these wallets is to generate the information needed to process and complete blockchain transactions.

It is important to never misplace or forget your 'seed' or recovery phrase. It refers to the string of random characters that will help you regain access to your cryptocurrencies in case that you forget your PIN code.

Types of wallets

Due to the continuous diversification of crypto strategies, a reliable and safe wallet for your altcoins is your must-have tool. Generally, they are classified into three types- software wallets, hardware wallets, and paper wallets.

1. **Software wallets** are app-based and need internet connectivity. When the wallet is connected to the internet, it is called a **hot wallet**.

This type of wallet is best for active users who generally store smaller amounts of funds. Hot wallets bring high utility but are less secure compared to cold wallets.

They can be subcategorized into:

- **Desktop wallet**

  This kind of wallet offers functions and features that protect your virtual fund against attacks and thefts. However, you need to download the entire blockchain of the altcoin on your computer before you can utilize it.

  After downloading it, you can access a special file that stores your private key. The key will unlock your altcoin wallet. Once you are in, you can perform crypto transactions like trading, buying and selling coins, and transferring funds anywhere in the world.

  A desktop wallet provides better security compared to a mobile wallet and web wallet. It's best to use a computer that you don't typically use or an older model of laptop with a clean operating system and completely offline. Just make sure you have a backup if the computer unexpectedly dies.

  The popular choices among altcoin users are Exodus and Electrum.

- **Mobile wallet**

Mobile altcoin wallets are popular choices among on-the-go people who prefer to do transactions via their smartphones or other mobile devices. In essence, it is a mobile app that stores the users' private keys and allows access to their holdings whenever they need to perform transactions. It comes in handy when you need to pay for products or services of retail stores that are already accepting crypto payments.

The potential risks of using a mobile altcoin wallet include security threats and crypto thefts if you accidentally lose your phone or someone steals it.

Moreover, hackers target this type of wallet because it is the custodian of private keys, making it easy to access the holdings. This type of crypto wallet is prone to keyloggers, malware, and viruses.

Some of the most popular mobile wallets are Trust Wallet, Mycelium, Coinomi, Electrum, and Safepal.

- **Web wallet**

A web or online wallet is a cloud-based application that you can access using Google Chrome, Firefox, and other internet browsers. New users have to register on the app to get a private key and begin crypto transactions. Many people use this wallet because of its convenience and ease of use. It is the fastest way to complete your crypto transactions and does not lag between the server and app locations. It is ideal for storing small numbers of altcoins.

The downsides of this type of wallet include susceptibility to malware, DDOS attacks, insider hacking, and phishing scam. You may end up losing your funds because your private keys are stored online. If tonight the exchange is shut down or hacked, you will wake up without a single crypto coin.

To ensure higher security, always review the protective measures of the wallet to prevent loss of funds and breach in the system.

There are two kinds of web wallets – hosted and non-hosted.

- **Hosted wallets** hold the users' funds and private keys on the server. This type of crypto wallet is often the target of hackers, so make sure to review all the features of the wallets you are eyeing to. Providers of hosted wallets offer different levels of protection and are usually insured.

  Examples of hosted wallets are Binance, Coinbase, and CEX.io.

- **Non-hosted wallets** store your crypto assets but let you control your private key and seed words. This means that you have control over your funds and access it whenever you want.

  Examples of non-hosted wallets are MetaMask and MyEtherWallet.

2. Hardware wallets are offline wallets with private keys that are embedded into the device that serves as storage of your coins and tokens. They are also called cold wallets because they are internet-dependent. These physical devices are the most secure way to store your coins.

They are ideal for users who like investing significant amounts of funds and those who like to trade their crypto once in a while to make a profit. To access your holdings and make transactions, you need to connect your hardware wallet to your laptop or desktop via Bluetooth or a USB port.

3. One variation of offline wallets is the **paper wallet**. It is a less technical wallet and works by generating a public address and a private key. Users need to print out the generated information on a piece of paper. Whenever you perform crypto transactions, you need to enter the private key in your software wallet.

To ensure safety, store the paper in a safe place or memorize the private key. Some paper wallet providers use QR codes to execute crypto transactions.

However, there are several flaws that make it a less popular choice like not being able to transfer partial funds to another user. Currently, paper

wallets are considered very risky, unreliable, inconvenient, and obsolete.

Do you know how to back up your crypto wallet?

The simplest way is to back up the seed phrases or wallet.dat files. You can also create a QR code, print it, and store it in a safe place. Another option is to copy the master key to the text file, encrypt it, and store the file in another wallet (preferably a hardware wallet).

Guide questions when choosing a wallet?

1. How should I select a wallet?

- If you are a beginner, you can start with a reliable online wallet that offers low fees for crypto transactions. Coinbase and Exodus are great choices.

- If you are already an experienced user, the best choice is a hardware wallet. It will be easy for you to navigate its added features. Ledger and Trezor are excellent options.

- If you are a serious crypto enthusiast, pick a crypto wallet with enhanced features and added security protocols. The best choices are Coinbase, Ledger, Exodus, and Trezor.

2. What are the top factors that you need to consider?

- *The kind of altcoin you want* - Some wallets support limited types of altcoins. The best altcoin wallet has hundreds of coins and tokens, providing an excellent experience that fits all.

- *How frequent are you going to trade* – If you are an active trader, the good option is a hot wallet because it allows you to buy or sell your altcoins wherever you are. If you are into long-term trading and investing, best to choose a cold wallet.

- *The price of the wallet* – Understand that while a hot wallet is free to set up, you need to pay a fee whenever you trade your crypto. A cold wallet or hardware wallet comes at a price but secures your crypto better.

- *The advanced features* – Innovative features like instant crypto conversion, real-time market insights, advanced reporting capability, tighter security protocols, and more always make a difference when choosing a wallet.

- *Peace of mind* – You should choose the type of wallet that will not give you anxiety over your virtual funds in terms of security and safety.

3. How secure are digital wallets?

The security features and protocols of individual altcoin wallets are extremely important to consider during the selection. It is your primary security tool, so it is crucial to make sure that the wallet will deliver the standard security features. Some wallets have sophisticated protocols when it comes to security matters such as utilizing the two-factor authentication process.

Others utilize biometrics during the validation process to keep the holdings safe. You may also consider subscribing to crypto custody services. This option offers recovery of lost coins caused by hacking. It is for crypto investors who prefer to use insured altcoin wallets and have no issues about having their private keys in the custody of the provider.

4. What level of accessibility does the altcoin wallet offer?

Accessibility is the wallet's capability to bypass varied geological barriers. This means that you can use it anywhere and anytime you need to do transactions. If you are a traveler, it's best to get a non-geo-selective altcoin wallet. Take note that the accessibility level of the crypto wallet is also determined by its classification. Mobile and online altcoin are best in terms of the accessibility of holdings.

5. How do the updates in the wallet help users?

Wallet providers continue to upgrade their products to resolve issues and loopholes in the system that hackers and thefts tend to capitalize on. It is important to check if your provider updates the system and its functionalities. This also speaks of the credibility of the wallet to protect your holdings. Look at how frequently they update the existing altcoin wallets and the convenience that the new features or improvements that it gives to users.

6. What are the added features that you should consider?

Providers of crypto wallets are now exploring ways other than just holding digital assets or securing the private keys of users. For one thing, the most popular wallets are now adopting innovative payment features, exchange tools, tracking tools, and a lot more.

Fun Trivia

*Mt. Gox (Magic the Gathering Exchange)
was the world's biggest exchange
in 2014, handling about 70% of
bitcoin transactions. But it went bankrupt
after reporting the loss of
850,000 bitcoins.*

What I recommend: 5 best software wallets

1. Coinomi Wallet

Coinomi is a very popular choice and trusted by millions of altcoin users. It is a Hierarchical Deterministic (HD), multi-chain, security-first wallet for both desktop and mobile users. Its security has never been compromised or hacked.

Pros

- supports over 1,700 crypto assets
- offers instant exchange of supported assets via the shapeshipt.io built-in exchange
- superb security protocols
- generates seed or protective phrase for the wallet
- offers greater anonymity/privacy
- offers free-of-charge services
- stores and encrypts the private key on the mobile device

Cons

- not open-source
- does not support fiat currencies
- not yet compliant with FCA or other crypto regulators

2. Exodus Wallet

Exodus is both a desktop and mobile crypto wallet that is best for altcoin traders. This free wallet can help you diversify your crypto portfolio and trade through their website or mobile app. It is sleek and very responsive, ranking high on the list of best altcoin wallets for beginners. Exodus allows you to purchase, exchange, or manage your altcoins in one single application.

Just remember that this wallet is non-custodial so it is up to you to safeguard your password and recovery phrase. You wouldn't want to lose your access to your holdings forever.

Pros

- a multi-currency desktop wallet that supports Windows, Mac, and Linux
- easy to set up, convenient to use, and free
- provides trading apps and live price charts
- supports more than one hundred coins and tokens
- intuitive interface
- encrypted, cold storage
- has a built-in shapeshift.io exchange that allows a single-click exchange of
  one coin/token to another crypto
- gets updated regularly (every 2 weeks)
- offers total control over the users' private keys and even encrypt them for them
- has advanced security protocols that keep hackers and malware threats away

Cons

- not completely open-source
- charges a higher conversion fee
- less secure compared to the hardware wallet

3. Guarda Wallet

Guarda is a universal, non-custodial altcoin wallet. It means that you need to secure the safety of your password as well as the recovery phrases. It is regarded as one of the excellent hot wallets for beginners and those with smaller holdings.

Pros

- works excellently on Windows, iOS, and Android systems
- comes with a dedicated Chrome extension (also with Linux, Mac, and Ubuntu app)
- free to set up
- easily connects to various partner exchanges
- very convenient to use
- offers private key access
- allows easy buying and exchanging of cryptocurrencies
- makes the process of fund transfer safer
- rewards crypto by holding coins

Cons

- supports a small number of cryptocurrencies (just over 50 coins and tokens)
- less secure than a cold wallet

4. Indacoin Wallet

Indacoin wallet is mobile-based, multi-currency storage that is available in both Android and iOS devices. This wallet allows users to exchange altcoins within the wallet. You don't need to move your crypto assets out to complete the process and help you manage the assets using one app.

Pros

- supports more than 100 crypto coins and tokens
- offers direct purchase or conversion of altcoins
- availability of recovery option
- allows you to buy altcoins using a credit/debit card and trade them
- easy to use and simple interface, which makes it perfect for beginners
- available in over 100 countries

Cons

- less secure because it only uses a 4-digit PIN
- Android app

5. Gemini Wallet

Gemini Wallet stores your assets safely in their institutional-grade cold storage and their insured hot wallet. The bulk of holdings are stored in the offline cold storage and easily accessible when needed by the users. It employs industry-leading infrastructure to ensure top-notch protection and security of the wallet. It is beginner-friendly.

Pros

- insurance coverage against Digital Assets theft (hot wallet)
- high-security storage
- continuous upgrade of wallet infrastructure to optimize users' experience and support new currencies
- offers native SegWit addresses
- easy-to-use

186

- 24/7 expert support
- availability in the 50 states of the U.S. and over 50 countries in Europe, Asia, Africa, Oceania, and South America

Cons

- restricted methods in buying and selling crypto (via bank or wire transfer only)

Did you know that?

Top 10 crypto exchanges typically earn around $62 million every month. Exchanges from the Top 50 earn an average of $26 million and Exchanges from the Top 100 earn $13 million.

What I recommend: 5 best hardware wallets

1. Ledger Wallets

Ledger is a popular choice when it comes to cold storage. This Paris-based company leveraged its proprietary technology in developing infrastructure and security solutions, including hardware wallets. Since its inception in 2014, Ledger wallets have sold over 1 million units in 165 countries and counting.

To ensure the highest standard of security protocols, Ledger uses BOLOS, a unique operating system that they integrate into the wallet's chip. Their flagship wallets are the bestselling Ledger Nano S and Ledger Nano S.

- **Ledger Nano S** accepts a variety of altcoins and ICO tokens. This hardware wallet comes with tamper-alert software that is perfect for both beginners and advanced users. You need to have it with you to ensure transaction approval. It also offers a desktop app called Live to offset the inconvenience and allows users to execute transactions or track them. It costs $59.

  Pros
    - supports over 1,100 crypto coins and tokens
    - portable and lightweight
    - easy to use
    - offers excellent value
    - sleek design
    - powerful functionality
    - highly-secure

  Cons
    - no private key access
    - navigation can be inconvenient and confusing
    - a bit complex setup and requires extra steps to buy or load crypto to the device
    - not an open-source

- **Ledger Nano X** is a premium crypto wallet that stores your private key offline. It has all the features of Ledger Nano S and more. It can store more assets and lets you manage your portfolio while on the go via Bluetooth. You just need to link the device to your smartphone to access it. It is primarily designed for HODLers. It costs $119.

  Pros
    - looks like a USB pen drive, making it easy to carry anywhere you go

- offers extremely high security that is audited and verified by the French National cybersecurity agency ANSSI
- employs custom build OS (BOLOS)
- comes with CC EAL5 + certified Secure Element (SE) chip
- has DeFi functionality
- attractive design
- offers a huge amount of space that can store up to a hundred applications
- easy to use and set up

Cons
- screen navigation is a bit complicated
- more pricey
- no private key access

2. Trezor Wallets

Trezor is a great choice when it comes to hardware wallets. It was built by SatoshiLabs, making it the first secure and legitimate wallet for Bitcoin. Now, it caters to a large number of alternative coins and tokens. It comes with an OLED screen and looks like a tiny calculator.

All Trezor wallets come with a PIN code that is stored in the system. This eliminates loss of PIN even if the device or computer you use to access the wallet faces some technical issues.

Moreover, Trezor wallet features an inbuilt system that blocks brute-force attempts to access the funds. It works by raising the waiting time by a power of 2 for every incorrect input of the PIN code. Each wallet has a 24-word seed and passphrase that are RNG (Random Number Generator) selected offline and are displayed on the screen. You will be given new numbers in every transaction you do.

- **Trezor One**

  Pros
    o offers very secure offline storage
    o supports a large number of cryptocurrencies
    o supports Mac OS X, Windows, or Linux
    o simple to use
    o open source
    o sleek design
    o best for active traders and HODLers

  Cons
    o on the more expensive side (costs $99)

- **Trezor T**

  Pros
    o Colored touchscreen
    o very easy to use
    o extremely sleek design
    o compatible with Linux, Mac OS, and Windows
    o supports more coins and tokens
  Cons
    o on the more expensive side (costs $159)

3.Prokey Optimum Wallet

Prokey Optimum is a good starter wallet for beginners because it is easy to use. But it is also a popular choice among advanced traders and investors who like its multi-functionality and high security. It costs $59.

Pros
- o supports more than 1,500 coins and tokens
- o compatible with Mac, Android, Windows, and Linux
- o setup is easy
- o connects easily with computers and mobile devices
- o secure firmware that offers safety
- o protects crypto assets from remote and physical hacks
- o transparent and open-source
- o Plug and Play

Cons
- o small screen
- o relatively new to the market

4.KeepKey Wallet

KeepKey is a robust hardware wallet that looks like a big phone or mini-tablet. It is a bit bulky and weighs about 55g. It supports more than 50 cryptocurrencies which include the most popular coins and tokens. This hierarchical deterministic (HD) wallet comes with a passphrase and PIN code. It costs $99.

Pros

- offers high security
- available on Windows, Mac, and Linux
- good value for your money
- large LCD screen
- integrated with ShapeShift

- well-built design

Cons

- no private key access
- has more user restrictions
- not pocket-friendly
- no Lock feature
- recovery seed is displayed only once

5.SafePal S1 Wallet

SafePal S1 is the first hardware wallet that Binance has invested in. Small as a credit card, you can take it anywhere you go.

Pros

- offers multiple layers of security sensor
- has a self-destruct mechanism
- 100% cold storage that does not require WiFi, Bluetooth, or USB connectivity
- supports more than 10,000 coins/tokens and 23 blockchains
- offers unlimited currency storage
- easy-to-carry and lightweight
- holds multiple crypto assets in a single device
- supports firmware upgrade

Cons

- made of plastic material, which makes it fragile

Exchange Wallets

Most crypto exchanges have built-in storage or exchange wallets. This makes trading more convenient and cost-saving. Transferring funds from exchanges to an independent crypto wallet and back again necessitates paying fees. Exchange wallets hold the users' assets as long they want and withdraw when they want to. They keep your trading funds safe and within reach.

Exchanges with secure wallets

Coinbase

Coinbase has a separate wallet service that is available in iOS, Android, and web browsers. The wallet was originally named Toshi before it became Coinbase Wallet. It was initially developed for Ethereum use and to have an interface that helps users to access DApps (decentralized applications).

Currently, the Coinbase wallet is one of the most trusted wallets in the crypto world. With millions of users across over 100 countries, this software wallet offers a higher level of security.

It has two types- the Standard Wallet which stores small numbers of cryptocurrencies and the Coinbase Vault which is ideal for storing a large number of coins and tokens. In addition, the Coinbase Vault offers two options- Group Vault and Individual Vault.

The advantages of using a Coinbase Wallet includes:

- It is a regulated wallet.
- It supports a wide range of crypto coins and tokens.
- It allows easy tracking of holdings via its proprietary platform.

- It offers an option to auto-send or receive funds.
- It is easy to use.
- Setup is free and simple.
- Recovery options are available
- iOS and Android compatible

Kraken

Kraken takes pride in having an integrated, strong, and very secure exchange wallet. It has a stellar reputation in the crypto industry and is one of the most trusted in Japan and European countries.

The majority of assets (95%) deposited by users are kept in cold storage or offline wallets to ensure their safety. The cold wallet devices are geographically distributed with 24/7 guards and security cameras. It only maintains enough funds in hot wallets within the system to sustain high liquidity and operations.

Here are the benefits you get when using Kraken Wallet:

- built-in crypto exchange functionality that allows users to trade anytime, anywhere

- allows fiat money withdrawal

- full SegWit wallet support

- extremely reliable and secure

- utilizes two-factor authentication

- employs API key permissions and account timeouts

- encrypts users' personal information

- reasonable withdrawal fee

Binance

Trust Wallet is Binance's official mobile wallet. It holds your crypto assets outside the trading platform and comes with built-in features that deliver a seamless experience.

This wallet offers the following benefits:

- It is multi-asset and all-in-one storage of your holdings.
- It supports over 40 blockchains and hundreds of thousands of coins and tokens.
- It is completely free with no hidden charges.
- Sending and receiving your cryptocurrency is fast and easy using QR codes, blockchain addresses, or address names.
- It is designed to safeguard your funds.
- It does not require personal data during the transactions, keeping your real identity hidden.
- Its decentralized nature allows you to have total control over your crypto funds and private keys.
- It comes with multiple card payment processors, letting you purchase altcoins and bitcoin without the need to leave the app.
- It supports crypto staking without any hassle.
- It has a built-in DApp (decentralized applications) browser on Android, allowing you to explore earning opportunities.
- It allows crypto swaps or exchanges.

Cex

CEX is a mobile exchange wallet that allows users to trade instantly and stores crypto for them. With the integration of a crypto exchange system, it allows you to trade your altcoins straight from the wallet, with no need to access a desktop or a laptop. It is ideal for day traders and active traders.

The benefits it gives include:

- client-level security measures (anonymity, strong data encryption)
- uses mobile and email verifications checking during the registration and initial logging in
- very strict Know Your Client requirements and regulations
- officially regulated
- stores most of the holdings in secure cold wallet devices

Bitfinex

Bitfinex offers 3 types of wallets to suit your needs – Exchange, Funding, and Margin.

- An Exchange Wallet is for buying and selling coins and tokens that the platform supports.
- A Funding Wallet is for providing funds or financing other margin traders. It is ideal for people who want to earn without active trading. This wallet allows you to offer your chosen terms such as amount to lend, duration, and desired return rate.
- A Margin Wallet is for margin trading, a type of trading that allows users to borrow funds from Bitfinex's P2P lending platform to leverage their positions.

Transferring funds from one wallet to another is free and simple.

Blockchain.com

Blockchain.com exchange offers lightning-fast trading of altcoins and supports 4 major currencies- USD, GBD, EUR, and TRY. Its proprietary wallet- Blockchain is one of the widely-used and trusted exchange wallets in the world.

It offers the following benefits:

- quick swap, buy and sell of coins and tokens
- allows the transfer of coins to the Interest Account to earn interests up to 13.5% every year, deposited monthly
- allows users to hold their private keys along with a Secret Private Key Recovery Phrase
- best-in-class crypto security
- supports clients in more than 200 countries
- is available in 25 languages

SPECIAL MENTIONS

Air-gapped crypto storage: Ellipal Titan

It holds the record of being the first air-gapped cold storage in the world, tamperproof, and with a full metal seal. It is waterproof, dust-resistant, and impact-resistant.

For data transmission, it does not need WiFi, Bluetooth, or USB. Instead, it uses generated QR codes, making it extremely safe and secure. The QR codes format is transparent, controlled, and verifiable. For sending and receiving crypto assets, you need to connect this wallet with the Ellipal app.

Ellipal Titan has a built-in camera that scans QR codes and a huge touchscreen display. It stores the private keys offline, away from the prying eyes of hackers.

Any attempt to break it open triggers the deletion of stored private keys and causes the chip to erase every single data on the system. It costs $169.

Interest-earning wallet: BlockFi

Opting to store your altcoins in BlockFi Wallet allows you to earn interest up to 8.6% annual percentage yield (APY) through their BlockFi Interest Account or BIA. The interest is paid every month and accrues daily.

There is no minimum deposit required and the wallet is open to everyone who wants to own cryptocurrency. The app supports iOS and Android devices, letting you access your funds anytime.

All-in-one wallet: eToro

eToro is a multi-functional crypto wallet with great features that store your coins and tokens safely. It is also considered one of the safest hot wallets because of its high-level security components that prevent unauthorized access.

This includes strong DDoS protection, standardization protocols, and multi-signature facilities. It also allows existing users to access the cryptocurrency market.

It supports more than 120 cryptocurrencies and quickly converts over 500 pairs within the system. It offers a security key service when you accidentally lose or forget your private key.

Wallet with a Visa card: Wirex

It is perfect for people who are always traveling and want to trade wherever they are. Wirex offers safekeeping of your altcoins as well as letting you spend your crypto wherever a Visa card is accepted.

It converts your crypto at point-of-sale and gives Cryptoback rewards when you use this wallet when you pay online or in-store purchases. For maximum security of your altcoins, enable two-factor authentication.

DeFi wallet: Crypto.com

It is a non-custodial wallet that allows users to access DeFi services. The streamlined app lets you swap and farm DeFi tokens using this wallet.

A DeFi wallet has features to help you increase your yields by up to 20x. Crypto.com wallet stores your private keys and crypto. It gives you full control over your assets and holdings.

This wallet provides a 12/18/24-word recovery phrase, helping you import your current wallet. When it comes to security, this innovative wallet encrypts the private keys locally on your phone or computer with Secure Enclave.

It also uses 2-Factor Authentication and Biometric Authentication.

User-friendly wallet: Jaxx

Jaxx wallet has a user-friendly interface with clear text, pleasant colors, and an easy way to view the history of all your transactions.

It is best for both beginners and experienced users who like convenient features like QR scanning, access to the private keys and seed phrase, internal crypto exchange, multi-currency facilities, and cross-platform pairing.

Jaxx wallet is free for download and offers three options to complete transactions with varying fees that go direct to the blockchain miners.

Custodial Storage for Institutions and HNWI

Some exchanges specialize in giving custody services to High Net Worth Individuals (HNWI) and institutions.

The top exchanges that cater to the big players in the industry are:

✓ Coinbase – Coinbase Custody places crypto assets by storing them in segregated cold wallets. To ensure transparency, regular audits are conducted. Fund transfers are also being catered and customer support is always available.

✓ Gemini – It has two kinds of custody for virtual assets. One is the Deposit Custody, the default account that stores the users' funds in cold storage. The other kind is the Segregated Custody Account for the hedge funds of the institutions.

✓ itBit – It has an institutional custody service that allows clients to obtain and verify reports of their assets whenever they want. The assets are kept in cold storage and segregated. It also provides 24/7 support.

✓ BitGo – BitGo Cryptocurrency Wallet is the first multiSig hot wallet that is designed for institutional investors. The wallet's platform integrates your crypto into your investment portfolio, letting you transfer funds safely and easily.

It has advanced security configurations and multi-user policy control. BitGo has a BitGo Custody, BitGo Business Wallet, and BitGo Pay as You Go options to match your needs.

FAQs

Which is the best wallet for your altcoins?

There is no such thing as the best wallet. It all depends on your purpose for owning cryptocurrencies. For beginners who are looking forward to buying different kinds of coins and tokens, the best choices are Coinbase and Gemini wallets.

Is it necessary to have a crypto wallet?

It is not compulsory to have a separate crypto wallet if you are already using exchange wallets. However, getting a separate wallet to store most of your assets will keep them away from potential risks.

How to obtain a crypto wallet?

There are various ways to have a crypto wallet, including using the built-in wallets of the exchanges.

What is the best advantage of a software wallet over a hardware wallet?

Software wallets work like banking apps, allowing you to access your account via your smartphone or desktop.

Are software wallets safer than exchange/web wallets?

Software wallets or apps/programs that are installed in your mobile phone or computer are safer than web wallets. This is because the hacker needs to access your device to access the software.

Use 2-factor authentication and a strong password to protect you against cyber thefts and attacks. Moreover, do not lose your phone.

Is a hardware wallet worth the investment?

I highly recommend a hardware wallet, especially if you are into trading who want to transfer your profits to more secure storage. It is also best for investors of altcoins who prefer long-term or HODL investing.

How safe are hardware wallets?

Compared to software wallets, they are more secure. Hacking them remotely is quite impossible. They are also invulnerable to computer viruses that harm the software wallets.

Do I need more than one hardware wallet?

It is better to have 2 hardware wallets. The other one should be your backup if the one you usually carry or use is lost or stolen.

Why are hardware wallets called cold storage?

The physical aspects of hardware wallets enable usage even without internet connectivity. It makes them cold storage.

What is a multi-currency wallet?

A multi-currency wallet is a type of wallet that can store more than one type of coin or token. Some multi-currency wallets allow users to convert one crypto into another via the integration of the ShapeShift feature.

What is a MultiSig wallet?

It means a multi-signature wallet. This kind of wallet requires input or authorization from two or more parties to complete blockchain transactions.

Chapter 9

Should You Invest in Altcoins?

If trading cryptocurrency is not your option, you can still explore the potential of virtual assets by investing in alternative coins or altcoins. They are the stable coins, security tokens, and utility tokens, other than Bitcoin.

Like other types of investment, altcoin investment is long-term focused and ideal for people who want to grow their investment portfolio over time. The traditional way of investing uses stocks, bonds, commodities like gold and silver, and other asset classes.

In a gist, investing in altcoins depend on the following factors:

- Your financial goals
- Your risk tolerance
- Your knowledge about the cryptocurrency market and altcoins
- The time you can give in researching and monitoring your assets
- Your starting capital

At a glance

Is altcoin worth a try?

As an investment, altcoins have their own allure that attracts smart people. The most obvious is the higher percentage gain that crypto offers. This is why you should be investing in an altcoin that you believe is a good investment instrument.

Unlike trading that you are speculating or gambling, investing for a long haul is a smart decision which you should buy and hold.

o   You should invest in a coin or token that you truly believe in and understand its true potential.

o   It is crucial to research the people behind the altcoin, its value proposition, its performance history, trading volume, solidity, and more. With due diligence and a comprehensive study of different types of altcoins, you will find the coin/coins that match your criteria.

o   Be wary of altcoins with low capitalization because they are prone to hacking attacks and market manipulation.

- o Calculating how the risk factors will impact your invested fund is a strategic move you need to do.

- o A worthwhile altcoin should offer the advantages you are looking for to ensure that your money is safe and will gain profit. You can begin by checking the top 10 coins in terms of market cap.

There is a continuing investor-driven demand for altcoins that significantly drive their value on the market. According to some market analysts, this investment trend works both ways- pushing the price up or plunging it down. It is up to the investors to speculate the direction of the altcoins. This short frenzy is also another indication to invest in altcoins, rather than trade and lose. Many altcoin traders are into long-term investment too, to diversify their strategies and holdings.

As more and more investors understand the true financial potential of altcoins and their real-life applications, the demand for altcoin investment is now growing steadily. In addition, the lower market shares of altcoin and lower prices compared to Bitcoin makes the yielding potential more profitable.

What are the risks of altcoin investing?

The main stimulus of investing in altcoins is the premise of 'room to grow' and is generally cheaper than Bitcoin. In the context of being cheaper, investors should remember that it correlates with lower market capitalization compared to Bitcoin.

In general, cryptocurrency is a volatile investment instrument. This encompasses all types of altcoins and tokens, including their big brother Bitcoin. There are many players in the market now and new types of altcoins are produced every day. Since there is no solid regulation about the creation of coins and tokens, the altcoin space is growing with alternative coins.

Altcoins are now occupying more than 40% of the total market cap of cryptocurrency. This makes it nearly impossible to directly say which among the many options is the best altcoin.

Another risk you have to consider is the lack of a regulatory body that governs altcoins. By being 'unregulated', there is a high possibility that you may lose your coins all at once and leave with nothing. You don't know where your money goes when you buy altcoins.

What you have in your digital wallet are numbers that represent the value of your investment and the guarantee that your invested fund is earning profits.

These risks should not be ignored and must be taken into consideration. Studying the security components and other risk-mitigating measures of the crypto exchange is very important to ensure that your holdings will be safe.

Guide questions that can help you decide to invest in altcoins

- Who are the people issuing and sponsoring it? What is their financial and technical background? How do they make money out of the transactions?

- What are your rights as an investor?

- When can you sell your investment? How can you sell it? What is the cost of selling it?

- Where is the invested fund going? How will they use it?

- What are the legal protections or safety nets that they offer in the event of malware, hack, or fraud attack?

- Who will refund your money when something happens? In case your rights are violated, are there adequate funds to commensurate you?

- Are they being audited on a regular basis? Who audits them?

- Do they issue financial statements?

Why are more investors choosing altcoins?

Altcoins quashed the Bitcoin monopoly of the crypto market, becoming optional coins for people who want to explore other investment tools. The altcoins rapid growth is due to their unique features which include having full blockchain technology, authenticity, and practical use in the market.

Altcoins cost less compared to Bitcoin, making them the perfect instruments for those who are still discovering the beauty of investment. Without paying the astronomical price, the promise of reaping huge rewards makes altcoins very attractive to financial-savvy individuals.

Other reasons are:

- **Altcoins grow fast**

  The rapid growth of altcoins gives pioneering investors a significant ROI.

- **Institutions and large companies start buying altcoins**

Ethereum, considered the second-largest crypto asset, is becoming the favorite of institutions and firms. In April, digital asset management company Coinshares reported that major institutions bought over $30 million worth of Ethereum. This brings the total holdings of institutional investors to $13.9 billion. Grayscale Investment Trust has also invested $1.5 billion in various altcoins including ETH.

- **The price surges of altcoins are higher**

  Altcoin prices can surge more than the 20% market, depending on the uptrend factors. Moreover, DeFi trends are beginning to influence the altcoin market directly because investors can see their higher economic growth rate.

- **Altcoins are supported by reliable and popular exchanges**

  Platforms with high liquidity and offers a wide range of altcoins like Binance, Coinbase, and Kraken prove the trustworthiness of the coins and tokens. Also, altcoins can be traded as Bitcoin pairs and purchased using fiat currencies.

- **Altcoins are legitimate coins for trading, hence good for investment**

  With the testimonies of people who profit in trading altcoins, the hesitancy to invest in them is becoming low.

- **Retail merchants and commercial businesses are now accepting altcoin payments**

Aside from Bitcoin, the two altcoins that businesses accept as a form of payment are Litecoin and Ethereum.

Did you know that?

Ethereum was proposed by Vitalik Buterin,
a crypto programmer
In 2013. During that time, he was only
19 years old.

Risks and Opportunities

The altcoins' market is not yet mature at this point in time and everyone is still speculating on the future of cryptocurrencies. But the growing interest of people in altcoins and the proliferation of crypto exchanges/brokers is a manifestation that those with sufficient market liquidity will stay.

For those who are willing to take risks and discover the potentials of altcoins, understanding the risks and opportunities that it gives is important.

Opportunities

- Altcoins are regarded as the 'enhanced versions' of Bitcoin because they are created to provide the bitcoin's shortcomings

- Altcoins offer a wide selection of coins and tokens that delivers different functions

- Stablecoins, which are one type of altcoins, have the potential to fulfill the goal of Bitcoin as an acceptable medium for everyday transactions

- Several altcoins like XRP and Ether are trusted by mainstream institutions, gaining great traction and high valuations

- Higher risks can equate to higher rewards (with a big 'IF")

- Allows investors to get in early on projects that can immensely grow and gives 100x ROIs in just a matter of months

Risks

- Compared to Bitcoin, altcoins' investment market is smaller

- The smaller market capitalization and lower trading volumes make altcoins more susceptible to pump and dumps

- The variety of altcoins in the market makes it difficult to make a decision which is the best one

- Altcoins are impacted by the price of Bitcoin and momentum

- The lack of defined investment criteria and metrics as well as the absence of regulation give altcoins thinner liquidity and a lesser number of investors

- Altcoins are easily manipulated by bag holders and whale (big) investors

- A long term investment is incredibly risky because some altcoins lose their value as time passes by

- The reality of 'dead' altcoins that sunk the investors' money

Is your crypto dead?

Knowing that dead coins exist in the realm of crypto space helps investors make calculated and informed decisions. The tempting illusion of profitable crypto projects is constant and it is up to you to conduct extensive background checks on the projects. It is important to check their availability on major and trusted exchanges, their profit statements, and their trading volumes.

To spot dead coins, observe the active activities of the projects on social media platforms. Websites like Deadcoins and Coinospy track down floating dead crypto projects.

Some of the known dead coins are:

- **Aeron (ARNX)** was once a tradable coin on the Binance exchange but delisted after some time, causing the prices to drop up to 90%.

- **BitConnect (BCC)** enjoyed success during its first years but started to lose its credibility when UK financial regulators questioned its legitimacy at the end of 2017. In 2018, BitConnect was labeled a Ponzi scheme by Texas regulators, causing its eventual shutdown and the crash in the BBC price by 9%.

- **Storeum (STO)** died because of its lack of store value, zero liquidity, and dwindling market. The price of STO was $0.000012, but only 18 entries were recorded in its order book.

- **VegasCoin (VEGCOIN)** was a typical example of abandoned projects.

- **0xBitcoin (0xBTC)** was initially performing well in the market. The price soared to $5 but suffered a loss as the value fell to $0.10. The core team of the project left when it happened.

What are dead coins?

Crypto coins that are called 'dead coins' are those that suffered disinterest and eventual death due to a lot of reasons. The common reasons for their death include abandonment of key people in the project, insufficient funding or low liquidity, turning out to be scams, limited to zero listings on popular crypto exchanges, low trading volume, joke projects, and more.

In the crypto world, about 3.6% of the list of dead coins do not attract funding to support their development or offer lucrative profit margins.

Around 3% accounts to joke projects, while 6 out of 10 crypto coins with inferior liquidity and negligible trading volume are usually abandoned by the developers. Coins are considered abandoned or dead if their trading volume within 3 months is below $1,000.

The 2017 ICO craze rocked the crypto world when the number of coins gained momentum from 29 to more than 850 projects. Sadly, about 80% of the initial coin offerings were scams and left a trail of dead coins.

Nevertheless, new developers are all set to create new altcoins. In 2018, over 1,200 projects were launched. After two years, the total number of coins and tokens in the market is around 8,000.

With the proliferation of the wide variety of coins in 2020, another scam called 'rug pulls' resulted in another batch of dead coins.

Cryptocurrency investing mistakes that beginners should avoid

The continuous inflow of corporations and institutional investors raises the awareness of investing in cryptocurrencies, especially altcoins. The fact remains that the prices of these coins and tokens are dependent on public perceptions and speculations.

However, gauging how the fundamental factors influence the future performance of coins remains the most popular approach. By not following the basic guidelines, the possibility of portfolio losses is great no matter what kind of investment method you are using.

I rounded up the 5 worst investing mistakes you need to avoid as a crypto investor:

1. Buying crypto on speculation

Beginners are prone to this mistake, leading them to buy high and join the crowd that aims to gain big profits without considering the potential prospects of the coin or the factors that drive their price higher. Always remember that the cryptocurrency market is volatile and no one can predict the movements of their prices.

2. Low prices do not mean that the coins are cheap

Do not buy coins based on the promise of the creators that they will be the next 'bitcoin' and make you a millionaire in the near future. While it happens, like in the case of Dogecoin that experienced unexpected growth and made the investors instant millionaires and billionaires. But not every 'meme' inspired cryptocurrency has utility value or acceptability factor. In short, a low price typically reflects the actual worth and demand of the coin or token and not a discount.

3. Be guided by your risk tolerance

Always remember that you should not invest more than you can afford to lose. Investing is a speculative approach, where you win and lose. There is no sure guarantee of winning all the time. To mitigate losses, allocate funds that equate to your level of risk tolerance. Never, ever pull out other investments for the sake of leveling up your crypto portfolio. The smart move is to stick to long-term investments and put up a small percentage of crypto assets.

4. Always have an exit strategy before you buy altcoins

Purchasing an asset without exit plan is very risky. It is crucial for investors to have a solid framework or investment plan in advance that will stop high losses and achieve their financial goals. You don't invest your money to lose but to earn, so during the period when the market climate is becoming tougher, your exit strategies help you cut losses.

Exit strategies are also the keys to win more. Having a deeper understanding of market psychology and market sentiment makes smart investors decide to sell during the uptrends instead of holding their coins with the expectation of better price growth. If you want to squash losses and take advantage of gains, you should know when to sell.

5. Putting your golden eggs in a single basket

It is one of the worst mistakes that beginners can make. The hype of entering the world of crypto can be exhilarating and can make you invest big on a single popular coin only. But this approach can ruin your future investing and wealth plans. The better option is to spread your investment across or diversify your assets portfolio. In this way, you can mitigate major losses.

Newbies have a tendency to consider every price dip as a buying opportunity. They also believe that it is a good strategy to buy during the bull run or before the prices of altcoins become higher. Following these misconceptions would entail a higher risk of losing your venture capital. The key is always understanding why a bear or bull run is happening before investing big.

Altcoin investing tips to help you dive in

In May 2021, the total crypto value was over $2.5 trillion as more and more individuals, institutions, and companies joined the wagon. In another study, over 14% of adult Americans now own cryptocurrencies.

And while there are people who invest money to speculate, many are considering long-term investing because they see altcoins as a hedge against inflation and assets with store values.

Here are two ways to do it right:

1. Prepare for volatility and risks

Each coin or token has unique features that influence its price direction. This is why you need to have in-depth knowledge about a certain altcoin before you invest your money.

- Know the rationale behind the coin or token's creation

- Know the creators and major supporters of the coin including its governance structure

Understanding more about alternative coins can help you better diversify your portfolio and add crypto to your other holdings. It is important to embrace volatility issues and prepare for the best or worst. Preparation is always the key to reduce or prevent losses.

2. Learn the dynamics of the risk-reward concept

If you are all set to dive into crypto investing, remember that moderation is the key to success. Limiting the percentage of crypto in your overall portfolio would not impact its risk-reward dynamics when the worst happened. One approach is through dollar-cost leveraging or investing a fixed amount regularly.

Quote

"Behind every crypto coin or token is a community."

FAQs

Are altcoins good investments?

Like Bitcoin, altcoin offers investment opportunities to those who dare but also risks that should be considered before taking the plunge. One key to preventing huge risk is trading well-established alternative coins with high liquidity and trading volume

Are stable coins really stable investments?

Stable coins are pegged to fiat currency or other investment commodities, making them a very good investment.

What are the coins that can help me diversify my investment portfolio?

Getting hold of any of the coins on the top 20 in terms of market cap, liquidity, and customer support. Bitcoin, Litecoin, and Etherum are always in the top 5.

Chapter 10

Other Key Concepts and Financial Lexicon in Crypto That You Should Know

Crypto Staking

Staking is a strategy that involves 'locking up cryptocurrency through Proof-of-Stake (PoS) consensus algorithm to earn passive income. The 'stake' serves as a validator to ensure the continuity, security, and integrity of the PoS network. In return, the validators or stakers receive newly minted coins.

How does it work?

- The participant supports the network by setting aside or locking up a certain amount of crypto coins/tokens.
- The staked coins will generate an active validating node on the blockchain.
- The higher the volume of coins, the greater the staking compensation or interest.

Many blockchains are now adopting PoS protocols as a response to the increased demand for cryptocurrencies. This innovative approach yields a higher annual percentage yield (APY).

You can stake crypto in 3 ways – via crypto exchanges, crypto wallets, and staking providers/pools.

1. Staking via crypto exchanges

- Binance offers flexible stalking or the staked funds are not locked and can be withdrawn by stakers anytime they want

- FTX locks staked coins within a certain period (fixed staking, but offers an option to instantly unlock them for a fee

- Bitfinex offers soft staking (flexible staking)

2. Staking from crypto wallets

The easiest way to stake your crypto is via altcoin wallets. The yields are much higher compared to staking in pools and exchanges. As long as you use a secure wallet, the staking risks are very minimal.

One example is Ethereum. You can stake your BNB (Binance Coin) using Trust Wallet and enjoy more than 23% APY based on the current computations. Using the same staking wallet, you can also stake TRX (Tron), CTX (Tesos), ATOM (Cosmos), KAVA, and ALGO (Algorand) to earn 6% to 12% APY.

Other popular choices are Ledger Wallet, Trezor Wallet, and Exodus Wallet.

3. Staking with dedicated staking providers or staking pools

- Staking providers offer a more comprehensive platform that allows crypto holders to lease nodes hosting and choosing coins they want to stake. It is best for large stakers. The most popular are Capital, Staked, MyCointainer, Stake, and stakefish. The most popular example is AllNodes.

- Staking pools work by allowing multiple stakers or validators to deposit their funds to increase the block rewards. By combining the computations resources to verify and validate new blocks in the network, the stakeholders get a share from the rewards. This option offers frequent staking income and more predictability.

What are the risks?

- Market risk – It refers to the potential adverse movement of the price of the staked coins/tokens.

- Liquidity risk – It is important to make sure that your crypto has a high trading volume and liquidity.

- Validator risk – It involves technicalities that can disrupt the staking process or the validator nodes.

- Validator cost – The costs you pay for running validator nodes (electricity/hardware) or percentage of the rewards can reduce your staking returns

- Lockup period – This staking option does not allow access to your assets for a specific duration of time.

- Rewards duration – Opting for long reward duration prevent stakers to reinvest the rewards, so choose assets that can give you daily staking rewards

- Theft or loss - Using a custodial staking platform that does not guarantee strong security is a red flag, so make sure that you go for staking wallets/exchanges/providers that are trusted and well-established.

The hottest coins that offer big staking rewards are Ethereum 2.0, XTZ (Texos), ALGO (Algorand), ICX (ICON), ADA, DOT, ATOM (Cosmos), and NEO.

Decentralized Finance (DeFi)

DeFi is a peer-to-peer, digital financial services technology that allows crypto trading, interest accounts, and loan transactions.

It offers the following core benefits:

- True decentralization that dispenses third party interventions, censorship resistance, and global participation

- A non-custodial system that allows users to store their private keys and be in total control of their assets

- With blockchain as technological infrastructure, there is contract automation and immutability as well as low-cost, quick transactions

- Improved transparency protocols in the ecosystem that results in market and price efficiency.

- Favors network effects that generate innovations and combinations of projects in layer 2 and 3 applications

This blockchain-based concept of finance uses smart contracts rather than traditional financial instruments. Smart contracts refer to the set of special codes that automate the agreements between borrowers and lenders or buyers and sellers of digital currencies.

DeFi makes the assets open to the public decentralized network, allowing anyone to use the blockchain system instead of using middlemen. It utilizes technology to eliminate intermediaries and allow peer-to-peer transactions. All DeFi transactions and activities are done without the help of banks, exchanges, brokerages, and other financial institutions.

Other use cases that utilize DeFi:

- Lending and borrowing crypto to earn interest (via Aave, Dharma, Compound)
- Betting on the outcome of the events (via Augur, Synthetix, TokenSet)
- Buying Stablecoins that are pegged to a currency or commodity (via EOSDT, MakerDAO)
- Creating and exchanging asset derivatives like precious metals or fiat currencies (via Synthetix)
- Decentralized exchange of crypto (via Oasis, IDEX, Kyber)
- Insurance (via Etherisc)
- Taking part in a lottery (via Synthetix)

Quick facts

➢ The DeFi components are Stablecoins, a software track, and use cases

➢ The infrastructure and use cases of the DeFi ecosystem are still under development

➢ Oversight and regulation of decentralized finance are still lacking

➢ In the future, many believed that DeFi would replace the current rails of modern finance systems

➢ The primary exchange or network that supports decentralized finance activities is the Ethereum

➢ DeFi revolves around dApps or decentralized applications.

➢ Grayscale and other major asset management firms are starting to invest in DeFi technology

➢ As of March 2021, the total locked-in value of DeFi smart contracts was over $41 billion

Decentralized Applications (DApps)

In cryptocurrency, DApps or Decentralized Applications are digital protocols that run on a peer-to-peer (P2P) computing system or blockchain network.

They are often called smart contracts that distributed ledger technologies (DLT) like the Ethereum blockchain have popularized.

All DApps are executed and stored in the blockchain system.

Examples of DApps;

- Uniswap – decentralized crypto exchange
- Freelance – smart contract platform
- Augur – prediction market platform
- Blockstack – a platform that is designed for decentralized apps development
- Steem – a platform that rewards publishers with crypto token or coin
- Cryptokitties – Ethereum-based game

DDoS Attack

DDoS or Distributed Denial of Service attack happens when nefarious parties take advantage of the network by sending multiple requests. The goal is to overwhelm the website's capacity limit to handle transactions and from functioning properly.

DDoS is primarily accomplished using a network of remotely-controlled bots or zombie computers. Typically, the attack is focused on certain layers such as Layer 3 (the network layer), Layer 4 (the transport layer), and Layer 7 (the application layer).

Attackers target popular crypto exchanges in attempts to steal crypto or ask for crypto ransom.

Cybercriminals also use DDoS as a diversionary tactic while stealing data or installing malicious software to the website.

Quick facts

> In 2017, Bitcoin's system was allegedly attacked. It caused performance slowdown and left consequences in

terms of processing volume and data storage. Since all blockchain transactions are irreversible and permanent, the false transaction during DDoS attacks would be stored on the system.

➢ Hongkong-based Bitfinex is a victim of several DDoS attacks (*source*: Twitter feeds showing seven attempts in 2016, seven attempts in 2017, and one attempt in 2018)

Initial Coin Offering (ICO)

ICO or Initial Coin Offering is one approach to raising funds for a blockchain project. It works by offering digital tokens.

Most ICOs are for ventures that are experimental, at an early phase of development, or have not started yet.

ICOs are high-risk, speculative investments that are not for faint-hearted people. There is a record of projects that take a number of years before becoming commercially viable. Some failed.

Risks to consider:

- Value fluctuation
  The value of ICOs greatly depends on their popularity, perceived value, ease of use, and underlying blockchain technology.

- Fewer safeguards

  ICOs are not regulated and highly speculative which can turn out to be scams, especially if it represents an overseas entity. ICOs are available online, sold globally, and paid with cryptocurrency, so when the issuers disappear after the fundraising, they are actually scams. Investors have little or no chance to get back their invested money.

GLOSSARY

A

Algo-Trading

Algorithmic trading is a trading system that uses automation to process the crypto orders of buyers and sellers. It uses algorithms or computer program rules.

Algorithm

It is a set of rules or processes that the computer follows to calculate operations or solve problems.

Arbitrage

Arbitrage is the strategy of taking advantage of the difference in the selling price between two exchanges. You buy a crypto coin or token from one exchange and sell it to another exchange for a profit.

Airdrop

Airdrop is a method of distributing tokens. It works by sending the crypto to a wallet address. It is often utilized for marketing functions like app downloads, referrals, and reshares.

Apeing

It is an approach that a crypto trader uses to buy a token from a project launch without in-depth research about it.

Ashdraked

It is the term used to describe the complete loss of the invested capital through a shorting approach.

ASIC

Application Specific Integrated Circuit or ASIC is a silicon chip that is designed for a specific task. In the context of crypto mining, the ASIC performs a calculation by finding values that deliver the necessary solution once it is placed into the hashing algorithm.

Atomic Swap

It refers to the crypto transfer from one user to another without the intervention of an intermediary or an exchange.

AMM

AMM or automated market maker refers to the system that gives liquidity to the crypto exchange.

B

Bag

It is cryptocurrency slang that describes a huge quantity of a certain coin or token.

Bagholder

A bagholder is a crypto owner or investor who buys and holds a large amount of a certain token or token.

Baking

It is a process that Tezos use to append new transaction blocks to its blockchain.

Basket

A basket is a collection of virtual currencies that are managed and considered as a single asset.

Bear Trap

It is a coordinated attempt of a group of traders to manipulate the price of a specific cryptocurrency.

Bearwhale

Any person that holds a large number of crypto and uses them to get a massive profit or drive their prices down.

Block

Block is a file with transaction data that is completed at a given time and becomes a part of the blockchain network.

Block Explorer

It is also called the blockchain browser or an application that allows users to check the details of the blockchain blocks.

Block Reward

Block rewards come in the form of coin and transaction fees that are given to miners after the transaction block has been successfully hashed. The reward composition depends on the cryptocurrency policy.

Blockchain Trilemma

It refers to the 3 issues that typically affect blockchains. They are security, scalability, and decentralization.

Bug Bounty

It is a reward given to someone who completed tasks research, design work, identifying code vulnerabilities, and more.

Bubble

It is a situation where the crypto is traded at a price that exceeds its intrinsic value.

Burned

Burned coins or tokens are those that are intentionally and permanently removed from the list of circulating crypto.

Buy Wall

It refers to the extremely big limit order that a trader places on an exchange.

C

Candlestick Chart

It is a graphing method that displays the changes in the crypto prices over time. A candle chart has 4 points of information:

- Opening price
- Closing price
- High
- Low

Capitulation

It refers to the process of selling crypto at a lower price, causing a significant loss. Traders capitulate when they believe or lose hope that the price of a certain currency will increase.

Central Bank Digital Currency (CBDC)

CBDC or Central Bank Digital Currency uses token or stablecoin to represent the digital form of a country's fiat currency. The idea is to create a legal tender that is regulated by a central bank.

CEX

Centralized exchange (CEX) is a type of crypto exchange that is owned and operated in a centralized manner.

Chain Split

It describes the separation of the original coin or fork into multiple independent projects.

Change

It is a concept used in cryptocurrency that utilizes the UTXO model. Change involves sending back coins to the crypto holder after using the unspent output to create a transaction.

Consensus

Consensus is the process that peers or nodes agree together and allow the transaction to take place. It is very important in the maintenance of the distributed ledger systems.

Coin

It is a cryptocurrency that operates independently. It also describes a single unit of the crypto.

Coin Mixer

It allows users to combine transactions to various addresses, making them untraceable and impossible to trace back the original sender or receiver of the cryptocurrency.

Coinbase

It is the number of coins generated from scratch in mineable cryptocurrency as a reward to miners for mining new blocks.

Confirmation

Every 10 minutes, a new block is mined. The block confirms the new transactions. Large transactions may require several verifications from a number of blocks. Once the transaction is confirmed, it cannot be double-spent or reversed.

Contract account

It is an account with associated code and crypto balance.

Core Wallet

It is a type of wallet that can hold an entire blockchain.

Crowdfunding

It enables companies, especially startups, to collect funds from supporters of the crypto.

Crypto Debit Card

A card that allows holders to pay for commodities and services using their crypto coins or tokens.

Cryptojacking

It involves using the computer of another user to mine crypto without permission.

Cypherpunk

A movement promoting crypto use and privacy-focused technologies in advancing political and social reforms.

D

DeFi Aggregator

It brings trades from different DeFi platforms in a single place.

Dead Cat Bounce

It is the term used to describe a temporary recovery after the prolonged price decrease.

Decentralized Social Media

It is a blockchain-based social media platform.

Deterministic Wallet

It is a crypto wallet where addresses and keys are generated from a single seed.

Difficulty

The difficulty is a concept that outlines the hardness of block verification during the mining process. In Bitcoin, the difficulty of Proof of Work mining changes every 2016 block. This is to adjust and keep the standard 10-minute block verification time.

Distributed Ledger

It refers to the system of recording the distributed information in different devices. The crypto blockchain is a distributed ledger that tracks all transactions.

Dumping

It is a collective sell-off of large quantities of crypto that are sold in a short period of time.

Dusting Attack

The goal of this attack is to discover the true identity of the owner of a crypto wallet, which in turn can be utilized in a phishing scam.

E

Encryption

It is the process that combines plaintext or document with the 'key' or a shorter string of data to create a ciphertext (output). Anyone who got the key can decrypt the output back.

Emission

The speed of the production and release of new crypto coins.

F

FOMO

FOMO stands for 'fear of missing out' where traders buy or sell crypto to gain profit during a bull period.

FUD

It is the acronym for 'Fear, Uncertainty, and Doubt.' This strategy aims to influence the traders' perception of a crypto market or a specific coin by spreading false, misleading, or negative information.

Fiat On-Ramp

It is one way to get crypto coins from fiat currency.

Fiat-Pegged Crypto

It is an asset, coin, or token on a blockchain that is connected to a bank-issued currency.

Fish

It refers to the person with a small cryptocurrency investment.

Futures

They are standardized legal agreements to sell or buy a certain asset at a specified time and price in the future.

G

Genesis Block

It is the initial data block that is computed in the blockchain network.

Gems

The term 'gem' is used to describe unknown low-cap crypto coins that are undervalued but have great potential

Governance Token

It is a token that represents a voting right to influence the crypto ecosystem.

H

Hash

Hash refers to the function that accepts input and generates an alphanumeric string output called 'digital fingerprint' or 'hash value'. Each block in the crypto network has a hash value that validates the transaction.

Hashing

Hashing refers to the mining process that uses cryptographic hash functions to solve mathematical problems.

Halving

Halving is an event that impacts the supply and demands of mined cryptocurrencies like Bitcoin and Ethereum. It is basically the process of halving the mining incentives after a certain number of blocks is achieved.

Hybrid Consensus Model

The Hybrid Consensus Model uses both Proof of Work (PoW) and Proof of Stake (PoS) consensus. This mechanism brings balanced network governance by allowing blocks to be validated by miners and voters (stakeholders.)

Honeyminer

It is a crypto mining app that users can download on multiple devices.

In-the-Money/Out-of-the-Money

They are two trading mechanisms that give options to investors to use and harness the benefits of additional tools.

I

Infinite Mint Attack

It occurs when a hacker or an unwanted person mints a great number of tokens within the network's protocols.

Initial Dex Offering (IDX)

An IDX or initial dex offering is an option used by companies instead of an initial coin offering (ICO).

Initial Exchange Offering

It is a form of crowdfunding that start-ups in crypto generate funds by listing in the exchange.

Initial Token Offering (ITO)

An ITO is like an ICO but offers tokens that hold intrinsic utility value (either through usage or software in the ecosystem).

Instamine

It is a term used to describe the distribution of a large portion of crypto right after its public launch.

Intrinsic Value

In cryptocurrency, the asset's intrinsic value refers to its actual worth that is determined by a financial calculation instead of its present price.

J

JOMO

It stands for 'Joy of Missing Out,' which is the opposite of FOMO (fear of missing out).

K

Kimchi Premium

It is a phenomenon that makes the valuation in South Korean exchanges appear higher compared to other global crypto exchanges.

L

Ledger

It is the record of financial transactions that can only be appended when there are new transactions in the blockchain network. It cannot be changed or edited.

Light Node

It is a downloaded wallet that is connected to full nodes. It further validates the stored information on the blockchain.

Liquidity

It is the term used to signify how easily a coin or token can be sold or purchased without influencing the overall prices in the market.

M

Malware

Malware is malicious software or harmful computer program that can compromise the operations of a server, network, or computer.

Margin Call

The value of the investor account is less than the margin maintenance amount.

Market cap

Market capitalization or market cap is the total capitalization of the coin or token's price. It is used to rank the crypto's relative size.

Mempool

It is a collection of unconfirmed transactions in the node.

Merkle Tree

It is a cryptography tree structure where each leaf node is labeled with the data block hash while the non-leaf node has the hash of the label's child nodes. It helps in the secure and efficient verification of the blockchain content by propagating the change upward toward the top hash.

Mining Difficulty

It refers to the difficulty of finding the next block's right hash.

Mining Farm

When a group of crypto miners work together for a purpose or achieve a goal like energy use.

Mining Reward

It is a reward that miners get for mining a new block.

Mining rig

It refers to the equipment that miners use for mining crypto.

Moon

It is a situation that displays an ongoing upward movement of the crypto price.

N

Network

It is the nodes in the blockchain that work to process and validate transactions.

Nodes

Nodes are computers that connect the crypto network. The nodes work to relay and validate transactions while keeping the blockchain copy. There are two types of nodes:

- Full node – A computer that can fully download blockchain's complete data and fully validate crypto transactions.
- Lightweight node – This type of computer uses a different process of validation and cannot download the entire data of the network.

O

Open Source

It is a concept where participants believe in an open and free sharing of information for the greater common good.

Option

It is a contract that gives the traders the right (not an obligation) to buy or sell the underlying instrument or asset at a strike price.

Oracle

In the blockchain network, the oracle refers to the machine or human that relays the data to the smart contract, which in turn verifies the outcome of an event.

P

P2P

Peer-to-peer or decentralized interactions of two parties in the blockchain.

Permissioned Ledger

A permissioned ledger is owned by one person or group of people. Any access to the network or ledger is given by the owners. Permissioned ledgers run faster and are easier to maintain compared to public blockchains. The data of this type of ledger is highly verifiable and accessible to all parties.

Ponzi Scheme

It is a fraudulent investment strategy that promises returns to investors from funds that new investors contribute.

Private Blockchain

It is a distributed ledger (blockchain) with a closed network and is controlled by one entity. New participants require a verification process and have the capability to limit the number of people who can participate in the validation process.

Private Currency

It is a token or currency that is issued by a private company or person. Usually, a private token or currency is used within the private network only.

Proof of Authority

It is a consensus mechanism that grants a private key to a private blockchain. It allows the blocks to validate the cryptocurrency transactions.

Pump and Dump

Pump and dump refer to the investment scheme that a participant or participants group does to artificially raise the asset's value so they can sell their coins at a higher price.

R

Recovery Seed

A cryptographic security code that is composed of 12 to 14 random characters.

REKT

It is the slang for 'wrecked', which means that the investor has lost substantial money.

Rug Pull

A type of scam where crypto developers take the investors' money and abandon the project.

S

Seed Phrase

It refers to the single starting point in getting the keys of a deterministic crypto wallet.

Serialization

It is the process that converts the structure of data into byte sequences. Ethereum, for instance, uses RLP (recursive-length prefix encoding) encoding format.

Sharding

It refers to the splitting of the network into 'shards' or portions. Every shard comes with a unique set of smart contracts and account balances.

Shitcoin

A coin with no usage or potential value.

Slippage

The situation where traders have to pay a different amount for their purchased crypto because of the sudden price movement.

Smart Contracts

Smart contracts are self-executing coded agreements between crypto buyers and sellers. Once the predetermined conditions on the contract are met, the contracts automatically complete the process without intermediaries.

In a gist, smart contracts are relatively straightforward and trustless.

Smart Token

It is a token with value and has the key information necessary to simultaneously execute transactions.

Soft Cap

It refers to the minimum amount that ICO aims to raise.

T

Transaction Block

It refers to the set of network transactions that can be hashed or added to the blockchain.

Ticker Symbol

It is a unique letter combination assigned to crypto or stock, making them identifiable on trading apps and exchanges.

Token Generation Event

It refers to the time when a token is publicly issued.

TVL

It is the total value locked (TVL) that represents the number of assets being staked in a certain protocol.

Trade Volume

It is the amount of crypto that is being traded in the past 24 hours.

Trading Bot

It is a program that automates the crypto trading of assets on a trader's behalf.

U, V, W, X, Y, Z

Unspent Transaction Output (UTXO)

It refers to unspent transactions that are left after all the transactions are completed.

Vanity Address

A crypto public address where letters and numbers are chosen by the owner.

Vaporware

A crypto project that never happens.

Volatility

It is the statistical measurement of returns dispersion that uses the standard variance between returns and the market/security index.

Wash Trade

It is a type of market manipulation where investors make artificial activity by buying and selling similar crypto simultaneously.

Whitelist

It is the list of registered participants who are interested in ICO.

Whitepaper

A document that provided technical information and a growth roadmap of the crypto project.

Zero Confirmation Transaction

It means unconfirmed transactions on the exchange.

Conclusion

Thank you for reading my book.

After reading all the chapters of **Cryptocurrency Trading Guide to Altcoins & Bitcoin for Beginners**: *Learn about Decentralized Investing Blueprint, Cryptography, Blockchain, Mining, Ethereum, Litecoin to Create Wealth. Best Trading Strategies,* I hope you are more equipped and prepared to begin your journey to success.

My personal journey to crypto trading begins by learning the basics. I am a learner of life, of exciting rides to create more wealth. And I believe that every one of us has this thirst to gain more, be more, and earn more. Trading and investing are two ways to achieve it fast. But it is not for weak-hearted people. It works for people who are not afraid of the myriad of trading risks and are willing to experience loss when they hit the worst.

And for the more courageous, cryptocurrency is the new player in the game. It promises a great return on investments and grows your wealth in no time at all. But it has its own set of risks that can wipe off your capital or investment. Your ticket to success is to learn all the facets of crypto trading and decentralized investing.

As more and more individuals and companies are exploring the real-world application of decentralized investing and trading in blockchain technology, expect more amazing things to happen. You can be a mere observer or ride the tide and become a player.

Again, my gratitude for making this book part of your wealth journey. I wish you success and good riddance!

Thank You

Thank you so much for purchasing my book.

You could have picked from dozens of other books but you took a chance and chose this one.

So THANK YOU for getting this book and for making it all the way to the end.

Before you go, I wanted to ask you for one small favour. **Could you please consider posting a review on the Amazon? Posting a review is the best and easiest way to support the work of independent authors like me.**

Your feedback will help me to keep writing the kind of books that will help you get the results you want. It would mean a lot to me to hear from you.

Bitcoin & Cryptocurrency Investing:

Top 10 DeFi Altcoins to Change the World and Your Finances, Blockchain, Cold Storage, NFT & Mining Explained, Smart Contracts & Decentralized Finance for Swing Trading

"We see bitcoin as potentially the greatest social network of all."
~ Tyler Winklevoss

Disclaimer:

The contents of this book may not be reproduced, duplicated or transmitted without direct written permission from the author.

Under no circumstances will any legal responsibility or blame be held against the publisher for any reparation, damages, or monetary loss due to the information herein, either directly or indirectly.

Legal Notice:

This book is copyright protected. This is only for personal use. You cannot amend, distribute, sell, use, quote or paraphrase any part or the content within this book without the consent of the author.

Disclaimer Notice:

Please note the information contained within this document is for educational and entertainment purposes only. Every attempt has been made to provide accurate, up to date and reliable complete

information. No warranties of any kind are expressed or implied. Readers acknowledge that the author is not engaging in the rendering of legal, financial, medical or professional advice. The content of this book has been derived from various sources. Please consult a licensed professional before attempting any techniques outlined in this book.

By reading this document, the reader agrees that under no circumstances are is the author responsible for any losses, direct or indirect, which are incurred as a result of the use of information contained within this document, including, but not limited to, —errors, omissions, or inaccuracies.

© Copyright by Vitali Lazar

All rights reserved.

256

Table of contents

Introduction

"To make our world a better place, we need to build products that the corrupt cannot abuse. Bitcoin is the best example of that."
- Olawale Daniel-

Just mention Bitcoin in a conversation and you'll be hearing varied opinions from people around you. Why there is a fuss over this cryptocurrency? What makes it a hot topic that can stir contrasting views? How well do you know Bitcoin-it's history, uses, benefits, and journey to the top of the crypto list?

Let me give you insights and answers about Bitcoin through this book. **Bitcoin & Cryptocurrency Investing: Top 10 DeFi Altcoins to Change the World and Your Finances, Blockchain, Cold Storage, NFT & Mining Explained, Smart Contracts & Decentralized Finance for Swing Trading** is not your ordinary book.

It is your ticket to understand Bitcoin and leverage its features to achieve your investing goals. This is a no-holds-barred journey to Bitcoin crypto investing, so feel free to navigate and explore each chapter that is designed to help you understand Bitcoin better. It tackles the fundamentals of Bitcoin as well as strategies, tips, and information to guide you through the complex world of pure crypto and bitcoin-related stock investing.

Take note that while it will help you navigate cryptocurrency investing, this book does not guarantee your financial success. It is just a means, a journal of tips and strategies to help you gain confidence and knowledge on how to pursue Bitcoin investing. Your success in investing is in your hands. It is about knowing the right timing, the right asset vehicle, when to buy or sell your holdings, and a whole lot more.

Every investor wants profits, whether direct or passive income. When we buy something, we expect to get hold of a commodity we like, need, or want. In crypto investing, we pay for a virtual commodity with a value that rests on the users' adoption of its worth. Crypto investing, especially in Bitcoin, requires a strong might and risk tolerance.

If you want a "safe investment" that brings in guaranteed returns, do not invest in cryptocurrency especially Bitcoin. It is not an appropriate asset for those who do not like risks, because in just a fleeting moment, a significant downtrend in the market, you could lose a great portion of your invested fund.

But Bitcoin investing offers a path that can make you an overnight millionaire or even a billionaire, depending on the number of coins you have in your personal portfolio. Bitcoin remains a volatile, high-risk asset. But its volatility makes this crypto one of the most interesting, powerful, and profitable investment assets.

For conservative investors, Bitcoin investing is an attractive option but they hesitate on trying this option due to the risks and uncertainties that its nature brings. However, with the increasing growth of institutional and big investors, the level of hesitancy is beginning to wane. The crypto industry is evolving and is now connecting with the traditional forms of investment through Bitcoin-linked exchange-traded funds (ETFs) and crypto stocks of major companies. While indirectly, investors enjoy the opportunity of tasting the power of Bitcoin.

Bitcoin follows the principles of market efficiency and principles of economics. While it runs independently with its own technology, rules, and principles, it has shown liquidity, security, fungibility, and sustainability. The fact that its supply would be limited does not discourage investors but only makes it more interesting in their eyes. Indeed, Bitcoin has grown so much in terms of public acceptance, the number of loyal users and holders, and returns of investment. From an uncertain beginning, Bitcoin showed its strength and flexibility despite the price spikes and crashes. It always recovers from a bearish period with a higher price baseline and continues to dominate the crypto scene.

Bitcoin is a trailblazer that inspires creators to make their own cryptocurrency and spawns crypto-related projects. This alone makes it a powerful asset vehicle and currency in this modern world where the internet makes everything possible. It still has a lot of room to grow and potentials to explore.

More than 10 years ago, Bitcoin does not possess any real monetary value. But look at it now, one bitcoin is more than the value of one dollar or any fiat currency. It is like gold that holds such a large value, even without physical form. It is just a concept in the digital sphere, but because users embrace its speculative value, it has grown so much bigger.

Satoshi Nakamoto, the person behind this project is truly a man of vision. He has created one of the best inventions in the 21st century. His legacy is tantamount to the future of the financial world and the future is beginning right now. Bitcoin has opened the door for another gold rush- this time in digital form. Its raucous journey has turned ordinary people into wealthy ones and rich people losing a lot of money due to not-so-smart investment moves.

History showed that it took four pieces of bitcoins to make a penny. This was what happened during the first Bitcoin transaction when Laszlo Hanyecz bought 2 Papa John's pizzas in Florida for $25 or equivalent to 10,000 bitcoins. Today, to get hold of 1 bitcoin, you need to pay thousands of dollars.

While it is waiting for the time where its primary purpose will come true- as a medium to pay for daily transactions just like the fiat currencies, Bitcoin has already gained traction as a hedge against inflation and a store of value. While Bitcoin's price is still highly-volatile, the trust of institutional investors and attempts of regulatory agencies to make applicable rules are making the crypto market more mature.

The narrative also changed. In the past, the price fluctuations stemmed from the speculative moves of traders and retail investors. Nowadays, the market price of Bitcoin is influenced by a set of factors in the mainstream economy.

This book **Bitcoin & Cryptocurrency Investing: Top 10 DeFi Altcoins to Change the World and Your Finances, Blockchain, Cold Storage, NFT & Mining Explained, Smart Contracts & Decentralized Finance for Swing Trading** will take you on a journey and teach you how to effectively invest in Bitcoin. Each chapter is written to enlighten, prepare, and help you master the strategies of crypto investing.

Chapter 1 Hail to the King of Crypto: Bitcoin gives you the birds-eye view of the hottest cryptocurrency, how it works, its unique characteristics, and more.

Chapter 2 The Digital Gold Rush gives you a list of people who trusted and enjoyed the perks of investing in Bitcoin as well as the countries that accept it and forbid its trading plus a whole lot more.

Chapter 3 Is Crypto Investing for You? talks about the principles of crypto investing, the risks and rewards, and how its operating system blockchain works to your advantage.

Chapter 4 Bitcoin and Stock Market explains the correlation between Bitcoin and the stock market, the successful journey of bitcoin futures to the traditional trading markets, and the preview of crypto stocks to invest in before the next digital rush.

Chapter 5 Guide to Bitcoin Investing: Let's Gear You Up teaches you how to buy and sell Bitcoin, top reasons why and why you should not invest, ways and strategies to invest, and other investing concepts you can use along the way.

Chapter 6 Personal Portfolio Management helps you understand the benefits of a well-managed, diversified portfolio, the investment styles to use, factors to consider, how to manage your own portfolio, or hire a portfolio manager.

Chapter 7 What Should Comprise Your Crypto Portfolio? allows you to choose what to include in your portfolio, how to optimize the crypto evolution (Bitcoin, Ethereum, and DeFi), and pick the perfect asset for you from the top 10 DeFi altcoins that are making an impact on the world's financial sectors.

Chapter 8 Everything You Need to Ask About Bitcoin & Resources for Bitcoin Investors answers your questions about Bitcoin. There is also a list of the most useful resources for everyone who wants to invest in Bitcoin.

As the author of this book, I used my more than ten years of experience as well my share of failures and successes to produce this book. I was like you once- a beginner who kept reading, trying, positioning, finding the right asset vehicle, and believing that I can master the art of investing. I can proudly say that I found my pot of gold in investing and I want to guide you through this book.

It is my pay it forward gesture. I want you to know the key secrets of successful investors. All it takes is to open the first page and continue learning until the last page.

This book is for you. Press on.

Chapter 1

Hail to the King of Crypto: Bitcoin

"Bitcoin is a techno tour de force." – *Bill Gates*

In the span of more than 10 years, Bitcoin becomes a household name. But not all people know how it works, how it can be used for global transactions via the internet, and why it has become a new investment and trading craze.

In laymen's terms, Bitcoin refers to the digital currency that operates on its own blockchain system. It survives without the traditional backing of precious metals or fiat currency. It trades on exchange platforms and uses electronic wallets or hardware wallets for safekeeping purposes.

For beginners and casual investors, delving deeper than its face value is very important. The basics are relatively easy to comprehend. Let me take you on the journey of learning about Bitcoin, the most valuable cryptocurrency on the world's virtual markets today.

1. Bitcoin is an electronic representation of money that uses cryptography for verifying its transaction. Cryptography refers to the science of encoding and decoding details and information.

2. Bitcoin as an investment asset that offers inflation hedge and capital appreciation. However, the volatile nature of its market value makes long-term investment high-risk.

3. Bitcoin is a digital, decentralized, private, and scarce resource. It operates according to its set of codes. Its code is being run and processed by nodes or thousands of high-end computers across the globe. It is used for transactions without the intervention of a bank or middleman. Bitcoin code is limited to 21 million only.

Satoshi Nakamoto: The father of Bitcoin

The concept and development of Bitcoin are credited to Satoshi Nakamoto. But who's he, anyway? Until today, the real identity of the father of bitcoin remains elusive. Some speculated that the name was just a pseudonym of a person or a group of people behind the cryptocurrency.

Nakamoto authored the whitepaper of Bitcoin and designed the blockchain database among other things. His goal in creating this cryptocurrency is to put the control of currency in the people's hands and take it away from powerful financial elites.

He was active during the introduction of Bitcoin, then went off the radar after three years. His co-developer Gavin Andersen received a farewell email on April 23, 2011, saying that Nakamoto "moved on to other things" and that he knew that Bitcoin's future was in 'good hands.' Nakamoto assigned Andersen as the caretaker of Bitcoin. As of today, Andersen is getting more reclusive and has also given up his role as 'a core maintainer' of the Bitcoin code.

Trivia

Gavin Andersen wrote code for Bitcoin during its inception and became Satoshi Nakamoto's trusted right-hand associate.

And while Nakamoto is "out there doing other things", he is enjoying profits from his own share of bitcoins. He owns more than 1 million Bitcoins which is worth around $60 billion based on the current (2021) market price. His coins also equate to 5% of the total circulating bitcoins.

If Nakamoto sells part of his million coins, it would totally upend the entire crypto market.

Attempts to unmask Nakamoto

Mystery fires the active and wild imagination of people. When Nakamoto preferred to remain hidden while developing Bitcoin, many speculations and guesses surrounded him. There were rumors about him being a Yakuza member, a money launderer, or a participant of a cabal of programmers and developers. Some people even thought that he is a woman.

His mask of anonymity ignited many attempts to reveal his true identity. Some of the personalities that were associated with Nakamoto's persona include:

- One of the 'suspects' was Nick Szabo, a crypto expert who helped Nakamoto develop Bitcoin. The New York Times pinned him as Nakamoto, but he denied the claim. Some linguists even studied and compared his writings with Nakamoto's and believed that there were some semblances.

- In 2014, Newsweek identified Dorian Nakamoto as the man behind Bitcoin because of his successful engineering career and partly because of having the same surname. The publication also claimed that both Nakamotos have Japanese connections and lean on libertarian beliefs. Dorian strongly denied his involvement with cryptocurrency by issuing a public statement via the Associated Press. The next day, the 'mystery man' Nakamoto posted a brief statement in an online forum saying "I am not Dorian Nakamoto."

- When Australian scientist Craig Wright announced in 2016 that he was Nakamoto, the crypto community didn't believe him. He even presented academic credentials and references to the crypto paper that appeared on his own blog months before the Bitcoin whitepaper appeared online. In addition, there were also references about leaked correspondence and emails about "P2P distributed ledger" with his lawyers. But inconsistencies in his proofs became the subject of criticisms. Even when Bitcoin co-developer Andersen backed Wright's claim by saying that he was '98% sure', there was lots of backlash. Eventually, Wright retreated.

Cool Fact

UCLA Professor Bhagwan Chowdhry nominated Satoshi Nakamoto in 2015 for the Nobel Prize in Economic Sciences.

How well do you know Bitcoin?

Bitcoin is a cryptocurrency that utilizes cryptology to secure its system. It is a decentralized virtual currency that is created (mined), distributed, stored, and traded using a ledger system known as the blockchain.

Its decade of history of value is marked with cycles of impressive booms and turbulent crashes. Investors and traders watched in awe as Bitcoin's value soared high and then crashed down. Nevertheless, the volatility of this crypto did not stop the widespread popularity that inspired the creation of many alternative coins (altcoins).

Early timeline

August 18, 2008 – Bitcoin.org was registered. At present, this domain name is "WhoisGuardProtected." This means that the identification of the entity or entities that registered the name is private and confidential information.

October 31, 2008 – Satoshi Nakamoto sent a statement at metzdowd.com's Cryptography Mailing list that he has been working on a fully peer-to-peer electronic cash system. According to him, this new project would not require a trusted third party to operate. This information was included in the whitepaper entitled "Bitcoin: A Peer-to-Peer Electronic Cash System", which can be accessed on bitcoin.org. It is the Magna Carta of bitcoin's operation then and now.

January 3, 2009 – This date marked the mining of the first bitcoin block- Block 0 or the 'genesis block.' Written in the block was the message "The Times 03/Jan/2009 Chancellor on brink of second bailout for banks." The context of the statement has puzzled the public. Only Yakamoto and his peers knew its relevance.

January 8, 2009 – Bitcoin mining and operation officially began when Block 1 was mined.

Bitcoin mining

Bitcoin is produced through mining or the process where this crypto is released for circulation. The term mining in bitcoin is a reference to the method of gathering precious metals or the digital equivalent of finding cryptocurrency. The idea is akin to finding gold where anyone with a shovel can dig and look for it. In bitcoin mining, people with computer skills and knowledge can participate and look for blocks.

Crypto miners can join the network as transaction processors and validators. They need to solve complex puzzles to unlock new blocks. Using specialized computer hardware in computing difficult mathematical problems, miners need to complete the task and produce a 'hash' (64-character output) that will lock the new block to the network.

The new blocks are important elements in adding, verifying, and storing transaction records in the Bitcoin network. Each block on the blockchain network represents a file that can store 1MB of bitcoin transactions. On December 13, 2020, the blockchain size was already 308 gigabytes (GB).

The first miners to add new blocks to the blockchain earn bitcoins. To get the reward, miners should prove their role as a blockchain network through PoW or proof of work system. The proof of effort should include the energy and time spent to run their computers and solve the equations. The faster and more high-end the hardware of computers, the larger yields of block rewards they would receive.

Companies that are built for mining use specially-designed computer chips to process Bitcoin transactions and earn rewards. Large transactions that involve greater monetary value need more validations to guarantee security.

Did you know that?

The Bitcoin mining farms across the globe consume approximately 60 terawatt-hours of electricity every year.

Bitcoin halving

Bitcoin halving, as the phrase implies, is a major event where the coin incentives of miners are cut in half or reduced to 50% after reaching the 210,000 newly-discovered blocks quota. It aims to ensure that the circulating amount of bitcoin would not trigger pressure for exponential increase of market price.

The halving occurs every four years and will continue until the last batch of 210,000 bitcoins is mined. After mining the last block, expect Bitcoin to be more scarce and valuable.

During the initial stage of Bitcoin in 2009, the reward for miners was 50 BTC.

- The first halving happened in 2012, cutting down the incentive to 25 BTC for every block mined.
- The second halving occurred in 2016, slashing the reward to 12.5 BTC and completing 420,000 blocks.
- The third halving was on May 11, 2020, where miners earned 6.25 BTC for each block they unlocked. It marked the completion of unlocking 630,000 blocks.
- The fourth halving is expected to happen in 2024, considering that new coins are generated every 10 minutes.
- The final halving is predicted to take place between 2040 and 2140.

Consequently, halving brings dramatic effects because it often triggers a significant Bitcoin turbulence. It is characterized by surges in trading volume 1 month before and 1 month after every halving. Understandably, when halving is happening, there is a short supply of Bitcoin in the market. The law of demand and supply dictates that when there is not enough supply, the price of the asset will increase, In the case of Bitcoin, the value of the coins yet to be produced is expected to be higher.

- The history of Bitcoin halving showed that on November 28, 2012, the price per BTC was around $12 then skyrocketed after a year to around $1,217.

- When the second halving happened on July 9, 2016, the value of Bitcoin was $670 and then rose to $2,550 per BTC by July 2017. The price continued to rise and by December 2017, Bitcoin's market price peaked at an all-time high of $19,700 per coin. In December 2018, it fell down to $3,276, which was 506% higher than its pre-halving price.

- The third halving took place at around 3 PM EST on May 11, 2020. The price per Bitcoin was $8,787. Several weeks later, Bitcoin surpassed all its all-time highs and set its bull-run performance on February 21 with over $58,000 per coin price. But, it didn't stop there as the price soared to an astonishing $64,507 per BTC, which was 634% higher than its pre-halving value. On May 11, 2021, it settled to $54,276 (517% higher than the 2016 halving).

The diminishing rate of miners' subsidies is pre-determined by Nakamoto. It revolves around the idea that as the transaction fees in the network increase, the reward for discovering a newly-minted coin shall be decreased. Technically, this key feature of Bitcoin helps control crypto inflation and emission. Within the Bitcoin code lies the automatic adjustment in releasing new crypto coins, which consequently postpone the end date of emission.

Interestingly, there were two events that resulted in further Bitcoin price fluctuation. First, when Tesla CEO Elon Musk announced on May 12, 2021, that his company would not be accepting Bitcoin payments. The second event that plunged down the price below $40,000 was the restrictions imposed by Chinese regulators, banning payment firms and financial institutions from offering crypto-related services. These two announcements caused Bitcoin price drop.

Crypto experts in the industry viewed the recent halving as a robust factor that can impact its ecosystem in many ways. One of them is the decreasing number of miners because the economic mining rewards are getting smaller. It makes Bitcoin mining less compelling and unprofitable for efficient miners.

After the final halving, all Bitcoin miners will receive incentives in the form of transaction fees from people who sell and buy the crypto. This is to ensure continuous processing on the blockchain. As of August 2021, the circulating bitcoins were 18,799,131 million. It means that only 2,200, 869 million coins are waiting to be mined.

Trivia
Did you know that there is a micro-nation with bitcoin as its currency? It is the Liberland, a place between Serbia and Croatia. It was founded in April 2015 by Vit Jedlicka.

Blockchain: The core of Bitcoin operation

Bitcoin exists within blockchain technology. It was the first cryptocurrency that successfully used the innovative system of recording key information. To date, the Bitcoin blockchain application is still the best in the crypto industry.

Although in terms of scalability, it is relatively slow because Bitcoin blockchain can only process up to 7 new transactions per second. Its competitor Ethereum can process 30 every second while the Visa credit card system can complete 24,000 transactions per second.

People are also looking forward to the much-anticipated upgraded version of Ethereum or Ethereum 2.0, which is expected to handle up to 10,000 transactions per second.

In essence, blockchain refers to the trustless, transparent, and publicly accessible transaction ledger in the bitcoin network that allows ownership transfer using proof of work (PoW) and public-key encryption. It is a type of digital ledger of transactions (DLT) where inputs are duplicated, distributed, and validated across the whole computer network.

This public ledger is maintained by many computers across the globe. This network of state-of-the-art computers validates, encrypts, and stores transactions in blocks. The growing blocks as transactions continue are linked together with the use of cryptography. Recording of completed transactions requires the use of hash or cryptographic signature.

Why makes blockchain technology interesting?

It is one of the 21st most-hyped systems that was developed by Nakamoto to support Bitcoin's digital operation. At present, it has many versions to power altcoins. Developers are also integrating blockchain technology into different industries and businesses that need automated authorization, legal contracts, and records of transaction series.

Its secure and innovative features resolve trust issues. Since no one is running the bitcoin blockchain in terms of administration, all users are the ones who are making it active. No one can directly steal your coins unless you send them to a fraud person who is doing virtual business with you. In this case, it would be impossible to retrieve the fund you sent and the only one who can withdraw the money is the other party.

Another reason for the hype around this technology is its capability to prevent your bitcoins from being hacked, double-spent, or faked.

What are the properties of blockchain technology?

- **Distributed** – Network participants receive a copy of the digital ledger, ensuring the transparency of transactions.

- **Programmable** – It is programmable for a certain purpose with the help of Smart Contracts for transactions.

- **Anonymous** – The identity of users is either pseudonymous or anonymous.

- **Unanimous** – All the participants of the blockchain network agree to the validity of transactions.

- **Secure** – To ensure security, all records of transactions are individually encrypted.

- **Immutable** – All validated records cannot be reversed and changed.

- **Time-stamped** - The timestamp of every transaction is recorded permanently on the block.

The growing blocks on the blockchain significantly enhance the ledger's security. It means that if hackers attempt to tamper information or corrupt the entire system, they need to change all the blocks across the distributed versions in various locations.

Also, when one network participant sees tampered information, it would automatically halt the process and send it back as an error or invalid transaction.

How does Bitcoin Blockchain work?

Step 1: The sale or purchase of bitcoin is entered into the system, then transmitted to the thousands of nodes (network of computers).

Step 2: Each of these nodes would have its turn to confirm the validity of the transaction based on computer algorithms. The participant (or miner) who successfully produces a new block for the fresh transaction is rewarded with the transaction fee that the buyer or seller pays.

The fees vary according to the volume of purchased or sold bitcoins.

Step 3: Once the transaction is cryptographically validated and affirmed by the majority of the nodes, the sale will be encrypted to a block on the digital ledger.

Step 4: The block where the data is encrypted will be permanently chained to the previous blocks after using a hash (cryptographic fingerprint).

Trivia

Did you know that the concept of blockchain is mentioned in an academic paper in 1982? It was part of a dissertation that said: "the design of a distributed computer system that can be established, maintained, and trusted by mutually suspicious groups."

.

Peer-to-Peer (P2P) Network

In the Bitcoin network, the full nodes aka peers work with others to give essence to the peer-to-peer protocol for block and transaction exchange. It means that users can receive or send payments from other users on the network regardless of their locations. The transactions are purely P2P or do not need the approval of external authority or source unless they are doing business with a regulated institution or exchange.

Full nodes are capable of downloading and verifying each block and transaction before sending them to other nodes in the blockchain. There are two types of full nodes:

> Archival nodes – These are full nodes with the ability to serve historical blocks to their peers as well as store the whole blockchain.

> Pruned nodes- They are full nodes that do not have the ability to store the whole blockchain.

How does P2P operate?

Before a single full node can start validating a freshly-mined block and unconfirmed user transaction, it must be downloaded first and validate all existing blocks from block 1 to the last block in the network chain. This process is known as the Initial Block Download (IBD), where the node downloads all the previous blocks to prepare for the new transaction.

When a miner unlocks a new block, he can use either of the following methods to broadcast his successful discovery.

- **Standard Block Relay** – It is the approach where the miner acts as the relay node. It will send an "inv" (inventory) message to peers (full nodes and SPV). The inventory refers to the newly discovered block.

  The common responses of the peers include "*getdata*" message from block-first (BF) peer which means it is requesting the whole block, "*getheaders*" message from headers-first (HF) peer that also wants the full block, or "*getdata*" message from SPV (Simplified Payment Verification) user who wants a Merkle block.

The miner responds to every request by sending the new block according to the type of message its peers like "block" message, "headers" message, or "merkleblock" message then adding zero or more "tx" messages. The "tx" message contains a transaction in raw format.

- **Unsolicited Block Push** – The miner will send a "*block*" message to all full node peers. In this approach, it bypasses the standard block relay method knowing that none of the full nodes has the newly-discovered bitcoin block.

  For sending transactions to its peer, the full node will use an "inv" message. The receiving peer will forward it to the next node in the same format.

Key Point
In section 8 of the Bitcoin whitepaper, Simplified Payment Verification (SPV) is referred to as the method that the recipient uses to prove that the sender controls the source of funds without the need to download the entire blockchain.

Bitcoin forks

Bitcoin forks are the changes in the network's protocol or when 2 or more blocks display the same block height. When Bitcoin forks, it generates a new coin or token as well as a new network. This impacts the validity of the old rules, forcing miners to adapt to the new rules.

It also occurs when developers:

- disagree on the best way to handle Bitcoin's growth forward
- reverse catastrophic or hacking bugs
- add new features to the blockchain

The main classification of forks:

- **Hard fork** – A bitcoin hard fork is a radical change to the blockchain's protocol, resulting in 2 branches. One follows the protocol, while the other one becomes a new version. The forking process would upgrade the software rules and the mining procedures, causing the invalidation of new transactions.

  Hard forking needs consensus from the majority of coin holders to push through. For its adoption, there should be enough nodes to update to the newest version. Those who prefer not to update lose access to the new blockchain.

- **Soft fork** – A soft fork is a subtle modification in the software protocol and does not generate a new currency. It is also called UASF or a user-activated soft fork. It occurs by users' initiation instead of the miners or supercomputers who maintain the Bitcoin network.

  The user would adopt a specific action on how to interact with the blockchain. If other users follow suit and there is an adequate number, a fork follows.

During the forking process, new digital currencies are created with names similar to the mother crypto.

Examples are the following:

- **Bitcoin Cash (B cash**) – It was the first new coin that Bitcoin forking has created in August 2017. Its creation was a historical moment for Bitcoin and the whole crypto community. Bitcoin Cash is the 11th cryptocurrency in terms of market cap and is one of the most successful hard forks from its primary cryptocurrency. It offers 8 megabytes blocks.

  The Bitcoin Cash network has a hard fork that produced Bitcoin Satoshi's Vision (SBV). It was a project of Craig Wright, one of the noted individuals who claimed that he is Satoshi Nakamoto.

- **Bitcoin Gold** – This bitcoin was another result of a hard fork that happened in October 2017. The developers behind the hard fork felt that the mining functionality has become specialized in terms of hardware and equipment so they
  restored the basic graphics processing units (GPUs).

  Bitcoin Gold uses a pre-mine process, generating 100,000 coins as an aftermath of the fork. Most of these coins were in a 'special endowment' designed to help the future growth and financing of the Bitcoin Gold ecosystem as well as payment for miners.

- **Bitcoin Diamond** – Its objective is to enable cheaper and faster Bitcoin transactions.

- **Bitcoin Private** – The goal is to keep the transactions of users totally confidential or private.

Other notable forks of Bitcoin include:

- **Bitcoin XT** – This was the first significant bitcoin hard fork. It was launched in 2014 by Mike Hearn to include the new features he proposed like increasing the size of the block from 1 to 8 megabytes. It would mean processing 24 transactions every second instead of 7 transactions. In 2015, the software was running 1,000 nodes but was later abandoned by users due to disinterest.

- **Bitcoin Classic** – In 2016, another attempt to increase the block size was done by a group of developers. It ran 2,000 nodes after its launching but lost the majority of users who chose different options. It still exists and is supported by several developers.

- **Bitcoin Unlimited** – Another project was launched in 2016, the Bitcoin Unlimited. But while the developers of this project have released the code, they did not specify the kind of fork it needs. This fork gave users options to choose the size of the blocks up to 16 megabytes. It failed to gain positive users' acceptance.

Bitcoin clones

Not every fork results in a new cryptocurrency. There are software splits that copy the underlying code. Clones are technically not forks, but they are usually called 'forks' because they cloned the source code of Bitcoin, then began anew.

- **Litecoin (LTC)** – Considered the first clone of Bitcoin was initiated in 2011 by Charlie Lee. Its primary goal was to become the "silver" to Bitcoin's gold status. Instead of using the SHA-256 algorithm of Bitcoin, it follows the Scrypt algorithm. After several years, it had its own hard fork and produced Litecoin Cash.

- **Vertcoin** (VTC) – This Bitcoin clone aimed to leverage the mining process by keeping the mining resistant against Application-Specific Integrated Circuit (ASIC).

How did Bitcoin forks or clones affect the crypto community?

Forks, particularly hard forks, create a level of disruption in the community of users. The competing visions of developers usually make the miners, traders, and investors feel that they have no other choice but to make a decision to separate ways. More often, the fractured community would engage in heated debates and controversies. If there is too much disruption over the plan, it can prevent the fork from taking place.

This was the case with SegWit 2. X, a 2017 fork project. It didn't push through because of 'insufficient consensus for a clean upgrade of the blocksize'. Many feared that the upsize plan would create another hard fork and cause Bitcoin destabilization.

In relation to cloning the blockchain, there is a huge possibility that whale investors would try to purchase all the available tokens, knowing that they would cost more after the production of the new coin. This create artificial inflation of price and demand for the parent currency until the day of the cloning.

After the successful cloning, the whales have in their possession new tokens and parent tokens. Their next move is to dump them most of the crypto on crypto exchanges, causing a crash of value for the parent and forked token.

Does forking affect Bitcoin price?

Some programmers often considered
Bitcoin hard forks as an opportunity to
create money. However, the price is always

Unique characteristics of Bitcoin

User autonomy

Unlike the traditional fiat currencies that are vulnerable to external factors like economic crisis or major political developments, Bitcoin stands on its own. Its value is not affected by the usual problems in society or certain government policies. Only the holders and users of this cryptocurrency control the coins.

Pseudonymous

Users are not required to send personal information for identification purposes. The user can use a blockchain address to identify himself. The Bitcoin network also allows users to have multiple addresses in marking various transactions.

Immutable

All stored transactions in the blockchain of Bitcoin are irreversible. They cannot be altered or amended by any third party like a financial service agency, bank authority, or government entity. But if you mistakenly send a bitcoin to someone, you cannot file a charge bank. Your coin is gone forever unless the recipient returns the original bitcoin out of goodwill.

Secure

Since bitcoin is a virtual currency, there are fewer threat of theft. The only way to steal crypto is when a hacker knows the private keys of the user's electronic wallet. But in general, it is impossible to steal the coins. Up to this day, Bitcoin's blockchain remains secure to breaches and hacking, ensuring that transactions between two or multiple addresses are safe.

Low transaction fees

For international transactions, the service fees of Bitcoin are comparatively lower than conventional wire transfers. The standard methods usually have services costs and other fees. Bitcoin eliminates intermediaries and advocates direct transactions between the sender and receiver, making it a more hassle-free and cost-saving alternative. Moreover, transferring funds is faster due to the absence of a waiting period and authorization requirement.

Accessible

The power is in the hands of users. The ease of accessing bitcoins and using them for global transactions makes Bitcoin a must-have currency in this modern world. With only a computer or a smartphone, users can send or receive funds wherever they are. It empowers people who have no access to the banking system, credit cards, and other traditional modes of payment.

Mobile

As long as your device has Internet access, you can pay for your purchases or send/receive bitcoins wherever your location is. You don't have to go to the nearest bank to complete the transaction or visit a store to pay for the product. And what's more important is you don't have to supply your personal information to complete the online transaction.

Guide to storing BTC

Bitcoin needs a digital wallet. This wallet stores the bitcoins and the private keys that correspond to the blockchain address of the user. These keys are in the form of cryptographic information that helps you access your funds and transact business with another user.

Technically, a Bitcoin wallet is a program or device that is created for easy interaction with the blockchain. It is synonymous with a physical wallet, but instead of physical forms of money, it stores a set of private numbers (private keys) that unlocks the blockchain address of the user. When you sign in for Bitcoin transactions, you need to use these private keys to prove that you are the owner of the coins. It is crucial to keep your private keys confidential to prevent attackers from opening your address and move your bitcoins to their own wallets.

There are several types of Bitcoin wallets to match your needs. Each is different from each other in terms of accessibility, convenience, security, and other features. For instance, the full-node wallets support the Bitcoin network's decentralized nature. There are also mobile wallets with built-in QR code scanners or integrated crypto exchanges for convenient buying and selling of coins.

Types of Bitcoin wallets

- **Mobile wallets** –This type of wallet is an app that runs on the smartphone with private keys, making it virtually easy and quick to access the bitcoins. It is best for users who use Bitcoin for their daily transactions like trading and purchasing goods from retailers who accept crypto payments. Mobile wallet uses simplified payment verification (SPV) technology and relies on the Bitcoin network's trusted nodes for correct information.

The downside of mobile wallets is their vulnerability to hacking and malware issues. To prevent them from occurring, always enable the 2-factor authentication feature of your device and app. If you want a more secure authenticator app that is not prone to email hacks or SIM swap attacks, try FreeOTP, Authy, or Google Authenticator.

- **Web wallets** – Web wallets are online wallets of exchange platforms and are controlled by a broker/third party. They have several features that allow you to replicate your address across the devices you often use or link them to your desktop and mobile wallets. Like mobile wallets, web wallets allow users to access their Bitcoins while on the go.

  However, the people running the exchange platform have total control of your funds because they have access to your account's private keys. Another downside of using a web wallet is the risk of leaked emails and passwords which are half of your login credentials to access the funds.

- **Desktop wallets** – They are downloadable wallets that can be installed on your computer device. The private keys to access your bitcoins are stored on the hard drive or SSD. Compared to web and mobile wallets, desktop wallets are more secure because you have total control over your funds. But because they are accessible using the web, there is still a big risk. This wallet, however, is ideal for people who trade a little amount of BTC using their computers.

  If you choose to use a wallet with full nodes, you need large disk space and a quick internet connection. This kind of wallet offers granular control that other wallets lack.

✓ It delivers optimum performance by broadcasting the transactions directly to the system's memory pool.
✓ It features a replace-by-fee checkbox that lets you increase the transaction fees to make the transaction quicker.
✓ It has CLI and API in the interface, allowing app developers to incorporate the Bitcoin-related functionalities in the apps they use or build a proprietary wallet of their own.
✓ It comes with an intuitive drop-down box with speed control and transaction fee.

- **Paper Wallet**s – They are physical documents containing the public address where users can receive Bitcoin and the private key to enable transferring coins in the address. They are like QR-codes that you need to scan before adding the wallet keys to start a transaction. If you want to print the generated keys as a backup, store them in a safe place.

- **Hardware wallets** – They are also called **cold storage**. These are physical devices that securely store the private keys to your crypto account. They are regarded as the safest storage for Bitcoin and have immunity against computer viruses. When picking a hardware wallet, look for the brand with a screen that displays and verifies the wallet details. The screen serves as another layer of protection because it can confirm the address and amount of payment you will be sending. It is capable of generating a recovery phrase. Make sure that it comes from a legit seller of hardware wallets to avoid losing your Bitcoin. There are instances where fake hardware wallets were able to steal the stored cryptocurrencies of the users.

Security threats to Bitcoin wallet

The most common security risks that can jeopardize Bitcoin wallets include:

➢ Malicious software malware that can steal your private keys by scanning the hard drive of your computer
➢ Digital exchange platforms that steal bitcoins by conducting "exit scams"
➢ A Trojan virus that encrypts your hard drive files, allowing the hacker to find the links to your Bitcoin wallet and see how much you own, then make a demand to send the fund in anonymous account in exchange for decrypting your hard drive. This modus is known as ransomware.
➢ Losing your phone, tablet, iPad, or laptop where you installed your wallet

Ways to protect your Bitcoin wallets

Just like the wallet in your pocket or purse, it is important to keep your Bitcoin wallet safe at all times.

➢ If possible, use cold storage options that do not require internet connectivity to make transactions.
➢ Be cautious and always double-check the emails or notifications you receive. There is a kind of scam known as "phishing" where a fake website of a wallet provider would send a message. Once you give authorization, it can wipe out all your bitcoins.
➢ Avoid checking unknown websites that may contain malware and compromise your funds if you are using a mobile or desktop Bitcoin wallet.
➢ Never give your private key to anyone or send it through messenger or email
➢ Do not entertain requests of unknown users who would ask for a BTC and promise to return more coins. They are scammers.

Key Point

Losing your private keys means loss of access to your Bitcoin address and bitcoins. According to researches, about 60% of Bitcoin addresses are

Is there a physical Bitcoin?

Yes, there are physical coins that function as a bitcoin vault and a collector's item. They are preloaded with Bitcoin. The amount is fixed and the private key is protected by a tamper-evident seal. The most common are silver Bitcoin coins, but there are also golden or bronze coins. Each requires an upfront investment to own it.

You can also opt for physical coins that allow funding an amount of bitcoin to the address. These types of coins come with funding instructions. You can only spend them by breaking the protective hologram to retrieve the hidden private key. Once you redeem your coin, it will lose its digital value.

What is the real worth of physical bitcoins?

The value of physical bitcoins is often more than its actual worth because of their collectability and rarity when the minting of the range stops. Even without the Bitcoin value, the empty coins have their unique numismatic value. On eBay, the price for 125 unloaded Casascius coins is $4,995. A 2012 Casascius coin with 1 BTC value but was already peeled was bought by a private bidder for $1,999,99 on eBay.

The market of physical Bitcoin

The market is typically a niche for Bitcoin diehard enthusiasts and collectors who want physical coins for a series of collectibles, geek gifts, or conversation pieces. They are typically produced as limited series and when the last one was bought, they disappear from the market. The first physical Bitcoin coin was Bitbill. It came in the form of a credit card.

Some of the well-known physical bitcoins are:

- **Casascius** – Minted by Mike Caldwell in 2011, the Casascius coins came in different values such as 1 BTC brain coin, 0.5 BTC token, or 1,000 BTC gold-plated bar. The 25-Bitcoin denomination of Casascius coin is minted using brass material with gold electroplating.

  To cash in any of these Bitcoin coins, you need to remove the holographic sticker to get hold of the key to the wallet that contains the designated amount of bitcoins. This process is called "unpeeling."

  Unfortunately, Caldwell had to close his coin minting business in 2013 because he refused to register it at the federal level. The FinCEN or US Financial Crimes Enforcement Network classified his activity as "money transmitting." At the time of the closure, he already minted a total of 27,938 coins with different values.

  CasasciusTracker reported that this coin is still worth a lot. Out of the total number, the active Casascius in circulation were 19,924 as of September 21, 2021. About 8,014 have been redeemed by their owners. Assuming that all the remaining coins have a 1 BTC value, it means that they are worth more than 851 million based on the current price of Bitcoin.

- **Titan Bitcoin** – The company offers a variety of coins from the priciest to the cheapest options. This is to allow clients to choose the option that matches their budget. The denominations range from 0.5 to 1 BTC.

  The most expensive is the Titan One Gold coin. It is loaded with 1 BTC and 1 troy ounce of 24K gold. The cheaper option is the 1-ounce .999 silver coin with 1 BTC which costs $729. There is also a 12 nickel-silver alloy Titan Tenth coin with 0.1 BTC and is priced $96 per piece.

- **Alitin Mint** – This Springfield, Missouri company minted two popular coins. The first one was the Adam Smith coin with 2 BTC load and the second was the Joan of Arc coin with 1 BTC. Both were commemorative 2-ounce pure silver coins designed by the renowned sculptor John Andelin.

  Each variant has 600 minted coins. The Adam Smith coins are retailed for 2.92 BTC, while the Joan of Arc coins cost 1.45 BTC. Investors and collectors who bought this physical bitcoin in 2014 paid $378 per coin.

- **Cryptmint coins** – These .999 silver coins are sold for $99. They weigh 1 troy ounce with a diameter of 39 mm. Another option is the copper coins with a selling price of $42 apiece. There are 6 different QR back designs to choose from. They ship without preloaded bitcoin.

- **Ravenbit Satoshi coins** – Each Satoshi coin is 39mm in diameter and 3mm thick. Made of 85% copper, the front part of every coin has a person outline with binary codes that unlock the word 'Satoshi Nakamoto'. Each kit costs $25 and contains a coin, 2 security holograms, a display stand, and a pouch.

- **CoinedBit**s – They are novelty items without a Bitcoin value or physical wallet. Each collectible coin costs $14.99 for buyers in North America. For overseas buyers, the price is $19.99. They are made of pure brass with an 18K gold plating. Each coin has a 38mm diameter and weighs 1 ounce.

- **Antana coins** – These novelty coins are relatively affordable and created with names that are amusing. Every batch comes in a particular theme with a period of network statistic data. Some of the batch names were the "Transaction Malleability," "Goodbye Mt Gox", "Race for ROI", and "Pump and Dump". A complete set has 20 Antana bitcoins and is prized at 0.41 BTC, while individual coins sell for 0.02 BTC- 0.04 BTC.

- **Lealana coins** – Priced from 0.042 BTC-0.325 BTC are the unfunded gold-plated silver 1 BTC-Lealana coin. There is also a silver bitcoin set that contains 4 coins and is sold at 0.891 BTC.

Fun Fact

There are about 57 types of physical crypto coins. Most of them carry bitcoin value. This information came from Elias Ahonen's Encyclopedia of Physical Bitcoins and Crypto-currencies.

Is it legal to possess a physical Bitcoin?

Holding physical bitcoins is legal, provided that your location allows it. However, manufacturing or minting your own coins requires registration to ensure that your operation is not related to money transmission.

When buying physical coins in online marketplaces, make deals with legitimate sellers who will give you what you are paying for. Do your research diligently and have a ceiling of how much you can afford.

Key takeaways

- Bitcoin is the undisputed king of cryptocurrency, not because it is the pioneer virtual currency but because it has proven its worth.

- Satoshi Nakamoto's visionary and revolutionary concept of currency is now one of the valuable assets in the world.

- Bitcoin's blockchain technology has been copied and improved by modern creators who want to mimic or surpass the success of Bitcoin.

- The unique characteristics of Bitcoin that were once considered weaknesses are now its greatest strengths.

Point to Ponder

Should you buy Bitcoin or Gold?
In 2017, 1 bitcoin surpassed the price
of 1 troy ounce of gold.

Chapter 2

The Digital Gold Rush

"Bitcoin and its ilk are entertainment assets that provide 'psychic income.'"

Dennis Chookazian, Cryto analyst and futurist

Once an ambitious, futuristic project of pseudonymous Satoshi Yakamoto, Bitcoin proves itself to be more than that. It went beyond the skepticism and doubts, becoming the trailblazer of the future technology and giving virtual currencies a monetary role in the modern world.

Today, Bitcoin's network is growing stronger and has sparked the interest of new and big investors who want to diversify their wealth portfolio.

What's in store for Bitcoin now that it has established its mark in economic development?

Crypto analysts and experts believe that Bitcoin can be a strong instrument to resolve big global issues.

1. As a new form of investment, Bitcoin can utilize smart contracts and give investors easy exposure and access to stocks in foreign countries. This eliminates the need to find trusted brokers or intermediaries to sell the stocks.

2. As an instrument for money transfer or remittances of migrant workers. Transaction fees can be around 10 to 15% of the amount. With over $500 billion global remittances annually, it means that $50 billion or higher goes to the fees. Bitcoin can help reduce or eliminate the exorbitant fees.

3. As an enabler of functions of home electronics like televisions, refrigerators, washing machines, and so on. It works by sending a fraction of Bitcoin to the seller every month or week to make them run. It is a developing concept, but as I see it, everything is possible with Bitcoin.

Bitcoin is known for its ability to make people rich quickly. No other financial vehicles can match what Bitcoin has shown. It is also the fastest-growing asset in the world, where over 2% of the global population are now Bitcoin proud owners and still counting.

Not only that, more and more major players in various industries are showing their interest in cryptocurrency, in particular Bitcoin. Social Capital CEO Chamath Palihapitiya even made a fearless forecast that in the next 15 years, 1 bitcoin will be worth $1 million. If this happens, holding your investment for a while is a good decision. Your Bitcoin can make you an instant millionaire. But of course, it depends on how aggressive you are in accumulating bitcoins.

Did you know that?

Former child actor and entrepreneur Brock Pierce is the first person to get a crypto-based mortgage. He invested 3 million BTC to purchase a chapel in Amsterdam, The Netherlands.

Meet the world's Bitcoin billionaires and millionaires

Everyone who invests in Bitcoin wants to be a millionaire. Those who bought Bitcoin for under $10 when it was launched or less than $20,000 in the early part of 2018 earned huge profits after holding it for a time being. The sudden growth and demand of this cryptocurrency produced many Bitcoin millionaires and a handful of billionaires.

The Early Birds

These are people who bought Bitcoin during its early stage. Those who went all-in became billionaires, while others who were more conservative in their purchases became millionaires.

Cameron and Tyler Winklevoss

Many believed that former Olympic rowers and twin brothers Cameron and Tyler Winklevoss were the first bitcoin billionaires when the bitcoin price surged in 2017. They used the $65 million settlement from Facebook to buy bitcoins in 2012. After 5 years, their investment paid off, making them billionaires during the bull period.

The twins claimed to possess 1% of circulating bitcoins or about 100,000 coins that are worth $950 million. They also invested in other cryptocurrencies like Ethereum and various blockchain-related businesses. The twin's great interest in crypto prompted them to devise their own system of storing the private keys of their crypto assets. They eventually launched Gemini, the world's first regulated crypto exchange. The Winklevoss brothers also bought Nifty Gateway, the auction platform for digital art.

Michael Saylor

Before his company decided to invest in Bitcoin, MicroStrategy CEO Michael Saylor was already investing in cryptocurrency. He made his fortune in investing but lost most of it during the dot.com bust. But instead of stopping, Saylor continued investing in Bitcoin and soon enough gained more than what he lost.

One time, Saylor tweeted that he was "hodling" 17,732 BTC and bought each coin at an average price of $9,882. His fascination with Bitcoin even led him to invest $1000 every second. He is among the top 100 BTC owners according to BitInfoCharts and on the 2021 Forbes' Billionaires List of crypto tycoons.

Matthew Roszak

Matthew Roszak became interested in Bitcoin way back 2011 and began buying to diversify his investment. After a decade, his crypto portfolio is already worth $1.5 billion. He also produced the first-ever documentary in the crypto industry- 'The Rise and Rise of Bitcoin."

This 48-year-old entrepreneur is the chairman and co-founder of the blockchain tech startup Bloq, which offers consultancy on projects that involve digital assets. Roszak also co-founded Tally Capital, a cryptocurrency and blockchain-enabled technology investment firm with an impressive portfolio of major companies like Binance, Spacechain, Block. One, Blockstream, Spacechain, Orchid, Qtum, Tzero, Messari, and Civic.

Tim Draper

Tim Draper is a venture capitalist in Silicon Valley who purchased 29,656 bitcoins worth $18.7 million from the Silk Road black market stash that the U.S. Marshals seized in 2014. Apparently, each coin was worth $632 that time. Today, his bitcoins put him on the list of the crypto-rich people in Forbes Magazine.

He co-founded venture capital company Draper Fisher Jurvetson and has multiplied his worth by investing in cryptocurrencies, especially Bitcoin. Draper is also known for his VC investments in leading firms like Theranos and Tesla.

Barry Silvert

Barry Silbert is the founder-CEO of Digital Currency Group. This crypto conglomerate company invested in over 125 blockchain-related firms. His corporate portfolio includes Grayscale Investment, Genesis, and CoinDesk. Silvert's goal is to accelerate the global development of the financial system by establishing and supporting Bitcoin and other blockchain companies.

Michael Novogratz

When the crypto bull market happened in September 2017, Michael Novogratz claimed that he earned $250 million from his Bitcoin and Ethereum holdings. He purchased a private jet from the profits. After a year, he founded Galaxy Digital Holdings and invested $302 million to the company. His investment fund company trades, advises, and manages blockchain-related assets. It has a holding of 13,338 bitcoins which are valued at $122.5 million.

It is reported that 20% of Novogratz worth is in the form of digital assets and 30% of his fortune is tied to cryptocurrencies.

He started investing around 2015. In 2017, he disclosed that he has a $500 million crypto fund, including $150 million from his vast fortune. He is known for being a prominent predictor of Bitcoin's market price movements.

Dan Morehead

Dan Morehead founded Pantera Capital, the first investment company that focuses on bitcoin. In 2018, it was one of the biggest institutional crypto holders. His company launched the first crypto fund in the United States when the trading price of bitcoin was only $65. When the crypto boom occurred in 2017, there was a report that the bitcoin fund of Pantera Capital managed to gain 24,000% for their investors. The company's portfolio investments include Shapeshift, Polychain Capital, Brave, and Bitstamp.

Why do institutional investors change their minds about Bitcoin?

For many years, the idea of Bitcoin investing is far from the minds of people behind large companies. They probably wondered why retail investors willingly embraced the volatility of this cryptocurrency and added it to their portfolios. Perhaps the thought of adding Bitcoin into their corporate reserves was not even entertained, considering their foremost requirement is stability and security of funds.

Then, pandemic happened and there was a Bitcoin frenzy. The taboo discussion about crypto investing became a crucial matter among big names in the financial industry. Suddenly, the gradual adoption of major companies in different industries has changed the landscape of cryptocurrency. Digital coins and tokens have been recognized as investable asset classes.

As of July 2021, the top publicly traded companies owning the largest Bitcoin reserve include the following in no particular order:

MicroStrategy

MicroStrategy opened the floodgates of institutional investment. This prominent cloud software company purchased Bitcoin for $425 million in August and September 2020, adopting it as a primary reserve asset. It continued buying Bitcoin until 2021 and is now holding a reserve asset of 105,085 BTC, which is worth more than $3.3 billion.

On the eve of New Year 2020, MicroStrategy sold its 10.9% share of Bitcoin to Morgan Stanley, a leading wealth management firm and global investment bank.

Quick Facts

Did you know that in 2013 MicroStrategy CEO Michael Saylor said that the days of Bitcoin were numbered?
But then he saw its potential returns and eventually chose it as his company's reserve asset over gold.

Tesla

Tesla has invested $1.50 billion in cryptocurrency according to its file in the SEC. CEO Based on its SEC filing, the company's purchase reflected its updated investment policy to maximize returns and diversify cash on hand.

Tesla invested in various alternative reserve assets such as digital assets (crypto), gold exchange-traded funds, gold bullions, and other future-specified assets. During the first quarter of 2021,

Tesla sold 10% of its holdings to prove Bitcoin's liquidity as an option to cash. At present, it owns 42,902 BTC worth $1.37 billion.

Quick Facts

*Elon Musk is a known holder of Bitcoin, so it seems natural that his electric vehicle manufacturing
company would also adopt Bitcoin.*

Square Inc.

When payments company Square Inc. invested $50 million to buy Bitcoin, it further lit the interest of institutional players to look at cryptocurrency with bigger interest. During the 4th Quarter of 2020, the company reported an additional $170 million Bitcoin investment in its earnings statement.

In March 2021, Square Inc. reaffirmed its commitment to holding its Bitcoin in a long-term period by revealing a reserve of 8,207 BTCs worth $255 million. The company has no future plan to buy more Bitcoin but is making efforts to leverage its ecosystem by investing a $5 million fund for cryptocurrency education. Moreover, it showed its support to Bitcoin when it issued a white paper that defended cryptocurrency's impact on the environment.

In July 2021, Square Inc. announced that they would create a hardware wallet for Bitcoin.

Quick Facts

*CEO Jack Dorsey is a Bitcoin advocate who even
has his own Bitcoin node.*

Galaxy Digital Holdings

With over 16,640 BTC, Galaxy Digital Holdings is one of the biggest institutional holders that are working directly with the crypto industry. This crypto-focused merchant institution has partnered with BlockFi and Block. one. Its current Bitcoin holdings are worth more than $522 million.

Galaxy Digital Holdings founder Michael Novogratz is also an active Bitcoin advocate. When the stimulus measures to mitigate the effects of the COVID-19 pandemic were announced in April 202, he noted the strong interest of many firms in cryptocurrencies. He called the escalated attention as the 'Bitcoin moment'.

Coinbase Global Inc.

Crypto exchange Coinbase is one of the renowned firms that went public in April 2021. This move was considered a significant landmark in the cryptocurrency industry. Before its Nasdaq listing decision, Coinbase announced in February 2021 that its Bitcoin holding was around $230 million. By July 2021, the value of its 4,482 BTC went down to $143 million.

Voyager DigitalLTD

According to bitcoin treasuries.org, this renowned crypto brokerage firm has about 12,260 BTC worth $390 million. Voyager Digital operates by providing a one-stop digital trading shop that reported $60.4 million quarterly revenue in May 2021. It was 16 times bigger compared to the previous quarter.

Marathon Digital Holdings Inc.

Marathon Digital is a Bitcoin mining company with around 5,784 BTC worth $184 million in its treasury. It was established to become the 'biggest North America's Bitcoin mining firm' with the least energy expenses. Before it pivoted to crypto mining, Marathon Digital was a patent-holding company.

At the beginning of 2021, it added $200 million capital and ended January by purchasing $150 million worth of Bitcoin. Its long-term goal is to round up more than 103,000 Bitcoin miners to churn out around 50 to 60 BTC every day or an average of 1500 to 1800 BTC per month. As of June 2021, Marathon Digital was generating a monthly output of 265.6 BTC.

Hut 8 Mining Corp

With 3,522 BTC worth $112 million, Hut 8 is one of the major companies on the list. According to its SEC filing document, this Canadian-based crypto mining company "aims to grow the number and value of its bitcoin holdings to increase the shareholders' value." Also included is the explanation that it will be leveraging its held and self-mined Bitcoin reserve by partnering with the leading digital asset brokerages.

Hut 8 aims to mine 5,000 BTC by the year-end. It has invested in new crypto mining equipment and is riding on the favorable geopolitical landscape due to China's crackdown that reduced the difficulty of mining Bitcoin.

Bitcoin Group SE

Bitcoin Group SE is a venture capital company that is based in Germany. It is now holding around 3,947 BTCs which are worth $126 million based at the current price.

In October 2020, its Futurum bank and crypto exchange Bitcoin.de. have merged to become the first crypto bank in Germany. It came through after the German parliament allowed traditional banks to store and sell cryptocurrencies. It gave them a big opportunity to introduce the high returns and safety features of Bitcoin and other crypto to their institutional investors.

Riot Blockchain, Inc.

This US-based crypto mining company has 2,243 BTC holdings worth around $71 million. Riot Blockchain Inc. bought a Bitcoin mining facility for $650 million in Rockdale Texas in April 2021.

Its purchase of this 1-gigabyte facility was described in the crypto industry as an 'event of transformation'. It made the company North America's biggest publicly traded Bitcoin mining and hosting entity in terms of total developed capacity

Cool Fact

The U.S. United Wholesale Mortgage announced that they will be accepting Bitcoin and other cryptos as a mortgage payment.

The institutional investing landscape by waves

During the last two years before the pandemic, there was a growing interest and excitement about bitcoin among institutional investors. Bitcoin is seen by most of them as a hedge fund again inflation.

March 2020: The first wave

The sudden increase in the numbers of bitcoin that big investors bought was seen during the middle part of March 2020. Large companies and investors were reportedly buying a minimum of 1000 bitcoin. This phenomenon was described by industry experts as a move to secure hedge funds. Investing over $30 million in individual purchases means that the wealthiest and most powerful entities were busy safeguarding their holdings against potential risks.

Since crypto is deregulated and is not affected by economic downtrends, the money of the institutions is intact and secure. However, it was not surprising because many family-owned firms, hedge funds, and investment funds were already buying bitcoin. It was only highlighted when the CEOs of major companies and institutions became very vocal about their plans and decisions.

In April 2021, Coinbase confirmed that indeed, the big buyers were institutional investors. In its 1st quarter report, this leading crypto platform revealed that $215 billion out of its $335 billion in trades were made by the leading institutions and corporations.

The buying spree accelerated in October, then reached its peak in the early part of February 2021 when the price of 1 bitcoin reached $33,000. The last high-water mark was during the Bitcoin bubble in 2017 when bitcoin's price reached $20,000.

The first wave ended at the end of the month. The data revealed that many big investors were busy selling their bitcoins and earning huge profits. They believed that the price won't go beyond $33,000, so they sold their investment.

May 2021: The current wave

Since this May, the escalating growth of big investors rebuying bitcoins has become significant. There is no indication of slowing down, yet. It seems that Bitcoin has found its long-term position in the institutional portfolios.

Perhaps, one of the reasons for this stronger interest in this volatile crypto asset was due to the phenomenal price surge of $64,486 per BTC on April 14, 2021. Those who sold their coins in February were surprised by the development. And what made bitcoin more attractive during that period was its display of price durability.

In May 2021, bitcoin was trading more than $55,000. On May 11, it was fetching $56,800 then scaled down to $35,000 at the end of the month. The sudden change was due to the growing criticism regarding the environmental impact of bitcoin. But for institutional and big investors, this lull was an opportunity to jump back in their bitcoin buying spree.

They saw the April price of bitcoin as a good indicator of its strong market position, making them more confident to invest more. The mid-May price of $35,000 attracted them back. In addition, while the sharp and fast fall of bitcoin price in May was felt in the industry, many saw that bitcoin can survive amidst the system's loss of leverage. It has found its own leverage level that prompted the investors to trust its power of stability and sustainability. It triggered this current wave.

Did you know that?

The most valuable hard drive happened to be the one that British James Howells accidentally threw in 2013? It contained over 75,000 BTCs which is worth $2.25 billion or more.

Bitcoin price in institutional investment

Bitcoin's power to stay on top of the crypto industry lies in its proprietary blockchain data and its pricing durability. Institutional investors are more than willing to spend more than $36,000 for one BTC. As of September 2021, 1 BTC is priced at $43,000. They keep buying and haven't sold their holdings yet.

It is also interesting to note that these institutional investors can leverage their power in the crypto market, with their valuation influencing the price of Bitcoin. Also, with the largest financial firms and banks planning or offering access to bitcoins and other cryptocurrencies to their existing big clients, acceleration of institutional buying would be a common scenario for a long time.

Institutional investors consider bitcoin as digital gold, like precious metals to secure their wealth. They buy and hold bitcoin and altcoins to hedge their investment against constant inflation as well as diversify their financial portfolio. Also, compared to gold and other precious metals, bitcoin's evolving technology promises bigger growth potential. The technological innovations boost its current value and attractiveness to investors.

As of August 2021, Buy Bitcoin Worldwide data revealed that institutional investors are holding around $70 billion worth of Bitcoin or an equivalent of 1,476,568 BTC. This number is 7.85% of the 18,797,968 circulating supply of bitcoin in the market.

The gold rush is digital

The craze around Bitcoin becomes stronger as it reaches more than a decade of existence in the digital realm. Its decentralized approach is a big come-on for techie-driven economists, investors, and traders. It was like the 1848 gold rush where the elite group in the society wanted the asset in their possession, as gold represents power, fame, and status symbol.

Bitcoin is a game-changer, creating an unprecedented path that no other digital currency has done. While the journey to the top was tough, it displayed resilience and flexibility to be recognized in the digital world.

Whether you love or hate cryptocurrency, it is here and part of the modern world. The future is still unknown but there are expert predictions that crypto, especially Bitcoin, would continue shaping the virtual realm and go mainstream. By allowing users to buy, sell, exchange, or hold money without government or central bank authority oversight, crypto acts as the cutting edge of finance.

Trivia

In 2020, scammers who hacked the accounts of Barack Obama, Elon Musk, Kanye West, and other personalities received 400 payments all in Bitcoin currencies.

Ways organized crime syndicates exploit the digital gold rush

Aside from the traders and investors, there are groups of people or individuals who are leveraging the digital gold rush to accomplish their illicit activities. They conceal their organized crimes behind the anonymity feature of cryptocurrencies. In Latin America, unscrupulous people use Bitcoin in the following organized crimes:

- **Money Laundering** – Gangs are hiding behind the anonymous feature of cryptocurrencies.

  - The Unidad de Inteligencia Financiera (UIF) of Mexico is running after illegal crypto exchanges where money laundering is rampant.

  - In Rio de Janeiro, 12 people were arrested and charged with laundering extorted money from local businesses. The Civil Police said that they were using Bitcoin to hide their operations. They bought small amounts of bitcoins and stored them in different anonymous digital wallets.

➢ Venezuela is also raising questions about how the cash machines in Caracas can be utilized for illicit money laundering. According to the report of the Drug Enforcement Administration, anyone can deposit cash into these ATMs to buy Bitcoin. They believe that once the fiat currency is in the digital form, it would be easy to hide where it originated, allowing transfer from one user to another anywhere in the world.

- **Ransomware Extortion** – It refers to the data hostage operation of criminals who typically ask crypto payments as ransom. This extortion activity usually locks the target's computer system or steals its corporate data.

  One notable victim of a ransomware attack was JBS, the Brazilian meat processing firm that is supplying 1/5 of beef consumption in the United States. It paid the group "REvil" a ransom of $11 million worth of bitcoins.

- **Kidnapping** – Another syndicated crime where Bitcoin is being used as ransom payment is kidnapping. In Tia Juana Venezuela, the kidnapped victim Gustavo Torres Gonzales was murdered when his family did give the full amount of Bitcoin to the kidnappers. Another story of kidnapping happened in Argentina, where a merchant was finally released after 5 days of being held captive when the family paid the demanded ransom in Bitcoin.

- **Ciberburreros (Cyber mules)** – They are young people used by the criminal syndicates to purchase small volumes of crypto simultaneously. Since smaller transactions are not suspicious, the group behind them would be accumulating large holdings of digital currencies to use in criminal activities including money laundering. The pattern of their activities mimics the way the Sinaloa Cartel moved drugs in the U.S.

Did you know that?

*China is now controlling more than
75% of crypto mining networks, making
it the largest crypto miner.*

Getting onboard to the digital gold rush

It appears that 2021 is becoming the year of Bitcoin, making the pioneer cryptocurrency live up to being the 'digital gold.' While the world is battling the COVID-19 pandemic threats, Bitcoin has become an attractive cushion against inflation.

Goldman Sachs and Paul Tudor Jones recognized and endorsed it as digital gold, while the likes of MicroStrategy, Grayscale, and MassMutual welcomed it as part of their investment portfolio. PayPal also delved into the crypto world by adding Bitcoin and selected altcoins to its services.

Should you join the Bitcoin feeding frenzy?

The Bitcoin market is volatile. It started 2021 on a strong and high note and more bitcoins are changing hands. These are signs of a liquid, active, and healthy crypto market. Traders and holders of BTC who panicked with sudden dips of its market value sold their coins to many Bitcoin 'whales'. These investors have over 1,000 bitcoins in their possession and are always on the lookout for retail investors who are selling their crypto out of fear that the price crash would continue.

But a lot of institutional investors, crypto-analysts, and industry specialists are predicting a sunny outlook for this cryptocurrency over the next year or beyond. One leaked report coming from a senior analyst of Citibank revealed that Bitcoin has a high potential to reach another all-time high in December 2021 with a projected value of $318,000. If this happens, then Bitcoin is set to become the "gold of the 21st century."

Other predictions include:

- ➢ StormGain CEO Alex Althausen predicted that Bitcoin's market price would hit $100,000 by the end of the year.

- ➢ JP Morgan strategists believed that once Bitcoin beats its volatility, it could replace gold as the preferred safe-haven asset and achieve a long-term value of $146,000 per coin.

- ➢ Guggenheim's predicts that the price of Bitcoin would soar at $400,000.

Another interesting set of Bitcoin predictions for 2022 came from the Chief Economist Philip Gradwell of Chainalysis. He advised investors, in particular institutional sectors, to watch out for the following factors when advancing their investing strategies:

- ▪ Bitcoin will sustain its price floor of $36,000 until the summer of 2022.

- ▪ Bitcoin will continue its domination among large investors, followed by Ethereum.

- ▪ The next batch of Bitcoin investors would want the risks and flaws in the system resolved. Expect major activities in the system and crypto industry to elevate the status of Bitcoin and make it comparable with the gold-standard characteristics of conventional investment instruments.

- ▪ The liquidity of Bitcoin will surge as institutional investors buy and sell their crypto in shorter terms. In essence, more liquidity means a more mature Bitcoin market.

- ▪ As large investors aim for ESG investing or socially responsible investing, there would be actions and reforms in the crypto industry to reduce the environmental impact of their mining activities. To boost the confidence of investors in virtual currencies, Bitcoin Mining Council and other groups would actively address the ESG (Environmental, Social, and Governance) issues.

- There would be a stronger pursuit for regulations and perimeter settings.

- Skeptics and doubters who are afraid of catastrophic collapse will significantly decrease.

Trivia

When the IRS won the case against Coinbase, the exchange company was required to submit the list of 14,000 users with more than $20,000 cost of transactions between 2013 and 2015.

List of countries that say "Yay" and "Nay" on Bitcoin

After its 2009 debut, Bitcoin remains a hot subject of debate among regulators, enforcement agencies, and tax authorities. Until today, there is no single international law that can regulate the peer-to-peer transactions of Bitcoin.

However, the issue and question of its legality depend on the location and the activities of users. Some countries have enacted regulatory oversight that indirectly allows its legal use, while others prefer to wait-and-see what will be the consensus of the majority.

12 Countries that show   to Bitcoin

El Salvador

El Salvador formally adopted bitcoin as a legal tender when President Nayib Bukele signed the "Bitcoin Law" on June 8, 2021. Bitcoin officially joined the US dollar as El Salvador's legal tender on September 7, 2021. This historical decision made them the first-ever country to completely legalize the status of Bitcoin, recognizing its economic value.

- ✓ The Salvatorian government also purchased 400 bitcoins worth $21 million as a buffer fund.

- ✓ Chivo wallet, a Bitcoin wallet that is officially sponsored by the government has been downloaded by almost 46% of the population or about 3 million people one month after the law became effective on September 21, 2021.

The United States

Generally, there is a positive response toward Bitcoin in the United States. More and more prominent retail companies are welcoming bitcoin payment including Microsoft, Subway, and Dish Network (DISH). In addition, Bitcoin has successfully made its way to the derivatives market which adds to its sense of legitimacy.

- Bitcoin is categorized Bitcoin as a money services business (MSB) by the U.S. Department of Treasury and not a currency. It means that all payment processors and exchanges that conduct business with Bitcoin should register, report, and keep records of the transactions as mandated by the bank Secrecy Act.

- The Treasury's FinCEN or Financial Crimes Enforcement Network has been issuing guidance about this cryptocurrency since 2013.

- The Internal Revenue Service (IRS) has put Bitcoin under the property for taxation purposes category, in particular federal income tax.

- The Securities and Exchange Commission (SEC) considers Bitcoin as a security asset.

- The Commodity Futures Trading Commission (CFTC) sees it as a commodity.

The European Union

When the European Court of Justice (ECJ) issued a ruling on October 22, 2015, that the buy and sell of cryptocurrencies is a form of supply of services, it exempted Bitcoin and other digital currencies from paying value-added tax (VAT) in all member states.

Also, some of the EU countries are making bitcoin stances in their own jurisdictions.

- ✓ The United Kingdom's Financial Conduct Authority (FCA) is pro-bitcoin and wants to have a supportive regulatory environment on this cryptocurrency. Bitcoin is also placed under some tax regulations.

- ✓ Belgium's Federal Public Service Finance gave Bitcoin a VAT-exempt status.

✓ Finland's Central Board of Taxes (CBT) has classified Bitcoin as a financial service to exempt it from VAT. It is treated as a form of commodity rather than a currency.

✓ Bulgaria's National Revenue Agency (NRA) has included Bitcoin in its tax laws.

✓ Cyprus has no regulations over Bitcoin, allowing its operations in the country.

✓ Germany considers Bitcoin legal but subjects it to taxes that cover exchanges, users, enterprises, or miners.

Australia

Bitcoin is considered an asset under capital gains tax purposes by the Australian Taxation Office (ATO). By classifying virtual currencies as legal properties, they are subject to capital gains tax.

- The government of the "Land Down Under" allows crypto exchanges to operate freely anywhere in the country, as long as the operators register their business with the AUSTRAC (Australian Transaction Reports and Analysis Centre). They should also meet the required AML/CTF obligations and conditions.

- For initial coin offerings (ICOs), the Australian Securities and Investments Commission (ASIC) issued strict regulatory requirements to protect investors.

- In 2019, authorities banned the crypto exchanges that offer privacy coins or coins with built-in privacy features due to the speculations that they could be used by syndicated criminal elements.

Canada

With a friendly stance on bitcoin, Canada considers it as a commodity under the ruling of the Canada Revenue Agency (CRA). All Bitcoin transactions are considered barter and the generated income is viewed as business income. The taxable amount is dependent on whether the person is into investing or conducting a buy and sell business.

✓ In February 2021, the government approved the Bitcoin exchange-traded fund (ETF), making Canada the first one to give one.

✓ The bitcoin exchanges are under the money service business, placing them under the Anti-Money Laundering (AML) laws. This is to ensure that Bitcoin cannot be used as an instrument for money laundering acts of unscrupulous people.

✓ The Investment Industry Regulatory Organization of Canada (IIROC) and the Canadian Securities Administrators (CSA) compelled all crypto dealers and trading platforms to register under respective provincial regulators.

Japan

Japan has a progressive stance when it comes to regulating cryptocurrencies. Under the Payment Services Act, Japanese authorities recognize Bitcoin and other virtual currencies as legal property.

- All crypto exchanges should register with FSA (Financial Services Agency) and comply with the obligations of AML/CFT.

- The trading gains from crypto are considered as "miscellaneous income" and investors are taxed accordingly.

Singapore

In the island state of Singapore, cryptocurrencies are classified as property. All exchanges need to secure a license to operate from the Monetary Authority of Singapore (MAS) and follow the applicable regulations that are listed in the Payment Services Act (PSA).

- Singapore treats the gains of crypto companies as income and is subject to corresponding taxes.
- However, it does not tax long-term capital gains.

Mauritius

The country's Financial Services Commission considers Bitcoin and other cryptocurrencies as Digital Assets under the 2007 Financial Services Act. While virtual currencies are regulated, the authorities are still cautioning investors to be careful even though they are covered by the statutory compensation agreements protection.

Mexico

Since 2017, Bitcoin has been legal in the country. The plans to regulate this cryptocurrency as a Virtual Asset under FinTech Law are in progress.

Kyrgyzstan

Under the Kyrgyz Republic laws, Bitcoin is a commodity and not a currency or security. It is legal to mine, buy, sell, or trade this crypto on its local commodity exchanges. However, using bitcoin as a currency to settle domestic settlements is still prohibited.

Uzbekistan

This crypto-friendly territory has legalized crypto-trading and makes it tax-exempt by virtue of a decree that was signed on September 2, 2018.

Switzerland

All forms of Bitcoin businesses in this country are subject to the laws against money laundering. In some cases, Bitcoin entrepreneurs need to obtain a banking license before they can conduct their ventures. As of June 2021, there are about 100 Exchange Traded Products (ETP) in the country.

10 Countries that are UNFRIENDLY to Bitcoin

China

First on the list is China. The People's Bank of China (PBOC) has banned all Bitcoin transactions and crypto exchanges in the country. This is due to the no-approval transaction method that Bitcoin offers to users.

- All banks, payment processors, and other financial institutions are prohibited to deal or transact using Bitcoin.

- It has a continuing order to crack down on any crypto mining activities, forcing firms that are engaged in this activity to relocate or close their operations.

- In 2017, Binance which was launched in China relocated to the Cayman Islands when the authorities began their crackdown on cryptocurrency regulations.

Bolivia

There is an absolute ban on any use of Bitcoin and altcoins in the country according to El Banco Central de Bolivia.

Ecuador

In a national assembly, the majority of people voted against the use of cryptocurrencies including Bitcoin in the country.

Egypt

A religious decree that classified all Bitcoin commercial transactions as 'Haram" (prohibited under the laws of Islam) was issued by the Islamic legislator Egypt's Dar al-lfta.

Russia

While Russia does not have a standing regulation about Bitcoin, using it to pay for goods and services is considered illegal.

Vietnam
The government of Vietnam as well as the state bank stand on their decisions that Bitcoin cannot be used as a legitimate form of payment.

Saudi Arabia

All financial institutions in the country are warned by the Saudi Central Bank (SAMA) not to use Bitcoin because of its high-risk nature.

Qatar

Cryptocurrencies are prohibited in the Qatar Financial Centre and all banks cannot trade Bitcoin because of the threats involving hacks and financial crimes.

Bangladesh

All financial institutions in the country are prohibited to conduct any form of Bitcoin transactions. The Bangladesh Bank issued a statement in September 2014 that 'anyone caught using crypto would be charged and imprisoned under its anti-money laundering laws.'

Nepal

There is an absolute ban on any kind of cryptocurrency in this country.

Key Points

In the context of Bitcoin adoption, the 3 metrics must be present:
- *Number and presence of merchants that accept Bitcoin as payment.*
- *Size of the population relative to Bitcoin activities.*
- *Number and location of Bitcoin ATMs.*

Bitcoin Hotspots: Cities in the world that adopted Bitcoin
San Francisco (USA)

As the tech capital of the United States, it is expected to be part of the list since it is home to two prominent crypto trading platforms – Kraken and Coinbase. There are 65 Bitcoin ATMs in the city and 473 in the Bay Area. Merchants and business establishments in this major US city accept bitcoins as payment for goods and services rendered.

Vancouver (Canada)

Did you know that the first Bitcoin ATM in the world was placed at Waves Coffee House in downtown Vancouver on October 29, 2013? The city was also the home of the defunct crypto exchange QuadrigaCX, which became controversial when it lost the clients' fund amounting to $180 million after the news of the alleged death of the founder was released to the public.

At present, the Bitcoin community in the whole of Canada is growing stronger. People can buy Bitcoin from 221 locations in the country with over 50 merchants accepting it as payment.

New York (USA)

Known as the tech and financial hub of over 8.4 million people, this city is the major location of crypto startups and crypto-media firms like CoinDesk, CoinTelegraph, and Decrypt. Anyone can use their bitcoin in the metro area when paying merchants and crypto traders.

In Lower Manhattan, there is a Bitcoin Store and in Morningside Heights, CryptoART is a to-go place for crypto enthusiasts. New York is also the venue of Consensus, which is one of the crypto industry's biggest annual events.

Amsterdam (Netherlands)

Amsterdam is where Bitfury, the mining hardware maker is located. It is also home to the European HQ of BitPay, one of the leading payment service providers. Placed in the city's strategic locations are half a dozen ATMs where you use to buy or sell bitcoins.

Tel Aviv (Israel)

Tel Aviv is one of the best cities for crypto startups. It has 7 Bitcoin ATMs and 19 merchants who accept Bitcoin payments across the metro. Tel Aviv is also home to the 4,000-member Israel Bitcoin Meetup Group which is one of the most active in the crypto world.

Portsmouth, New Hampshire (USA)

Known as the "Bitcoin village", this tiny coastal city has a large crypto community. There are 21 Bitcoin ATMs as well as tellers in the city and nearby areas. Portsmouth's downtown section is home to the Free State Bitcoin Shoppe, Seacoast Repertory Theater, and other crypto-friendly businesses.

Ljubljana (Slovenia)

It is the biggest city and capital of Slovenia with about 200 merchants accepting bitcoin payments and 11 ATMs where anyone can use for easy selling or buying of cryptocurrency. Bitstamp, the well-known Bitcoin exchange was founded by Slovenians who eventually moved their operations to London and Luxembourg.

Miami, Florida (USA)

This major city of the United States is actively seeking blockchain businesses to invest in their area. It has 651 Bitcoin ATMs and tellers as well as 4 dozen merchants who accept crypto payment.

The city government through Mayor Francis Suarez is proposing to integrate bitcoin in their transactions such as allowing the residents to pay taxes and fees using this cryptocurrency and exploring the possibility of paying the salary of government employees in Bitcoin. It was the venue of Miami Bitcoin Conference, the oldest and biggest crypto convention.

London (United Kingdom)

With over 8.9 million people, London has 50 Bitcoin ATMs across the city and merchants accepting Bitcoin as payment for purchases of goods and services. Coinfloor, the pioneer Bitcoin exchange in the United Kingdom has its HQ in this city. People embrace crypto as part of their daily transactions with dozens of Meetup groups that support Bitcoin and altcoins.

El Zonte (El Salvador)

El Zonte is a fishing and surfing village with 3,000 people. It has been using Bitcoin since 2019 when California surfer Mike Peterson who was doing charity work in the area received more than $100,000 donation from an anonymous American in one condition- the amount paid in bitcoins would be used to establish a local sustainable Bitcoin ecosystem. This unknown donor became rich because of crypto trading and wanted to show the world that Bitcoin can positively change the society's way of living.

The initiative was dubbed Bitcoin Beach where residents use an app payment system for crypto exchange. They initially received a certain amount to use for routine activities like paying utility bills, buying goods, and other daily transactions. The experiment was successful and has become the inspiration of President Nayib Bukele to push the law adopting Bitcoin as legal tender. In 2020, El Zonte received a Bitcoin ATM from the government.

Cool Fact

El Salvador President Nayib Bukele is a millennial business-politician who describes himself as the "world's coolest dictator," and a Silicon Valley-like

Key takeaways

- The impressive rate of Bitcoin adoption within the span of 10 years is a clear and strong indication that cryptocurrencies are already part of society's economic and financial sectors.

- Bitcoin has changed the landscape of the global investment sector, attracting major and prominent institutional investors to explore its unique features and benefits.

- The transformation of Bitcoin from a highly-speculative investment instrument to a trusted portfolio stablemate is being considered by the governments that are still figuring out how to regulate this asset class.

- Bitcoin has created a list of millionaires and billionaires across the world, attracting more retail investors to invest in Bitcoin and wait for the next digital gold rush.

- More and more countries are becoming "friendlier" to Bitcoin.

Point to Ponder

Want to jump into Bitcoin investing?
Learn more in the next chapter.

Chapter 3

Is Cryptocurrency Investing for You?

"In cryptocurrency investment, long-term thinkers are less stressed."
– Olawale Daniel-

In Bitcoin investing, anyone who dares becomes filthy wealthy or loses his money. If you're the type of investor who worries about losing money or the myriad of risks that come with the nature of crypto, this investing in Bitcoin is not for you. It is for investors who have strong risk tolerance and are not afraid to fail at the beginning of their investment journey.

In a nutshell, cryptocurrency is in the category of "high risk, high reward" investment. The main appeal of crypto investing lies in the potential of amassing huge profits that can make you an overnight millionaire. But what if you wake up one morning and find out that your crypto coin has lost its value because of the loss of support and adoption from major investors?

Reality bites, but it is how the world of crypto operates- volatile, proactive, highly speculative, and full of risks.

To be successful in Bitcoin and crypto investing, there are 3 things you need to do:

1. Expect that crypto investing is like a roller coaster ride, so plan and prepare your strategies.
2. Start with small sums to buy crypto or fractional shares of investment until such time that you are more skillful and confident.
3. Track down the performance of your crypto investment so you will know when to sell it.

The fundamentals of cryptocurrency investing

As Bitcoin and other cryptocurrencies go mainstream, it becomes impossible for investors to ignore the lure of investing in virtual currencies. Many are considering buying Bitcoin or altcoins to add to their financial portfolio, seeing how these digital currencies are not affected by economic and political events that can crash the stocks and the value of fiat currencies.

But first, you need to learn the basics. You cannot just buy a cryptocurrency and then sell it when you want. You need to plan, prepare, and apply your knowledge with diligence.

Get familiar with cryptocurrency

Cryptocurrency or crypto is a digital currency that is created through encryption technology. It takes a virtual form of coin or token, which is intangible in nature. The unique encryption algorithms of crypto make it both a currency for online transactions and a virtual accounting system.

It is designed to be decentralized and cannot be controlled or manipulated by anyone, even the government. Compared to conventional currencies, cryptocurrency does not possess the fundamental tenets like being a medium of exchange, store of value, or unit of measurement.

The term 'crypto' in cryptocurrency refers to the complex cryptography that is used to mine or create every single coin. Bitcoin is produced by the mining process, where 'miners' solve complicated mathematical problems. On the other hand, other cryptocurrencies are generated as code by professional teams that build proprietary mechanisms for issuance.

Blockchain: The heart and soul of crypto

Cryptocurrency exists in the virtual sphere and is powered by **blockchain**, the core technology with extremely strong cryptography that secures all transactions. It has its own mechanism that operates without any human intervention, storing information in blocks and chaining them together in chronological order.

Technically, a blockchain is a database that collects and stores data electronically in groups or blocks. This innovative technology enables users to collectively retain control over their own funds and deal with each other without intermediaries like a bank, government, or third party. The peer-to-peer transactions are verified, time-stamped, and recorded by the computer networks of the blockchain system.

And because it is decentralized, blockchain is immutable. It means that every information that users input into the system is irreversible and permanently recorded. Access to view the transactions is possible but not the confidential details of the users.

How does blockchain work?

For example, Mr. A wants to buy a bitcoin.

- The purchase and sale transaction is entered in the public digital ledger (blockchain) and then transmitted to the nodes (network of high-end, powerful computers) across the world.

- The network of nodes will individually assess and confirm the transaction with the help of computer algorithms. This process of solving equations is called "proof of work."

- Once the transaction is cryptographically confirmed as legitimate, it will be added to the block in the ledger.

- The new block will be chained to other blocks to create a permanent history of all transactions.

Mr. A's transaction is complete.

Trivia

*The concept of blockchain was initially outlined by researchers
Stuart Haber and W.Scott Stornetta in 1991, but the real-world
application only happened in January 2009
when Bitcoin
was launched in public.*

The Cryptocurrencies: Bitcoin and Altcoins

The crypto variants are mostly forks of Bitcoin and the rest were developed from scratch. In terms of types of cryptocurrencies, there are two broad types:

1. Bitcoin

Blockchain-based Bitcoin is the first decentralized cryptocurrency and the most successful. It sends users transactions over its proprietary blockchain and utilizes public-key cryptography for verifying, signing, and recording them. It was introduced to the world on January 3, 2009, by the anonymous programmer Satoshi Nakamoto. Until today, the persona behind Nakamoto is still a big mystery.

Bitcoin's network is designed to stop developing new coins when the 21-million cap is achieved. As of this time, the total circulation is over $18 million. This limited supply is the primary reason that drives Bitcoin's market price.

One bitcoin is equivalent to 100,000,000 satoshis. A single bitcoin can be divided up to 8 decimal places, giving investors an option to buy fractions for a more affordable price rather than paying more than $56,000 for a single bitcoin.

How does it operate?

Users of bitcoin send or receive coins by inputting the public-key data that is connected to their electronic wallet. There is a fee to every transaction and it is used to incentivize the miners or the network of people that verify the transaction. The miner who successfully adds the transaction to a fresh block gets the reward. The higher the transaction fee, the faster it will be processed by the miners since it operates on a first-price auction system.

The block rewards in the Bitcoin system decrease over time. At present (2021), the reward for mining new blocks is 6.25 bitcoins. For every 210,000 mined blocks (around a 4-year period), the reward is halved. The next halving of bitcoin will be in 2024, where the block reward will be dropping to 3.124 bitcoins for every block.

Trivia

*Bitcoin (with uppercase "**B**") refers to the peer-to-peer decentralized system while the native cryptocurrency is called bitcoin (with lower case "**b**').*

2. Altcoins

Altcoins or alternate versions of bitcoins are cryptocurrencies other than bitcoins. They represent almost 60% of circulating more than 12,000 cryptocurrencies in the market as of October 2021. The price movements of altcoins usually copy the trajectory and trading signals of Bitcoin.

In the context of market capitalization, the largest altcoins are the Ethereum and Binance Coins. At present, there are more than 5,000 circulating altcoins in the world.

Altcoins are divided according to their consensus mechanisms and functionalities.

- Mining-based – These altcoins are produced by mining using Proof-of-Work (PoW). This method refers to the process where new coins are created by solving difficult equations or problems. Some examples are Litecoin, Zcash, and Monero.

  The alternative to this type of altcoins is the pre-mined coins. They are cryptocurrencies that are listed in the market before their distribution. Ripple's XRP is a good example.

- Stablecoins – These crypto are created to reduce the volatile nature of coins. They work by anchoring the value of the altcoin to the basket of financial products like fiat currencies, other types of crypto, or precious metals like gold or silver. The basket of goods serves as a reserve fund to redeem the crypto holders of their loss when the coin faces problems or fails to deliver the promise. Examples of stablecoins include MakerDAO, and USDC, and Facebook-backed Diem.

- Tokens – There are two kinds of token-utility and security. Utility tokens can be used to purchase services within the network, redeem rewards, or pay network fees. Filecoin is an example of this type of token.

  Security tokens are typically offered to potential investors via ICOs or initial coin offerings. They possess digital provenance and promise equity to the owners. Dividends are paid to the holders regularly. The price of these tokens appreciates over time.

- Meme coins – They are inspired by a joke on other crypto and gained popularity when famous crypto retail investors and personalities used the power of social media platforms to promote them. Dogecoin, for instance, experienced a 91% growth surge within 24-hours when Elon Musk of Tesla shared photos of his Shiba Inu puppy on Twitter.

Is cryptocurrency investing worth a try?

Crypto investing is a highly lucrative venture if you have a strong risk tolerance and willing to wait until the timing is right. The value of cryptocurrencies goes up because of speculations or when new investors are willing to pay more than the price the sellers set.

In order to profit from your investment, you need to wait for the demand to be strong and people want to own your coins no matter what the stake is. For Bitcoin buying and selling purposes, you need to register in a trusted crypto exchange.

For long-term investment goals, Bitcoin and Ethereum are two cryptocurrencies that are made for this purpose. They operate on the concept that if you invest now, you will gain incredible financial rewards in the future. The window of time is longer, but your ROI will give you financial freedom. This has happened to early investors of Bitcoin, who held their coins for a time being and sold them for huge profits.

Trivia

According to the 2021 report of crypto exchange Gemini, 14% of adults in the U.S. are proud cryptocurrency owners and 63% are under the category of "crypto curious."

Is it a wise investment?

The Bitcoin network is now valued at over $100 billion and there's no stopping its dominant role in the virtual world. As a pioneering crypto coin, Bitcoin's resilience has been established in its decade-plus existence. Its trailblazing ability has opened doors of possibilities and opportunities for traders, investors, and retailers across the globe.

Once regarded as the "money of the future", it is now accepted as payment for retail and trade transactions. For that reason alone, Bitcoin has proven its worth and power to penetrate the traditional market. Moreover, its popularity gave birth to the emergence of other cryptocurrencies or altcoins.

As an instrument of investment, cryptocurrency is highly speculative because of the absence of the underlying intrinsic value. Investors typically look into the intrinsic value of an asset or financial instrument to gauge if it is worth a try. It also them understand if the cost of getting it is overvalued or undervalued as compared to the asset's market value.

Cryptocurrency does not have an underlying value. It does not track the value of a natural resource or the growth potential of companies. Its value lies on users' and investors' trust and is not pegged on gold, metals, or fiat currency. In a nutshell, the return of your investment is determined by the people who are willing to pay more for your crypto coin in the future.

Bitcoin has established itself as a wise investment, creating a list of self-made millionaires and billionaires after betting for the power of crypto. But then, not all investors had the same fate. The dot.com era has become a dreaded part of the crypto history when investors lost so much when some crypto coins failed to deliver their promises. Hence, the importance of doing due diligence and not investing what you cannot afford to lose. Like any speculative game of chance or investment, crypto investing is either about winning big or losing big.

Is cryptocurrency safe?

In the world of investment, there is no such thing as 'safe'. It is a volatile, yet exciting world where risks and returns are the most important concepts. So, if you are asking me if crypto investing is safe, the answer is a resounding 'no', but it offers life-changing results.

The risks

- Vulnerability – One of the biggest concerns of potential investors is the cybersecurity issues that can wipe out their money in a blink of an eye. There were cases of security breaches and hackings in the past that cost investors millions of dollars. While exchange platforms are claiming strong security measures to protect their clients' investment, the threat is always there.

- Security of storage – Despite being virtual, cryptocurrencies need safe storage to protect them against theft or cyber hacking. This is where 'cold storage' becomes a better option than 'hot' or online storage, which essentially is leaving your money in crypto exchanges or brokers. Once your crypto coins are stolen, it is gone forever.

- Highly competitive arena – As cryptocurrencies become more mainstream and accepted as a mode of payment for various transactions, more and more crypto projects present themselves, attracting investors to support them. As competition becomes fierce, scams and fraudulent projects become more prevalent. If you have invested in a new crypto project, there is no guarantee that it will succeed.

- Price volatility – Warren Buffet once regarded the ecosystem of cryptocurrency as a bubble. The lack of inherent value is one big drawback, resulting in strong price volatility. History reveals that Bitcoin has suffered losing about 80% of its value when the market trends spiraled down, while Ethereum has lost almost 95% of its value in just a year.

- Decentralization – Cryptocurrency operates on its own, with the help of blockchain technology. No one controls, administers, evaluates, or supervises crypto operations. Until such time that the proprietary technology of crypto is recognized or adopted by the governments, the risk remains a strong concern.

The rewards

- Long-term store of value- Because of the mathematical algorithms cap, the value of cryptocurrency is not affected by inflation. In addition, because of its cryptographic nature, no authority can confiscate the coins or tokens unless the owner gives authorization. Its censorship-resistant and deflationary features make it extremely attractive to investors who worry about bank failures, inflationary events, and disasters.

- The potential of high returns– Undeniably, investors buy cryptocurrency because of the promise of big profits. If you do it right, you can say goodbye to your 9-to-5 job, and open your dream business, or live the life you want. In just one stroke of luck, your cryptocurrency can change your financial status.

- Confidentiality and transparency– For people who want to protect private financial information, crypto is the answer. This prevents becoming a victim of data breaches. In terms of transparency, crypto arms investors complete freedom and total control to conduct their transactions without any third party.

Why are you investing in crypto?

The most fundamental question to ask yourself is why you want to invest in cryptocurrency. Your 'why or whys' would be your guideposts in your investing journey.

- *Why cryptocurrency when there are other investment vehicles that offer lesser risks and more stability?*

If you aim for **portfolio diversification**, cryptocurrency investment is a smart decision. Bitcoin is the all-time favorite, but there are many altcoins (alternative coins) that are performing well in the industry. However, before buying an altcoin, make sure that you have studied its profile to ensure that like Bitcoin, it guarantees stability during the test of time.

The increasing **cryptocurrency adoption by** financial giants in the industry is boosting the trust and confidence of investors. PayPal and Square make it easier for their users to buy and sell crypto coins and tokens. Tesla and other institutional investors bought Bitcoin and other types of cryptocurrencies to solidify and diversify their portfolios.

Blockchain is the future of technology. For more than a decade since Bitcoin was introduced, its underlying technology blockchain has been recognized in the industry as a game-changer that benefits other industries like healthcare, shipping, and more.

By eliminating the traditional players in the computer network and intermediaries, the common transaction risks are eliminated. For investors who believe in the power of new technology to shape the future, crypto investing is a very attractive option.

How to invest in cryptocurrency safely

If you choose to invest in cryptocurrency, the first thing to remember is to be strategic to avoid mistakes. Like any kind of investing, success is not guaranteed. And because cryptocurrency carries greater risks compared to investing in stocks, you need to have a certain ceiling on the amount of money you can afford to lose.

Make sure that you have an emergency fund or savings for your personal/family needs if something happened after you invested your extra fund in cryptocurrency. This is to avoid cashing your investment when the prevailing price in the market will not give you profits or worse, less than the amount you pay for the crypto coin.

- ✓ Research and learn about the popular and most beneficial cryptocurrencies before making a decision to purchase. Of course, Bitcoin and Ethereum are the best choices, but there are very promising altcoins that can give you short-term to long-term profits.

- ✓ Take time to get familiar with the industry or world of digital currencies- how it operates and works for investors and users.

- ✓ Explore and study how blockchain technology empowers cryptocurrencies.

✓ Join online forums and communities of crypto enthusiasts to become more updated about the market trends and the latest news about crypto.

✓ Read the white paper of the cryptocurrency, which is accessible on the website. If there is no available white paper or if it seems a bit odd because of misleading or absence of crucial information, move to the next crypto on your list.

If you're thinking of buying crypto in an ICO (initial coin offering), reading the company's prospectus is important. Remember that for any crypto project, the widespread adoption of investors is important. Failing to gain good numbers of supporters and users is a red flag and can lead to loss of investment. But while there are failed crypto projects, many have survived the 'birthing period' and are now thriving well in the market.

Check the following information:

o *Who is the owner (or owners) of the company?* If the people behind the project are well-known and trusted names in the industry, it is a good sign.

o *Who are the major investors of the company or project?*

o *Is the company raising money to produce the crypto or already developed?* The status level of the project/product is important to consider.

o *What will you have in exchange for your investment? Is it a coin, token, or a stake in the company?* (Stake ownership involves receiving a share of earning, a token is a utility currency that allows you to vote or redeem for a special purpose, and the crypto coin is a currency you can use for digital transactions

By doing these things, you will better understand how your investment will work for you. In the end, the best investment is the one that grows over time and promises great returns when it's time to sell it to another investor.

Are you ready to invest?

When you have covered all the fundamental steps that smart investors do prior to investing, your next move is to know when to buy your first crypto coin or coins. The digital world is fast-paced and volatile, hence the right timing is the key to your purchasing success.

The prices of crypto tend to follow a certain pattern. More often than not, other cryptocurrencies follow the general trajectory of Bitcoin. To date, Bitcoin remains the leading virtual currency in the industry. Monitoring the price movement is crucial to investing. Any news or rumors of price manipulation, exchange hack, fraud, and so on can crash the selling price of crypto. Purchasing hot new crypto before it sells like hotcakes due to popularity and growth of value is a nice move.

To protect yourself and your investment, here are additional tips for your perusal:

> ➢ Check everything before leaping. It basically means that before you invest your hard-earned money to buy this hot commodity called crypto, learn how it works, how to buy and sell it, and how to leverage its value.

> ➢ Choose the right digital wallet to protect your crypto. There are different types of electronic wallets to suit your preferences. You can go for a hot wallet or cold wallet. Hot wallet requires Internet connectivity to access your crypto, while cold The software wallets are also categorized as mobile wallets, desktop wallets, or web wallets. Hardware wallets are the best option for

HODLers (long-term investors) and those who want more secure storage for their investment.

➢ Prepare your backup strategy. In any kind of investing, you need a plan and plan B to mitigate loss.

Key Point

*Financial experts describe cryptocurrency
as a transformative
technology with tremendous potential and
power to
revolutionize various industries.
It is often compared to what the Internet has
done way back 1990s.
The breakthrough technology created a
ripple of change as
well as new industries and new types of jobs
across the globe.*

2020: The turnaround year for cryptocurrencies

No one has ever predicted that Bitcoin and other cryptocurrencies would have a blast in 2020. The virtual currencies, even the strongest ones like Bitcoin, were all trying to push through the prolonged price slump. During that time, institutional investors were not keen on adding crypto to their financial portfolio and the market liquidity was low.

And the pandemic happened. Investors, private and corporate, became extremely comprehensive about the multiple rounds of central banks' stimulus spending and began looking for ways to stabilize their investments. Crypto investing turned to be a great option and shook the price stupor. As the demand continued escalating, the price of Bitcoin and altcoins skyrocketed. There was a general price growth of 200%.

But as I said, the crypto market is volatile and unpredictable. In September 2020, Bitcoin price went up from $10,764 to $64,829, and then again spiraled down to more than $40,000. Fast forward this 2021, the year is another breakthrough year for cryptocurrency. Amidst the ongoing pandemic, they continue to grow strong in terms of prices, adoption, and popularity among investors. Once again, Bitcoin dominated the scene and was followed by Ethereum.

Being the largest crypto in the context of market cap, Bitcoin has become a strong indicator of market trends and movements. Speculations can crash its standing and price or boost its popularity, demand, and price.

Monitoring the market price of popular crypto as well as the fastest-growing new cryptocurrencies or tokens is a must-do for investors. The market of virtual currencies is highly volatile, displaying uptrends and downtrends that can impact your profit or loss.

The future of cryptocurrency

Potential or speculation – these two terms are common in the world of cryptocurrency. Investors and traders see the potential of crypto while speculations influence the uptrends and downtrends, the demand and supply, and the prices of the crypto coins or tokens. No one can accurately predict the future value of cryptocurrency. As a speculative investment, it does not offer have a solid history to base predictions. Even the self-proclaimed 'crypto guru' or experts can never tell how will Bitcoin or other cryptocurrencies behave in the coming days, weeks, months, or years.

Key takeaways

- Traditional and cryptocurrency investing are basically similar. The goal is to buy an asset/coin with strong potential to grow its value in time.

- Both have risks and rewards, albeit crypto investing is much more volatile and riskier.

- The future of Bitcoin and other cryptocurrencies remains speculative and in the hands of their holders.

- Before investing, it is crucial to understand the risk factors and the unique volatility of cryptocurrencies.

- Know your reasons why you are investing in Bitcoin or any other crypto and make them your guiding wisdom.

Point to Ponder

Keep learning and growing your worth.
Investing in bitcoin-linked assets in the
Stock market is one way to do it.

Chapter 4

Bitcoin and Stock Market

"A bitcoin ETF ratifies crypto relevancy in today's economy."
– Chris Kline (COO and co-founder of Bitcoin IRA)-

Is there a correlation between Bitcoin and the stock market?

Correlation refers to the statistical relationship (causal or not or the degree to which two random variables are linearly associated. For years, experts have been trying to discern the correlation of Bitcoin with the stock market. Many times in the past, when the prices of stocks skyrocketed, Bitcoin followed or vice versa.

However, during these pandemic months when the global stock markets are experiencing some setbacks, Bitcoin has recovered immensely and displayed new all-time highs. The recovery occurred without the backup of uptrends in the stock markets. This is an indication of a trend break, which is a characteristic of their correlated way. Sometimes they follow the same route, other times they move differently.

➢ Bitcoin is technically an uncorrelated "safe haven" asset.

➢ While Bitcoin has shown a correlation with the stock markets, gold, and other asset classes, it is independent and has its own pattern of uptrends and downtrends.

➢ Bitcoin gradually decoupled from the stock market since December 2020 and demonstrated an inverse correlation.

Take a look:

- The Vanguard Total World Stock ETF Price Development Chart for a 5-year period (October 6, 2021) showed that world stock markets and Bitcoin moved in the same direction from 2017 to the first part of 2021. Then, the pattern broke. Bitcoin suffered a slump during the beginning of 2021. The international stock market continued its good performance. In October 2021, Bitcoin showed a positive recovery. The stock market was still down.

- In the 10-year comparative chart issued on October 7, 2021, by Vanguard Total World Stock ETF, there were two instances when the stock market and Bitcoin were non-correlated. One was during the end of 2014 up to 2016 and the second was at the start of 2018. Bitcoin had serious corrections during both times while the stock market displayed slight movement.

Correlation is a two-way relationship for Bitcoin and stocks

The relation between Bitcoin and the stock market is two-way. While there are events and factors that impact the Bitcoin market movement, the growing interest of large institutions and their own market forces can also play a significant role in the global stock markets.

Factors that tie Bitcoin to stock prices

- **Emergence of digital-savvy investors -** They are bridging the gap that separates stock from cryptocurrency.

- **Similar participants** - It reaches the point where the crypto market and stock market have the same players or participants, making the correlations inevitable.

- **Institutional adoption** – The correlation continues as more major companies and institutions include Bitcoin on the balance sheets.

- **Bitcoin futures contracts** – The successful launching of Maryland Based ProShares Bitcoin Strategy ETF BITO has opened a safer venue for investors to indirectly invest in the popular cryptocurrency.

Quote

"It was a blockbuster, smash, home run debut."
– Eric Balchunas (Senior ETF Analyst, Bloomberg) on BITO-

On Spotlight: ProShares BITO

It is official, ProShares Bitcoin Strategy ETF with ticker symbol BITO is a certified blockbuster after hitting a massive $570 million in assets in one day and over $1 billion in assets under management (AUM) in two days when it made its debut on the New York Stock Exchange. It broke the 18-years, 3-day record of SPDR Gold Shares (GLD) as the fastest exchange-traded fund to reach a billion-dollar threshold.

Finally, it was a home run performance for Bitcoin futures after the grueling months of waiting for the Securities and Exchange Commission (SEC) to approve their application. ProShares, a Maryland-based provider of specialized exchange-traded products has successfully launched their bitcoin ETF BITO.

It hit a major milestone of getting into the mainstream on October 19, 2021. This pure Bitcoin future ETF has opened the floodgates for other cryptocurrencies to follow. Once again, Bitcoin has proved its winning ability to attract investors by offering a safer option for those who are wary of direct investing.

What does it mean for investors?

1. Bitcoin has gone mainstream through stock markets, expect the altcoins to follow its footstep because BITO is just the "tip of the iceberg."
2. What happened has a historical significance which was a major step to the traditional financial platforms.
3. The great news around the success of BITO drove the Bitcoin price to another fresh all-time high of $66,974 in October 2021. According to CoinDesk, Bitcoin has gained 110% by market value even before the year ends.

Should you join the BITO $1 billion pool?

As the first U.S. bitcoin-related exchange-traded fund (ETF), ProShares Bitcoin Strategy ETF (BITO) offers investors a chance to gain capital appreciation from future contracts. It provides a pure form of cryptocurrency exposure using a brokerage account, which means you gain exposure to the asset without needing to hold or trade it.

This allows conservative investors who prefer IRAs, brokerage accounts, and other traditional vehicles to have exposure to bitcoin in a transparent, convenient, and liquid way. Take note that BITO is not a direct investment in Bitcoin. The performance and the price of bitcoin futures are different from the '**spot**' price of bitcoins. The spot price is the current price of physical bitcoins in the exchange platforms or brokers.

Futures contracts are Bitcoin's derivative and are not directly linked or backed up by physical bitcoins. Also, their prices do not necessarily correlate with the bitcoin's price.

- *If the price of Bitcoin increases by 30%, the bitcoin futures ETFs may rise only 20%. The explanation of this is – "bitcoin futures are contracts with expiration and need to be repurchased," which gives a margin of tracking error between the underlying asset (bitcoin) and the ETF.*

In context, BITO is almost similar to the U.S. Oil Fund (USO) as it also invests in futures contracts without necessarily tracking the prevailing oil price. Instead, it tracks down SPDR Gold Shares (GLD) that directly invest in an underlying asset or product for more accurate price tracking. Futures-based products can also replicate the underlying market's performance and as the asset managers roll the contracts forward, they incur costs hence the expense ratio charge during their maturity period.

The futures contracts that this ETF invests in are traded and subject to the internal rules of the Chicago Mercantile Exchange. Being a short-term investment vehicle for cash position, the exchange-traded fund (ETF) BITO can also invest in U.S. Treasury Bills and Repurchase Agreements.

Bitcoin futures are also subject to unique risks which include lack of liquidity and price volatility. Like any other asset class, its principal value and returns may fluctuate so the value can be less or more than the original value.

Before you buy shares, always remember the key rule in investing- "only invest the money you that you can kiss goodbye if unexpected happens." In the end, bitcoin futures contracts are the middle ground that bridges the gap between traditional investing and cryptocurrency.

Other differences between buying Bitcoin from BITO

Fees

- When you buy physical bitcoin, you will be charged with certain fees.
- When you purchase specialized ETFs like BITO, expect an expense ratio of 0.95% for every $10,000 investment.

Regulations

- Bitcoin operates on its own rules.
- Bitcoin-linked ETF BITO comes with better protection. Brokerage accounts are covered by the Securities Investor Protection Corporation (SIPC), providing up to $500,000 insurance when the firm shuts down because of financial difficulties that lead to missing assets of customers and bankruptcy.

Market hours

- Bitcoin is not subject to any kind of market hours. You can purchase, sell, or trade your bitcoins whenever you want.
- BITO can be purchased within the market hours of brokerages or exchanges. If you place your order during an off-market hour, it will be fulfilled when the stock market opens. Also, BITO transactions are not available during evenings or weekends.

Quote

*"I don't think SEC is in a big hurry
to move forward and allow direct
investment in Bitcoin anytime soon."*
-Ben Johnson-
(Morning Star's Global ETF Research Director)

The journey of bitcoin futures to the stock market

It took about 8 years of failures to finally have a crypto-tied ETF in the stock markets. But the idea that Bitcoin and ETFs would eventually meet has been there all along since these two areas of investment provide a conducive growing environment in terms of profits. Exchange-traded funds (ETFs) are a popular form of investment in the stock market and Bitcoin is known for generating huge profits.

But the journey is not easy and has some growing pains. The SEC's hesitancy to embrace crypto assets is based on the concerns of potential manipulation and fraud as well as lack of regulations over the Bitcoin market. Many companies have tried to seek approval for their bitcoin ETF applications from this regulatory body, but generally, the U.S. regulators are extremely careful in reviewing them. Most of the unapproved applications are based on spot markets or direct investing in cryptocurrency. The first attempt was filed in 2013 by the famous twins Cameron and Tyler Winklevoss. Their petition to launch Winklevoss Bitcoin Trust was disapproved by the SEC in 2017.

The shift happened sometime in August of 2021 when SEC Chairman Gary Gensler announced that the agency would be considering the futures-backed bitcoin ETFs under the provisions of the Investment Company Act of 1940. It resulted in a flood of applications.

What you should know before investing in bitcoin futures ETFs?

After the successful launching of BITO, the interest of investors escalated. It was like Christmas in October when large-volume and high-frequency traders/investors wanted to be part of the bigger picture.

While this ETF correlates with bitcoin, it does not mirror the value of the cryptocurrency. It will be tracking the future contracts' price which can be incredibly unpredictable like the physical coins. It is important to be mentally and emotionally prepared for volatility issues.

Bitcoin futures and bitcoin cryptocurrency are different from each other. When you invest in bitcoin futures, you are buying or selling bitcoin. You are buying or selling the asset from a broker or exchange provider in the future at a specified date and price. It can be immensely dangerous if the bitcoin futures ETFs occupy a huge portion of your financial portfolio. Start small and see how it will perform, then gradually increase if you enjoy the challenge of massive price swings.

When the set date arrives, investors must buy or sell the underlying asset at the specified price. If the amount of bitcoin during that day is high, you get a good profit. This is known as *"trading at a premium."* However, if the bitcoin's price is low than what you are expecting, you lose some money. It is *"trading at a discount."*

Bitcoin ETFs and Bitcoin Futures explained

Bitcoin ETF mimics the movement of the world's popular digital currency price. This investment vehicle tracks the performance of bitcoins. It also allows investment diversification without the need for investors to own the asset, do the complex trading process by themselves, or practice safe storage of bitcoins. It is a perfect alternative for people who only focus on the gains or losses of investing.

> ➢ Generally, ETFs offer a simpler option to buy and sell individual assets or stocks representing a larger basket of commodities that help investors diversify their holdings.

Bitcoin futures provides investors to gain exposure to the digital gold of virtual currency without holding it under their safekeeping. It works like the traditional futures contracts for a stock index or a commodity, allowing investors to speculate on the future price without holding the underlying asset.

Investors of bitcoin futures can take cash settlement rather than physical bitcoin delivery during the contract settlement. The first entity that offered this type of contract was the Cboe Options Exchange on December 10, 2017. However, it stopped offering new bitcoin futures contracts in March 2019.

Here are the active exchanges that offer cash settlement or physical bitcoin delivery:

- **CME or Chicago Mercantile Exchange** offers cash for monthly futures contracts. It started the bitcoin futures platform on December 18, 2017. It also offers *options on bitcoin futures* and *Micro Bitcoin futures* (one-tenth the size of bitcoin).

- **Intercontinental Exchange and Bakkt** offer monthly or daily bitcoin futures contracts for *physical delivery*. In the context of futures or options contracts, physical delivery refers to the transfer of the underlying asset of the contract on a predetermined date from the hands of the seller/provider to the buyer.

How does Bitcoin Futures work?

When you invest in Bitcoin Futures, you are buying cash-settled, **front-month** futures contracts or agreements to sell/buy the asset in the future at a predetermined price at a predetermined date, instead of investing in bitcoin directly. The term "front-month" means that the contracts will be maturing soon and once they do, the ETF will be buying up contracts for the next month.

Let's take CME Group bitcoin futures as an example:

- Contract unit is 5 bitcoin (BTC) and paid in US dollars
- Listed contracts for 6 consecutive months and 2 additional Decembers
- Margin requirement is 50% cash of the contract amount
- Settlement method is financially-settled

Let's say the price of bitcoin when you purchase your bitcoin futures contract is $10,000. Since each contract unit has 5 bitcoins, your total investment would be $50,000. The required margin at CME is 50%, so you have to deposit $25,000 and finance the remaining balance of the futures contract by using leverage.

Take note that the value of the futures contract follows the price of its underlying asset, which in this case is bitcoin. CME uses the Bitcoin Reference Rate to calculate the bitcoin's volume-weighted average price every day between 3:00-4:00 p.m. London time. The average price is calculated from different exchanges.

During uncertainties like price fluctuations, you have the option to sell your future contract to another investor or hold onto it. When the contract matures, you let it expire and collect your cash or roll it over by buying a new contract.

How can investors leverage their bitcoin futures?

For the variety of players in the ecosystem of Bitcoin, futures contracts deliver different purposes. Each purpose is unique to the particular group of participants.

- Investors can short their bitcoin futures as a hedge. This means that even if the price of the bitcoins moves adversely, they still make profits in the spot market.

- Active traders and speculators in the stock market who enjoy moving in and out of future trades can use the contracts for long and short-term profits.

- Bitcoin miners can use futures to lock in the prices and guarantee a hefty return on their investments.

Pros and Cons of bitcoin futures

Pros

- ✓ **Better liquidity in futures markets** – The futures markets have more liquidity and deeper volume compared to the crypto markets.

- ✓ **Door for institutional investors** – It is another venue where institutional investors can buy Bitcoin to add to their financial portfolios. Bitcoin futures are traded on the Commodity Futures Trading Commission-regulated exchanges.

- ✓ **Lower fees** – Bitcoin investing can be expensive due to the cost and transaction fees. Bitcoin ETF is a low-fee option than buying physical bitcoins or investing in Grayscale Bitcoin Trust (GBTC) which is known for an annual 2.0% charge

- ✓ **Safer option** – Bitcoin ETF eliminates the issues of complex security and storage procedures that are typically required from investors of physical bitcoins. Bitcoin wallet is not necessary because futures contracts are cash-settled.

- ✓ **Short-sell ability** – Investors can easily short sell their ETF shares if they see that the value of bitcoins will decline in the future.

- ✓ **Less risk exposure** - Future contracts have price limits and position limits, enabling investors to avoid risks.

Cons

- ○ **Cost of carry** – The price of futures is dependent on the current spot price and the pre-delivery cost of carry which can be positive or negative. The cost of carry is subject to the supply and demand that stem from the anticipated pricing of future events.

- ○ **Contango** – The state of Bitcoin contango refers to the situation where the forward price of the futures price is higher than its spot price. It usually manifests when there is a strong expectation that the price of the commodity will rise over time.

Other Bitcoin ETFs and Futures-based crypto funds

A. Bitcoin ETFs

There were 13 Bitcoin ETFs applications waiting for the stamp of approval from the SEC in July 2021. ProShares ETF BITO was the first one to get the much-awaited "Yes" of the body. Three days after the successful launch of BITO, Valkyrie Bitcoin Strategy ETF went public, too. On November,

- **Valkyrie ETF** (BTF, $24.30)

  This Tennessee-based alternative asset manager specializes in both traditional and digital assets. It has been selling trusts for crypto including Bitcoin, but its BTF is the first crypto ETF. Valkyrie is also eyeing to launch more bitcoin futures ETFs in the coming days.

  In a way, BTF is like BITO since it invests in CME Bitcoin futures through the Cayman Islands subsidiary and it charges an expense ratio of 0.95%. However, actively-managed BTF failed to receive the same warm response that BITO had during the launching as it only accumulated $5 million in assets under management (AUM).

- **VanEck Bitcoin Futures ETF** (XBTF)

  This is the third bitcoin futures ETF that went public. It started trading under the XBTF ticker on November 15, 2021, on the CBOE Exchange. It has a 0.65% net expense ratio and is actively managed.

  It is currently the cheapest bitcoin-linked exchange-traded fund with a structure like a C-Corporation. According to the firm's top executives, it may offer a more efficient tax incentive for investors who are opting for long-term holdings.

B. Futures-based crypto funds

- **Amplify Transformational Data Sharing ETF** (BLOK, $48.62)

  It is currently the largest ETF in the market today with actively-managed $1.3 billion worth of assets with a 0.71% expense ratio. It primarily invests in equities and offers more "direct" exposure in companies that develop blockchain technology or use it for their business operation.

  It has 47 holdings with the top 10 comprising 45% of assets. As of November 15, 2021, the list includes:

  - Silvergate Capital Corp Ordinary Shares - Class A SI
  - Galaxy Digital Holdings Ltd. GLXY
  - Coinbase Global Inc. Ordinary Shares Class A COIN
  - Hut 8 Mining Corp. New Com CA HUT
  - Nvidia Corp NVDA
  - Riot Blockchain Inc
  - Marathon Digital Holdings Inc. MARA

- Hive Blockchain Technologies CA HIVE
- Bitfarms Ltd/Canada CA: BITF
- CME Group Inc.

Other BLOK holdings outside the list but directly track the performance of Bitcoin include the 3iQ CoinShares Bitcoin ETF and the Purpose Bitcoin ETF. BLOK's expense ratio is 0.71%.

- **Siren Nasdaq NexGen Economy ETF** (BLCN $46.12)

This passively-managed index exchange-traded fund (ETF) boasts $291 million in assets. BLCN holds more stocks than BLOK. It has 63 holdings of companies with over $200 million in market capitalization and exhibits characteristics of a "blockchain company." It has a 0.68% expense ratio.

BLCN utilizes a "blockchain score", the proprietary screening method of index that scores the company's ability to get the most out from the blockchain technology.

As of November 15, 2021, the largest holdings that account for 20% of the overall assets, came from the following companies.

- Bakkt Holdings Inc. Ordinary Shares - Class A BAKKT
- Silvergate Capital Corp Ordinary Shares - Class A SI
- Marathon Digital Holdings Inc. MARA
- Galaxy Digital Holdings Ltd. GLXY
- Overstock.com Inc. OSTK
- Microstrategy Inc. Ordinary Share A MSTR
- NCIVIA Corp NVDA
- Coinbase Global Inc. Ordinary Shares Class A COIN
- Advanced Micro Devices Inc. AMD

○ Accenture PLC Ordinary Shares Class A CAN

- **Bitwise 10 Crypto Index Fund** (BITW $50.25)

  With $1.2 billion assets under management, BITW tracks the performance of 10 investable crypto in the Bitwise 10 Large Cap Crypto Index which accounts for 70% of the entire market of cryptocurrency. It is weighted by market cap so it is not surprising that 65% of its portfolio are Bitcoin accounts, followed by Ethereum (25%), and Cardano (4%).

  The over-the-counter availability of BITW that started in December 2020 made it highly popular and in less than one year, the $120 million in assets increased ten times. NITW's expense ratio is 2.50%.

- **Simplify US Equity PLUS GBTC ETF** (SPBC $26.89)

  SPBC has 111.0 million in assets with a 0.50% expense ratio. It offers 100% investment in equities and 10% Bitcoin exposure. By providing both in the stock market and crypto, Simplify US Equity has become a popular asset management company. It mostly invests in iShares Core S& P 500 ETF (IVV), partly in E-mini S&P 500 Futures, and Grayscale Bitcoin Trust.

- **First Trust Indxx Innovative Transaction & Process ETF** (LEGR, $43.03)

  This equity-based crypto ETF tracks the Indxx Blockchain Index, which in turn follows the performance of blockchain-linked companies. It also uses a weighting method to gauge the blockchain companies in terms of size, trading minimums, and liquidity.

- A score of 1 is for firms that are actively developing blockchain
- A score of 2 is for companies that are actively using blockchain
- A score of 3 is for those that are actively exploring blockchain

This ETF has $135.3 million in assets with an expense ratio of 0.65%. It has an approximately $94 billion median market cap, being a large-cap heavy fund.

- **Bitwise Crypto Industry Innovators ETF** (BITQ, $23.95)

As equity-focused crypto exchange-traded funds, it tracks the Bitwise Crypto Innovators 30 Index. It has $80.8 million in assets with a 0.85% expense ratio. For companies to be listed in the index, they should have 75% net holdings in bitcoin (other kinds of liquid cryptocurrency) or 75% of revenue is generated from the crypto ecosystem.

Hot crypto stocks to invest in for the next Bitcoin rush

When Bitcoin's price dropped to $30,000 in late May from $64,000 new-high in mid-April, it dragged down a lot of crypto stocks and altcoins. Then it had a quick rebound to around $40,000 and the current price is playing between around the range of $30,000 and $40,000. This development sustained the high interest of traders and investors in virtual currencies, bitcoin-linked ETFs, and blockchain technology-backed companies in the stock market.

The digital reforms are partly due to the pandemic, with many companies leveraging the secure authentication technology or blockchain and accepting Bitcoin as payment for the services or goods.

Stock markets have also leveraged the potentials of these digital currencies by offering bitcoin futures to investors who are looking forward to diversifying their portfolio as well as earning short-term to long-term profits.

Here are the top cryptocurrency stocks that investors should have to prepare for the Bitcoin boom:

1. PayPal Holdings (PYPL $288.12)

According to the survey of Mizuho Securities to 380 PayPal users, 17% answered that they are using the platform to purchase or sell their crypto. Putting it in a large perspective, this 17% translates to 67 million people out of its 392 million users across the world.

In a letter sent to their shareholders, hedge fund and investment company Pantera Capital shared that PayPal is buying over 100% of newly-issued bitcoins and Square's Cash App. This is a clear indication that crypto functionality is now recognized in the finance world and Bitcoin as a digital store of value.

Wall Street experts collectively believe that PayPal will be averaging an annual growth of 24.1% growth in the next 3-5 years. PayPal's market value is now $333.5 billion with a 1,206% earnings growth rate quarterly. Its profit margin is 22.8% while the return on equity - trailing 12 months (TTM) is 29.4%.

2. Square (SQ $238.70)

This card-reading hardware payment company has purchased 4,709 bitcoins amounting to $50 million. It is also a leading company in the stock markets that allow investors to buy, deposit, withdraw, and store bitcoins through its Cash App. It also added Auto Invest, a feature that allows dollar-cost averaging on a set schedule of weekly or daily purchases of stocks or bitcoins.

Square's current market value is $108.7 billion. It has allocated $170 million to bitcoins during the 1st quarter of 2021. During the 3rd quarter of the year, Cash App earned $3.5 billion in bitcoin-related transactions. Square's profit margin is 2.7% while the return on equity is 17.4%.

3. MicroStrategy(MSTR $533.00)

With a market value of $5.4 billion, MicroStrategy is the brainchild of Michael Saylor. He was only 24 when he started this company, making him one of the pioneering tech founders in the industry.

Once a small player, this data analytics company managed to get to the trillion-dollars list after making a strategic move to replace the cash with Bitcoin on the balance sheet. It spent approximately $3 billion to buy crypto, which resulted in a 370% growth in assets.

While enjoying the Bitcoin boom during the past months, MSTR moved further by transferring the volatility of the digital currencies to shares of stocks. It is moving forward with full steam, offering crypto stocks that you should be watching closely to leverage your investment potentials.

4. JPMorgan Chase(JPM $151.12)

JPM's CEO Jamie Dimon is not keen on Bitcoin. During the 2017 boom, he called Bitcoin a "fraud" and last year he said it is still "not his cup of tea." He is known as one of the most outspoken skeptics of digital assets on Wall Street.

However, he is supportive of blockchain technology and even letting the clients of the house of Morgan invest in Bitcoin Fun that NYDIG has created. In late July, JPMorgan has quietly rolled out access to 5 funds – the Grayscale Bitcoin Trust, Grayscale Bitcoin Cash Trust, Grayscale Ethereum Classic Trust, Grayscale Ethereum Trust, and Osprey Bitcoin Trust.

Recently, Dimon said that *"their clients are interested and he doesn't tell clients what to do."* If this is a sign of an eroding resistance in Bitcoin and other cryptocurrencies, Wall Street is waiting for him to concede.

5. Advanced Micro Devices (AMD $83.82)

AMD played well during the recent digital gold rush and has gone up near $100 per share during mid-January before settling in the range of mid-$80s. Nonetheless, it remains strong enough with its 242.6% quarterly earnings growth rate.

The company benefits from the high demand of crypto miners for high-performance computer processors. It reported a 93% year-over-year revenue increase during the 1st quarter of 2021. Stock analysts are optimistic about AMD with its market value of $101.8%, profit margin of 25.2%, and 60.6% return on equity.

6. Nvidia (NVDA $762.29)

Bitcoin mining has created a constant demand for the most high-powered computer processors, making NVIDIA's market value rise up to $474.9 billion with a quarterly earnings growth rate of 108.5%. Its profit margin is 27.7% while the return on equity is 33.4%

Nvidia also released its new generation of processors exclusively for crypto mining. During the first quarter of 2021, its crypto mining cards have generated a revenue of $155 million. And while it is not the purest crypto stock, NVDA always enjoys the boost from Bitcoin's boom.

7. Coinbase Global (COIN $226.01)

This brokerage company has been selling and trading bitcoins and other major altcoins then collecting fees for the transactions. It always makes bigger revenue and profits whenever the price of Bitcoin drops, making the "buy the dip" crypto buyers excited to get hold of this crypto coin.

It also launched Coinbase Prime, which has opened more opportunities to institutional investors. The unit ties data analytics, custody services, and trading together. COIN stocks are likely to become bigger and stronger.

Coinbase Global has a market value of $59.2 billion, 2,313% quarterly earnings growth rate, profit margin of 36.8%, and a 54.2% return on equity.

8. Grayscale Bitcoin Trust (GBTC $27.79)

With $21.9 billion assets under management, this investment company allows you to buy GBTC shares and tracks down the Bitcoin's price you hold but like ETFs, you cannot cash in the shares of stocks for physical bitcoins. GBTC is also not traded on any major exchange platforms, but "over the counter."

Key takeaways

- Bitcoin had early patterns of correlation with the stock market. An inverse correlation eventually decoupled them.

- The successful launching of ProShares BITO was a major milestone for Bitcoin-linked futures.

- Aside from Bitcoin futures, investing in hot crypto stocks is a ticket to leverage the opportunities in the next bull market.

Point to Ponder

The increasing number of bitcoin futures ETFs in the United States is a sure sign that crypto is now being accepted by the regulators and the crypto market is maturing.

Chapter 5

Guide to Bitcoin Investing: Let's Gear You Up

"It's money 2.0." – *Chamath Palihapitiva*

The impressive 763% growth of Bitcoin valuation within a span of one year made it the much-sought 'digital gold' among today's investors. The debates over its future in the investing sphere have ceased at this juncture, thanks to the large institutional investors and high-profile people who jumped into the bandwagon.

Undoubtedly, Bitcoin momentum is building up and attracting more individuals and companies. The recent developments and meteoric rise of its value have convinced many people that it is the just beginning of a golden journey for Bitcoin holders.

Investing in Bitcoin has become a fast wealth-building vehicle. But remember that just like traditional investments, it has its pitfalls and traps that can lead to losing instead of winning. It is easy to get excited as you explore the new realm and its opportunities, so here are some tips to live by:

1. **Start small** - The first and most important rule is to 'buy bitcoins within your limits' or the amount you can afford to let go without affecting your savings or living expenses. Create a budget for Bitcoin investing. The safest ceiling is not more than 10% of your financial portfolio. Perhaps, investing $10 every week is a healthy start. It is also fun seeing your Bitcoin investment grow week after week.

2. **Know your risk tolerance** – Bitcoin remains a high-risk investment asset, so it is necessary to check your risk tolerance before you start investing in cryptocurrency. If you are not comfortable buying volatile assets or you cannot afford to invest a lot of money, then go for the other investment options.

3. **Diversify your financial portfolio** – Wise men say, 'never put all your golden eggs in one basket.' It is true in investment, so always protect yourself and your family from investment loss by portfolio diversification. You should have low-risk primary investments (index funds, government bonds), medium-risk investments (corporate stocks, real-estate stocks), and high-risk investments (Bitcoin, altcoins). Bitcoin investment is your portfolio's 'icing on the cake' that has a potential promise of giving you a 'sweet luxury and fortune' and if it doesn't, your future is still fine.

Bitcoin as an investment asset

Bitcoin is an investment asset class of its own, proving its capacity to grow in value after going 20-fold times since 2018. But its magnitude does not end there, since this 'king of crypto' can transcend the borders of investing. It helps investors diversify their portfolios and is paired concurrently with other assets.

A. Bitcoin and Real Estate

There is a new concept in real estate called 'tokenization.' It refers to the process of producing a virtual token to represent the ownership of interest. The token exists on the Bitcoin blockchain, offering real estate investors to have more investment options and earn substantial profits. This unique convergence of Bitcoin and real estate companies has great potential to revolutionize the existing domestic and global markets.

Real estate tokenization gives an opportunity to people to explore the crypto world by allowing fractional ownership of residential or commercial property. To buy a real estate token, investors must participate in an initial coin offering. It operates by dividing the property value into multiple virtual tokens where individual and institutional investors are waiting to purchase a piece of the pie. The tokenization process utilized smart contracts.
Benefits of tokenization

  > **Increased liquidity** – Real estate investment is an illiquid asset or has low-liquidity characteristics because of significant capital requirement, tedious paperwork, and involvement of various parties. With tokenization, the property gets fractionalized and allows small investors or beginners to be part of the leading industry that generates real nice revenue.

➢ **Immutable proof of right or ownership** – Tokenization eliminates the battle over rights and ownership of the property. With data in the blockchain ledger, no one can tamper the documents. It is also easy to access once the fractional or sole ownership has been declared.

➢ **Market access** – When it comes to real estate investment, there is no denying that it is a game for the rich and famous who want to own remarkable properties. However, with tokenization, everyone interested can have a fraction of the asset and hold or sell it to interested buyers from any part of the world.

➢ **Less expensive** – Since the transaction requires less administrative work and intermediaries, the whole process costs less than conventional real estate transactions.

➢ **Transparent** – All details of the transaction, contract clauses, due dates, and other necessary information are programmed into a digital token, making them transparent to sellers and investors.

➢ **Easy management of the property** – Tokens and smart contracts in the blockchain streamline the process of lease renewal or monthly payment collection. With real estate tokenization, registered investors in the database get timely payments from tenants.

Wise thoughts

Real estate tokenization has an incredibly bright future. It is only a matter of time before all assets are blockchain- based assets.

-Graeme Moore-
Polymath head of tokenization-

B. Bitcoin IRAs

Bitcoin IRAs are special retirement accounts that offer higher returns as well as diversify the retirement portfolio. But then, before jumping on board and adding this type of retirement plan, remember that anything related to Bitcoin has risks and volatility issues. It is also crucial to understand what a Bitcoin IRA is.

In a nutshell, a Bitcoin IRA is a self-directed individual retirement account that allows people to invest in a variety of alternative asset classes (precious metals, real estate, and cryptocurrency.) It works like other IRAs, but with a little DIY. The Bitcoin IRA providers can partner with a crypto exchange or let you trade your Bitcoin in a 3rd-party crypto exchange.

Some of the popular providers of Bitcoin IRAs are BitIRA, Alto, Bitcoin IRA, Equity Trust, IRA Financial Trust, BlockMint, and iTrustCapital.

C. Standalone Bitcoin

The collective craze around Bitcoin is hard to ignore. And while it is also difficult to predict if it will be bigger than it is now and become a store of value or a global reserve currency in the future, it is now widely accepted as the 'digital gold' of modern times. Many are chasing the opportunity of massive profits that it offers while the others are still in quandary between the thrill of becoming rich or ruin.

When someone asks me if Bitcoin is a good investment, my answer is always in the affirmative. Because I do believe that like any other form of investment, the key to successful management is diligence. The way you handle your investment asset defines success and failure.

Traditional investors and institutions have already realized Bitcoin's ability to disrupt the conventional methods in the financial world. Many chose to adopt and integrate crypto into their vault of riches instead of facing irrelevance. As we are seeing it, the elite group and people with a healthy appetite for risks are leading the pack of Bitcoin supporters. They believed in its future and those who risked years ago have already reaped their millions or billions. As long as the global markets favor and chase Bitcoin, it will continue its phenomenal performance and attract more investors. Soon enough, when the last bitcoin is mined, it will be harder to buy and the demand will grow despite the presence of other cryptocurrencies.

To buy or not to buy Bitcoin

Investing in Bitcoin is a personal choice. The stronger is your appetite for challenges and risks, the higher is your interest to buy bitcoins.

Top reasons why you should buy Bitcoin

The main attraction is Bitcoin investing is you can generate a monumental return on profits, more than 100% of your capital investment. The more bitcoins you have in your portfolio, the higher is your opportunity to capitalize on market surges and sell them to crypto investors. You can generate huge profits as high as 300% if you have a large volume of Bitcoin by capitalizing on the market uptrends.

Bitcoin is also incredibly liquid because of the presence of online crypto exchanges, brokerages, and trading platforms worldwide. It is now easier to trade bitcoins for another asset like gold or cash, with low transaction fees. Bitcoin is an outstanding investment vessel whether you are looking for long-term investment or short-term profits.

It is being adopted by big businesses and institutions, becoming more mainstream. With modern software, carrying out Bitcoin transactions becomes automatic and fast which is favorable for entrepreneurs and merchants.

This crypto is immune to inflation. It is not affected by the changes in the monetary and fiscal policy that causes the dollar valuation to decline and result in a high inflation rate.

Bitcoin's blockchain technology is infinite and your investment is secured as long as you do not lose your private keys to access it. It is reported that about 3.7 million BTCs were lost because the owners can no longer access them.

You can also try Bitcoin trading, which is simple and instant. Simply buy your desired volume of bitcoins and hold them in your digital wallet. When you want to sell them, place an offer to let the users of the exchange know that you are disposing of your coins. But for this, you must be careful when to enter and exit the market.

Finally, it brings new opportunities for ordinary people to invest. For so long, investing is an activity that is limited to financial specialists and individuals with big capital to spend. Bitcoin is relatively young and this newness is a strong factor that causes volatility and unpredictable price swings that can bring massive profits.

Top arguments why you should not buy Bitcoin

Bitcoin price is always going back and forth. While there was an astounding 7,875% return for those who sold their coins until May 2021, the guarantee that it would perform similar valuation growth for another 5 years is unlikely. But then, it all depends on several factors including wider adoption of investors. You could lose your assets if you do not practice due diligence and precautions.

Cryptocurrencies, including Bitcoin, are susceptible to the "pump-and-dump" schemes. Beware of predatory investors who are on the lookout for amateurs on Bitcoin investing. Their modus is to convince the newbies to invest more money to cause surges that would rapidly increase the Bitcoin price. And while the unsuspecting investors are busy buying bitcoins, the predatory investors would sell their coins during the surge and earn huge profits. When the preys stop buying, the price of Bitcoin will be extremely low so they have no choice but to hold them until the next surge. Pyramid schemes are also rampant in the crypto industry, so be conscious of 'so-called investors' who will try to attract your attention to be part of their crypto team by offering huge returns.

The risk of hacking is always present. One way to have peace of mind is holding custody of your account's private key. And don't ever lose it or you will be saying goodbye to your bitcoins forever.

Many governments are trying to crack down on Bitcoin-related businesses. China totally banned cryptocurrencies, while others have a friendlier stance but are still finding ways to regulate them. The crackdown and other regulatory policies that authorities are placing to protect investors in their jurisdictions cause the value of Bitcoin to decrease.

4 Steps to follow when buying bitcoins

Step 1: Decide whether you will buy from a Bitcoin exchange or a Bitcoin stockbroker.

Step 2: Decide where to store your Bitcoin.

Step 3: Buy your bitcoins.

Step 4: Manage your Bitcoin investment based on your long-term plans.

Pro tips:

- ✓ HODlers who want to make mid-term or long-term investments mostly use crypto exchanges to buy Bitcoin.

- ✓ Speculative investors who want to explore various types of trading, TA instruments, and investment tools use crypto exchanges. They see brokers as a medium for their mid-term or short-term goals.

✓ When choosing a cryptocurrency exchange for long-term investment, consider the advanced options (DeFi tokens, crypto indices), bonuses and commissions, and cool perks they offer.

Bitcoin brokers versus Bitcoin exchanges

Bitcoins are available through crypto exchanges and brokers. They make profits from the service fees paid by their clients.

- **Bitcoin brokers** offer cryptocurrencies and other derivatives like options, futures, and CFDs. They act as mediators between the market and the traders or investors. Crypto brokers usually offer lower trading and withdrawal fees.

  Brokers allow investors to trade their virtual assets without owning them. The brokers allow the crypto sellers to set the price and fee. They can hold the funds for you and collaborate with other brokers to ensure a sufficient supply of bitcoins and other cryptocurrencies. To leverage the demand, they are more likely to sell virtual coins and tokens at prices that are similar to other brokers.

  Examples of digital currency brokers:

  ✓ **Robinhood Markets, Inc. (HOOD)** – It is the first investment broker that sells bitcoins. This broker firm does not charge commission fees for purchases and trades of cryptocurrencies. It makes profits from passing the trading volume to other brokerages or trading platforms (payment for order flow).

  ✓ **eToro** – Its social trading platform allows crypto users to match the trading moves of experienced traders.

✓ **TradeStation** – It offers bitcoin and altcoin trading.

- **Bitcoin exchanges** are platforms that sell Bitcoin and other cryptocurrencies. They act as intermediaries, enabling the trade and charging fees for their services. Fees for deposits, withdrawals, and trades are usually high. Most of them have their own exchange wallets, giving you an option to leave your digital assets for their safekeeping. You may also store your crypto outside the platform for better peace of mind.

In these platforms, there are multiple sellers and buyers who are simultaneously placing their offers to purchase or dispose of their cryptocurrencies. They match sellers with buyers, allowing any buyer to select the price that fits his budget and offers an intention to buy. Once the seller agrees, the order will be fulfilled and the transaction is completed.

Users can input a limit order or a market order when buying or selling bitcoins. If the buyer or seller chooses the limit order, the exchange will trade coins above the current bid price or below the current asking price. On the other hand, a market order authorizes the exchange platform to trade bitcoins in the marketplace for the most profitable price.

To deposit funds, users can use different options such as direct bank transfers, bank wires, bank drafts, money orders, debit or credit cards, and gift cards. For withdrawal purposes, check the options they provide which may include bank wire, credit card transfers, PayPal transfer, cash delivery, bank transfer, or check mailing.

There are two types of exchange:

1. *Centralized exchange* – They are online platforms that let you create an account by providing login details. You can transfer funds (fiat or crypto) from your bank account to fund your crypto wallet and make a transaction. In this type of exchange, the governing organization creates and sets rules regarding the information to be shared in the platform, what can be traded, and the withdrawal limits.

   Examples of centralized exchanges are *Binance, Coinbase, Gemini, and CoinMama.*

   ✓ **Coinbase** – U.S. buyers mostly prefer using Coinbase because it can easily be linked in the bank accounts. It also has a wide choice of altcoins. Every transaction is charged with a 0.5% spread (or the adjustment in the sale or purchase price of your investment) and a service fee which is variable depending on the mode of payment and location.

   ✓ **Binance** – It has the biggest collection of available cryptocurrencies and charges a 0.1% fee plus withdrawal fee. It also offers a wide range of cryptocurrency-to-cryptocurrency trading pairs. Binance is best for advanced traders and investors.

   ✓ **Coinmama** – It has 8 available cryptocurrencies in its selection, which include bitcoins. Coinmama requires a $60 minimum purchase. For each transaction, you will be charged a 5.9% transaction fee. If you're using a credit card for your purchase, you will be charged an additional 5% fee.

   ✓ **Gemini** – This crypto exchange offers bitcoin, bitcoin cash, and several altcoins. It requires users to purchase a minimum $60 purchase. The transaction fee for every transaction is 5.9% and an additional 5% fee if you purchase crypto using a credit card.

2. *Decentralized exchange* (DEXs)– These exchanges operate without any central authority and allow peer-to-peer trading. You can make transactions from your crypto wallet, directly sending or receiving crypto from another user. This eliminates the need to transfer assets to the platform, which lessens the risk of potential frauds and hacks. Technically, DEXs are pooled assets on the blockchain like Ethereum. One thing you need to know is you cannot trade Bitcoin on Ethereum-based assets. But you can select a pair of Bitcoin and Ethererum (or another altcoin).

This exchange type allows the smart contract to set the rules. A smart contract is technically a programming code that allows the system to execute transactions by itself.

For example, it automatically guarantees an Ethereum investor to obtain Bitcoin and vice-versa. Examples of decentralized exchange are *Ether Delta, PancakeSwap, Uniswap, and Bitshares* (BTS).

Table of comparison

	Crypto Exchange	**Crypto Broker**
Features	Best for average users	Best for experienced users
Use of fiat to buy crypto	Yes and No	Yes
Market depth	Limited market	Higher potential
Liquidity	Average level	Deeper level
Number of cryptos	High	Low
Safety	Funds are semi-protected	Protected
Regulations	Depending on your location	Regulated
Spread	Wide	Tight
Customer service	Limited only	Well-experienced

Other ways to get hold of Bitcoin

✓ **Peer-to-peer (P2P)** – It is the direct buying of bitcoins from owners who want to dispose of their holdings. You can check sellers from P2P exchange services such as LocalBitcoins.com, Bitquick, or Bisq. You need to create an account to post a request to obtain bitcoins. With the account, you can also sell your coins when you want to monetize them. Once your account is confirmed, you can start browsing the buy and sell listing offers and select a seller. However, you need to be extremely careful when opting for this option to avoid scammers. Only buy from legit sellers with positive reviews and high ratings.

✓ **Bitcoin ATMs** – Just like the conventional ATMs, they can be found in strategic places around the United States. They allow quick and hassle-free buying and selling bitcoins. It works by inserting cash into the machine to buy a certain amount of bitcoin. Once the transfer is confirmed, the coins will be transferred to the user's online wallet. However, using this option is more expensive since you will be charged with a purchase fee as well as a conversion fee (fiat to bitcoin). Typically, the average purchase fee is 8.4% of the amount you pay for bitcoins. While sales of bitcoins at ATMs are charged 5.4%.

✓ **Investment funds** – Digital currency asset manager Grayscale Investments offer Grayscale Bitcoin Trust (GBTC), letting you buy bitcoins from discount brokers.

✓ **Bitcoin futures** – It is for advanced investors who want to buy or sell bitcoins at a specific price on a future date.

✓ **Gift cards** – Gift cards can be traded for Bitcoin or used to purchase bitcoins. It works by buying a gift card from a retailer and logging in to any platform that accepts gift cards in exchange for bitcoins.

✓ **PayPal** – PayPal Holdings, Inc. (PYPL), a popular payment processor, is now offering Bitcoin. This option is safe and convenient because you can easily connect PayPal to your bank account or debit card or use the balance in your PayPal account to pay for your purchase from 3rd-party crypto providers. In addition, paying Bitcoin for the services or products you are purchasing is made possible via PayPal's "Checkout with Crypto" feature.

For a $100 to $200 crypto purchase, there is a $0.50 flat fee or a percentage of the total amount in dollars. The downside of buying Bitcoin or any crypto via PayPal is that it does not allow the transfer of bitcoins from its proprietary wallet to your personal wallet or an external wallet.

The transaction process: Deposits & Withdrawals

There are two ways to deposit and withdraw funds from the crypto exchange. One is using fiat currency and the second is cryptocurrency. But not all exchanges allow direct fiat deposit and only allow crypto deposits. Withdrawal and deposit fees are also higher when you use fiat. Crypto deposits have lower transaction fees.

Brokers usually offer a variety of deposit options such as cryptocurrencies, e-wallets, bank account, credit card, and debit card with no additional fees. For withdrawals, the fee is between 0% to 3% only.

The transaction fees

For every transaction, users need to pay fees which can be a percentage of the traded amount or a flat fee. Each crypto exchange or broker has its own transaction fees structure. Some of them charge higher withdrawal or trading fees or give discounts when you use their own token. Other exchanges based their fees on margin or a spread on top of the coin's market price.

Other factors that can influence the transaction fees are your payment method, location, security measures of the platform, and active trading features.

There are three fees to consider – deposit fees, trading fees, and withdrawal fees.

- **Deposit fees** depend on how you want to deposit your fund. Some exchanges do not charge bank transfers but charge a minimum of 3% of the amount to be traded when you use a debit or credit card for payment.

- **Withdrawal fees** typically depend on the percentage of the amount to be withdrawn or a flat fee.

- **Trading fees** are set by the exchange. There are also exchanges that publish their fees on their website while others would provide a quote during the trading.

Another factor to consider is the maker-taker fees of exchanges that offer active trading features. These fees are determined by price fluctuations in the crypto market.

If you set a certain price to buy a crypto and the market reaches that point, you will be charged with a "maker" fee. On the other hand, if you purchase coins at the prevailing market value, you will be charged with a "taker" fee which is higher than the other fee.

PRO TIP

Check the type of fees that will be charged to you when you buy or sell your bitcoins before you sign up. It is also best to factor in the cost to prevent spending more than your budget.

The sign-up process: Registration & Verification

Registering an account varies in *crypto exchanges*. There are platforms that only require a valid email address while others ask for additional verification proof like scanned ID, selfie while holding an ID, completing a KYC (know-your-client) process or even a video call. It is the option by exchanges that accept fiat currency mode of payment and to confirm the request of clients who want a higher limit of withdrawal/deposit.

Verification of the account may take several hours after signing up or even a few days. Some exchanges have a longer verification period and others do not accept new accounts due to a long queue of requests.

The signup process with *brokers* is easy. However, they would require verification requirements since brokers' transactions are subject to regulations. For hassle-free validation, submit an ID and proof of current address like a utility bill. The verification process is quicker and once your account is verified, you can deposit funds and make some transactions.

The payment process: Connect your preferred payment option

Once the verification is complete, the exchange or broker system will ask you to connect a payment option (bank account, or debit/credit card).

You can also use your PayPal to buy bitcoins. There are two methods to get hold of Bitcoin through this payment processor. The first option is to use your PayPal account that is linked to your bank account or debit card. The second method is to buy Bitcoin from a 3rd-party provider and use the balance in your PayPal account to pay for it. However, only a few sites allow this option. Also, only 4 cryptocurrencies can be purchased through PayPal. They are Bitcoin, Litecoin, Bitcoin Cash, and Ethereum.

Is it safe to buy Bitcoin using credit cards?

There are two reasons why it is not advisable to use a credit card when purchasing bitcoins.

1. Not all crypto exchanges accept credit cards because of the risk of fraud and the higher processing fees. Transactions using credit cards necessitate paying additional charges, which the exchange will pass to users.

2. Purchases using credit cards are more expensive because the issuers consider the crypto purchase a cash advance transaction,

hence charging higher interest rates and fees. In addition, there are credit card companies that limit bitcoin purchases to $1,000 per month.

Bitcoin investing 101: What do you need to start investing?

At this juncture, you have become more familiar with Bitcoin and crypto investing. Understanding how they work and paying extra consideration to risks and rewards are very vital to successful investing. Unlike the traditional financial instruments and equities, the value of Bitcoin is parallel to the people's interests. The higher the interest of investors, the bigger the demand that makes the price increase exponentially. Bitcoin has shown this phenomenon several times, creating new highs.

The basics are very simple. You just need the following to prepare:

- Secure internet connection
- Bank account information
- Personal identification documents
- Capital investment

Note: Personal and financial information is applicable when you are buying your coins from a crypto broker.

3 Popular strategies for investing in Bitcoin

Investing in Bitcoin is not very different from buying stocks and other financial assets. There are some similarities but also differences, in particular with the investment timeframes.

1. **Hold Bitcoin Long Term** – Some investors buy Bitcoin and want to hold them for a longer period because they

believe that their value would appreciate in time or become a store of value like precious gold. However, these investors are inclined to sell their coins when they believe that the time is right and the returns satisfy their desire for profit.

2. **Buy and 'Hodl" Bitcoin** - The term 'hodl' is a misspelled hold, which originated from the bitcointalk forum in 2013 when one of the investors mistakenly typed in hodl rather than hold. He was saying implying to 'hold on for dear life.' It eventually became a popular investment philosophy and strategy that requires crypto investors not to sell their coins amidst price fluctuations.

Hodlers are hard-core believers and maximalists. They believe that Bitcoin or other cryptocurrencies are here to replace fiat currencies in the long run. They do not do trading that is based on short-term swings of Bitcoin price. These investors simply hodl their bitcoins, avoiding the prognostication and volatility.

Moreover, they counteract the two destructive tendencies in investing – FOMO and FUD. Each represents a certain mental state and extreme emotions, causing a roller coaster of feelings that can help or hinder the success of traders/investors. Both have fear as the underlying emotion, which can be your best ally or worst enemy. FOMO is why prices go up and FUD is why the prices plunge.

- FOMO is the acronym for Fear of Missing Out. It leads investors to have a buying spree to avoid losing the golden opportunity. Somehow, the dominant emotions are making havoc over their prudence and logical reasoning. They disregard the possible dangers and are only focusing on the thought that they should buy right now!

- FUD is the acronym for Fear, Uncertainty, and Doubt. It leads to selling bitcoins at a low price. Sometimes it is called SODLing. The emotions typically come from negative or clickbait news and communication. A clickbait information is a calibrated message to generate traffic and also 'panic' among investors because of erroneous and shocking tactics. Most of the time, this misinformation comes from a bearish or confusing cryptocurrency market context.

3. **Trade Bitcoin based on their short-term volatility** – This strategy exposes the investors to greater risk but it offers faster compound profits. Bitcoin is volatile and is synonymous with unpredictable, violent valuation swings. Investors who enjoy short-term profits by buying coins on the dip and selling them at the peaks often go with this investing strategy.

   In essence, it is a technique where investors hold on to their digital currency assets for less than one year and engage more often in buying and selling them. They are the 'active investors' who are targeting to earn huge profits in a short span of time. The downside of this strategy is the risk of losing a part of the investment if not careful.

   This strategy requires knowledge, planning, and skills. You need to be aware of the fundamental principles, methods, and timing to make the trading experience rewarding in terms of financial and satisfaction aspects.

How long should you hold your Bitcoin?

The answer lies in your reasons and expectations. The primary goal of investment is to give you the opportunity to grow your finances by getting profits. Essentially, investing is a kind of business. You buy bitcoins during the bearish period and sell them when the market is bullish.

When you buy an asset, you typically choose a specific investment vehicle for one or more reasons. Perhaps you are investing because you are anticipating a big personal or family project 3 years from now. You want to have a consistent passive income or just to satisfy your speculation about this cryptocurrency.

People who invest in Bitcoin and other crypto enter the investing market with a vision to increase their net worth. Their goals keep them in the investment market even during bearish moments.

- Investors who invest in speculation do not observe a definite period to hold their investments. They can hold them for several hours, days, weeks, or even months before selling to the next investors who want to get hold of bitcoins and make future profits. These investors are always alert and would quickly sell the assets the moment they see that they would get a hefty ROI or buy more crypto.

- Investors who buy Bitcoin as a form of saving to finance a future project aim to sell the asset when it is time. The proceeds will be used solely for the special project. It doesn't matter so much if the amount of profit is not much as long as the intended amount for the project is covered.

- Investors buy Bitcoin as a source of consistent income. They hold their coins until the need comes and sell all or part of their crypto-asset to engage in another income-generating venture.

How long to hold your Bitcoin also depends on your perception of the crypto market. If there is continuing uncertainty and you are becoming anxious, you can decide to sell your investment and buy again in the future. There is no sense staying if you are emotionally down with the current downtrend scenarios. Besides, you can buy coins again during the bear period. In addition, if you already made a good profit and want to exit the market, then go for it. At the end of the day, always remember your investing goals and the reasons why you invest in Bitcoin.

Investing tip

BTFD (Buy the Fucking Dip) is when investors are selling their crypto coins out of fear.
This is the perfect time to start buying bitcoins.

When is the right time to buy Bitcoin?

Investor A purchased his Bitcoin a few days before the price in the market declined. Investor Z bought his Bitcoin when the price had gone to 50% of the original value and close to the period when the price became bullish.

The results?

- Investor Z made a 100% ROI of his investment because he bought the crypto asset at the right time.
- Investor A is still holding his Bitcoin and waiting for the price to go higher to earn a reasonable profit.

In retrospect:

The time you make an investment by buying your coin and how the crypto market behaves immediately after are other factors that will help you that influences the length of time you will hold your Bitcoin.

Therefore, your success is largely dependent on 'timing the market.' It means buying your coins when the price is low and selling them at the highest possible price when the market is strong. This is the simplest, yet most effective strategy. Never allow your emotions to overcome your logical reasoning.

Ways to Invest in Bitcoin

There are several direct and indirect methods to start investing in Bitcoin.

- **Buying and stockpiling Bitcoin**

  This is the simplest and fastest way to get hold of this crypto asset. Buying a standalone coin from a crypto exchange gives you ownership of Bitcoin. You can "physically" store your bitcoins in cold storage or use the encrypted wallet of the exchange platform.

- **Participating in mining Bitcoin**

  It means investing in companies that are involved in large-scale computing operations to mine Bitcoin. You earn profits and skip the complex part of the job.

  Another way is to let your computer be utilized as a public ledger node and receive Bitcoin for your participation.

- **Purchasing funds from Greyscale's Bitcoin Investment Trust (GBTC)**

  Greyscale offers investors to buy and hold Bitcoin in investor accounts, brokerage, Roth IRA, and certain IRA. This investment platform has made Bitcoin accessible to the masses, democratizing the notion that this popular crypto is for investors with huge capital. The funds offer diversification at relatively lower cost and allow investors to get exposure to the blockchain.

- **Buying shares in companies that use Bitcoin blockchain technology**

In this method of Bitcoin investing, you are buying the corporate stocks of publicly traded companies that incorporate blockchain technology to complement their products or services or are focused on developing blockchain-based industrial infrastructures. It has been a hot option because of the crucial role of this innovative technology as the database for digital and crypto transactions.

Here are some companies offering stocks with underlying blockchain technology that you need to check out:

- ✓ **Amazon** – Aside from being the largest e-commerce platform in the world, it also operates the cloud infrastructure platform Amazon Web Services (AWS). This service allows clients to create their own blockchain network and manage them through Amazon Managed Blockchain.

- ✓ **CME Group** – Being the largest options exchange in the world that offers derivative securities for foreign exchange, indexes, and stocks, CME Group has also created an active Bitcoin futures contract market.

- ✓ **IBM** – IBM Blockchain has been providing transformative solutions to clients like True Tickets, Kroger, and a lot more. It helps customers establish dependable chains amidst the current pandemic and other challenging issues. Its AI and cloud initiatives also attract a considerable share of the information technology market.

- ✓ **Square** – The Cash App payment platform of this financial tech company offers peer-to-peer transactions that allow Bitcoin buying and selling much easier. During the 3rd quarter of 2020, about $1.6 billion worth of Bitcoin has been purchased through Cash App. Square also has established Square Crypto with a team of expert bitcoin developers with exciting projects under its sleeve like building open-source venture

- ✓ **Overstock.com Inc. (OSTK)** – This leading online retailer was among the first businesses that accepted Bitcoin payment. Its subsidiary Medici Ventures has been investing actively in projects that are blockchain-related for years. It also converted Medici as a fund that will be used to create blockchain startups. The fund has an 8-year timeframe and is managed by Pelion Venture Partners.

- ✓ **NVIDIA Corp (NVDA)** – This firm designs and creates high-end processing chips and graphic cards that are mostly used by supercomputers and servers of the crypto mining industry. It also produced exclusive chips for mining cryptocurrencies, offering more exposure to blockchain technology.

- ✓ **VMware Inc. (VMW)** – In 2020, the company successfully launched VMware Blockchain that helps clients manage extremely complicated workflows and multiparty applications.

- ✓ **Coinbase Global Inc. (COIN)** – COIN stocks have been on the high because of its great "cryptoeconomy" potential that is built on blockchain.

- **Investing in bitcoin futures ETFs**

  Exchange-traded funds (ETFs) seem to be a safer option to invest your money. On October 19, 2021, the first SEC-approved bitcoin futures joined the ranks of other commodities or assets in the stock market. ProShares Bitcoin Strategy ETF BITO BITO tracks CME Bitcoin futures. During the futures contracts maturity, ProShares will collect a $95 (0.95%) fee for every $10,000 investment.

Key takeaways

- Several factors impact the value of Bitcoin- adoption as a payment system, store of value, finite supply, and reduced inflation.

- Getting started in Bitcoin investing is simple through crypto brokers or exchange platforms. The challenge is what kind of crypto to buy.

- Practicing safety measures, like getting cold storage (hardware wallets), is recommended to protect your Bitcoin.

- Investing in companies with Bitcoin in their hedge portfolio and using blockchain in their infrastructure or services is a viable option.

Point to Ponder

One secret of successful investors is having a well-balanced crypto portfolio. Learn how to build one.

Chapter 6

Personal Portfolio Management

"A good portfolio is more than a long list of stocks and bonds. It is a balanced whole with protections and opportunities with respect to a wide range of contingencies."
– Harry M. Markowitz
(Father of portfolio management and Nobel Prize-winning economist)-

A personal portfolio is a blueprint or a big-picture organized plan to manage the financial future. It is comprised of all the investments and a variety of asset classes you hold. A balanced, well-diversified personal portfolio is the key to financial freedom while your style of portfolio management will help you achieve it.

Portfolio management is about designing and managing the strategies to achieve the investment objectives. Essentially, the goals include getting a good deal of profits out of the acquired assets and asset allocation or choosing the type of investment vehicle that would give a short-term or long-term ROI.

Diversification is also a vital element to produce more income or hedge against inflation. Investors who are fascinated with cryptocurrency added Bitcoin in their investment portfolio, whether through bitcoin futures ETF or blockchain-linked stocks.

Benefits of portfolio management

> ➤ It keeps the portfolio's performance in perspective.

> ➤ It helps you monitor the risk levels and rebalance your portfolio when necessary

> ➢ It guides you figure out your financial priorities.

> ➢ It helps you make regular investments to reach your investing goals faster.

What is portfolio management?

In a nutshell, portfolio management is the science and art of choosing investment assets and overseeing this group of investments to meet the financial goals and match the risk tolerance of the investor (individual, institution, or company).

It is about weighing the opportunities and threats or the strengths and weaknesses of different kinds of assets in the market to build a solid financial portfolio. Ultimately, the primary objective is to maximize the expected return of the investment within the set timeframe and risk exposure level. Investors can choose to manage their personal portfolios or hire a professional licensed portfolio manager.

Large investors usually have portfolio managers to take care of their portfolios. These managers use their market knowledge and professional skills to manage the portfolios with the help of software or apps that would simplify the process.

The crucial factors that they work on include:

- Average risk and reward by asset class
- Risks associated with the investments
- Risk measurement
- Understanding the investor's "risk tolerance"
- Relationship between risks and returns
- Returns correlations between assets

- Accounting for fees in planning the portfolio
- Options' valuation
- Diversification of portfolio

Different models of investment portfolios

Generally speaking, investors with bigger capital and want a long-time horizon would prefer to invest in high-return, high-risk options. Those with smaller investment funds and want a shorter time span would go for low-risk, low-return assets.

○ **Conservative portfolio** – This model allocates more funds to lower-risk assets (money market securities, fixed income securities). It aims to protect the portfolio's principal value hence being called sometimes a "capital preservation" portfolio.

Opting for a conservative portfolio means that you are not totally avoiding the exposure to some growth stocks because they also help offset price inflation. You may choose to buy an index fund, equity from blockchain-linked companies, bitcoin futures contracts, and other alternative assets.

Profile example:

❖ 60% - 65% Equities
❖ 25%-30% Fixed Income Securities
❖ 5%-15% Cash and Equivalents

○ **Moderately conservative portfolio** – This kind of portfolio is ideal for investors who want to preserve the big part of the portfolio's total value but can take some level of risk. One strategy that works for this model is the current income where you invest in high-income securities such as coupon payments or dividends.
Profile example:

- ❖ 35% - 40% Equities
- ❖ 55%-60% Fixed Income Securities
- ❖ 5%-10% Cash and Equivalents

o **Aggressive portfolio** – It has a higher volume of equities which means the portfolio value fluctuates day after day. The primary goal of an aggressive portfolio is to gain long-term capital growth. It uses a capital growth strategy to achieve the investor's goals. As for diversification, adding fixed-income securities is a good idea.

Profile example:

- ❖ 50% - 55% Equities
- ❖ 20%-25% Fixed Income Securities
- ❖ 5%-10% Cash and Equivalents

o **Very aggressive portfolio** – This portfolio model is mainly composed of stocks. Investors who use a very aggressive portfolio aim for strong capital growth over a long-term period.

Profile example:

- ❖ 80% - 100% Equities
- ❖ 0%-10% Fixed Income Securities
- ❖ 0%-10% Cash and Equivalents

Remember that you can use them as a guide only and change the proportions of the assets to suit your preferences and investment needs.

Investment styles to consider for your portfolio

There are two primary types of portfolio management- active and passive. This is a fundamental decision to make as it will decide the direction of your investing success. If you choose this option, you believe that you can leverage the irregularities in market pricing and make excellent selections that are based not essential factors and not by chance.

1. Active portfolio management involves strategic planning when to buy or sell stocks and other forms of investment vehicles to beat the index performance.

- Investment funds that are actively managed typically have individual portfolio managers (team of managers or co-managers) who decide what to do with the assets. They use a combination of strategies, market forecasts, in-depth studies, and expertise to maximize the potential of the invested funds.

- Portfolio managers gather relevant data such as market trends, current news, political happenings that can affect the investment landscape, and economic situations. The irregularities can boost the potential ROI of the stocks and index funds.

- An active portfolio management approach uses brokers or fund managers to trade, buy, or sell stocks.

2. Passive portfolio management (also known as the set-it-and-forget-it strategy or an index fund management) duplicates the makeup of certain indexes to match their benchmark or market return. Investors who choose this option believe that investment markets are generally efficient and careful evaluation of available information about investment will lead to superior performance.

- It is ideal for people who prefer long-term investing in exchange-traded index funds.

- This strategy is structured like a mutual fund, a unit investment trust, or an exchange-traded fund (ETF).

- Passive portfolios have lower management fees compared to actively managed portfolios.

Did you know that?

About ten percent of Bitcoin supply
have been untouched for more than 10 years?
They are locked in dormant addresses
and worth over $23 billion.

Factors to consider in portfolio management

1. Investment goals

The first order of business- you need to know your reasons why you invest your money. Investment goals generally center on the risk-return profile of the investors or how much risk and volatility they can withstand. Once the ideal level is reached, you can start formulating the winning strategies.

Here are some general questions to ask yourself when setting your objectives.

- What do you want to achieve within your timeframes?
- Are you hoping to preserve your wealth and make a legacy to guarantee a good future for your family?
- Do you want to build a solid portfolio that will replace your paycheck when you retire?

Setting your objectives is the fundamental starting point of investment. Goals are vital points when designing your initial personal portfolio. You can always modify them whenever necessary.

2. Asset allocation

Another crucial element in investing is selecting the asset classes that will make up the financial portfolio and how much is the budget allocation for individual vehicles.

Asset allocation is about having a good mix of bonds, stocks, "cash" (certificate of deposits), bitcoin futures ETFs, blockchain-linked stocks, and other alternative investments (derivatives, commodities, real estate) in your portfolio.

It provides balance and protection against the volatility of some assets. Generally, conservative investors would go for stable investments like stocks and bonds while the more aggressive ones are likely to combine growth stocks, crypto-based stocks, and other volatile investments.

- If your main goal is growth, you can invest in assets that are likely to appreciate and offer a hedge against inflation. Opting for a wider asset allocation lessens the risks while achieving your objectives.

- When your goal is enjoying short-term income from your investments, you may choose to select assets that yield fast ROI and profits. However, opting for all--bonds or all-stocks portfolio may be a wise decision but over time, inflation can reduce your expected income. This can be resolved if you add other equities or assets that will protect your portfolio even if they do not directly generate income.

There are 6 common asset allocation strategies you can use to create a dynamic portfolio that brings beneficial overall returns:

a. *Strategic Asset Allocation* – It adheres to the principle of a proportional mixture of assets, taking into account the individual risk tolerance as well as time-frame. This method involves setting the targets and rebalancing the personal portfolio regularly to boost returns and cut back losses.

b. *Tactical Asset Allocation* – It is a tactical deviation within a short-term period that capitalizes or leverages the potential opportunities of exceptional investment. The flexibility would boost the market-timing aspect of the investment portfolio and rebalance the long-term positions of traditional assets.

c. *Insured Asset Allocation* – This method involves the creation of a base value that should be sustained. Investors or portfolio managers practice active portfolio management and rely on various resources (forecasts, analytical research, news, judgment, experiences) to make sound decisions when buying, selling, or holding assets. The insured asset allocation strategy is perfect for risk-averse people who want to secure their investments and achieve long-term goals.

d. *Constant-Weighting Asset Allocation* – This strategy adopts the approach of constant rebalancing of the portfolio. You purchase assets that have declined their value and sell them the value increases. The rule of thumb of this methodology is rebalancing when any of the asset classes show over a 5% deviation from the original value.

e. *Dynamic Asset Allocation* – It involves a constant adjustment of the mix of assets to adapt to the rise and fall of the markets. Technically, it is the opposite of the constant-weighting strategy because investors buy assets when their value increases and anticipate continued returns, and sell those with decreasing value in anticipation of possible further loss. Most of the time, the use of this strategy is influenced by the judgment of portfolio managers who speculate on the day-to-day performance of the assets.

f. *Integrated Asset Allocation* – It is a strategy that takes into consideration the risks of having a mix of assets and the expectations of market returns. In a sense, it encompasses all the key points of the other strategies.

3. Selection of uncorrelated assets

To reduce the risks in your personal portfolio, your best move is to diversify it by choosing uncorrelated assets. Overextended time, a lot of your accumulated assets may not be performing like before. By having a diversified portfolio of assets, you can attain your goals even if one of the asset classes did not perform well.

4. Tax implications

Investments are taxable so consider this when you are designing your personal portfolio. If you have diversified assets, they will be taxed accordingly depending on the classifications. This is where tax diversification comes in.

There are 3 "pools of money" in the United States – the taxable pool, the tax-deferred pool, and the tax-free pool. If your portfolio has a regular non-retirement account, traditional IRA, and Roth Ira, you have these three tax pools. A smart investor would always consider the tax implications to enjoy higher after-tax returns.

5. Diversification

The world of investing is uncertain. You may win or lose, which is why having a basket of investments that give you exposure to various asset classes would mitigate heavy loss. In essence, diversification spreads the risks and also the rewards within the asset classes. No one can accurately predict which assets would outperform the others, diversification will reduce volatility risk and cover the returns of all the subsets of assets or sectors over time.

5. Rebalancing

Rebalancing is simply the process of reverting the investment portfolio to the original asset allocation. It is typically conducted annually or at regular intervals. During the rebalancing, you can sell the high-priced assets and securities and buy lower-priced stocks or allocate the proceeds to bitcoin futures. Regular rebalancing will help you expand the growth opportunity and recapture the initial gains in potential sectors while keeping them aligned with your risk/return profile.

Phases of personal portfolio management

A. Planning

Like any kind of business, investing requires careful and smart planning. This initial stage of portfolio development requires making clear objectives, setting requirements, and selecting investment assets.

In determining the objectives, you should consider the returns after making investments, liquidity factors, time frame, and amount of risks. During this stage, scenarios like a market economy, inflation, changes in policies, regulations, and other vital factors should all be considered.

B. Implementing

When all the necessary requirements are set, the next step is implementing the chosen strategy. At this point, investors would be selecting the assets that would give them the rewards they want to achieve. Applying the diversification rule would help in minimizing the risks during financial crises and losses.

C. Controlling

Controlling means regular checking of the markets, doing analysis, and evaluating the portfolio's performance in the ever-changing investment climate. It also involves constant portfolio modification by selling overweight assets and buying underweight securities. While it can be challenging to make decisions due to the price fluctuations in the market, your experiences will help you master the strategies to effectively manage your personal portfolio.

Did you know that?

*Genesis Mining company sent Bitcoin
to a crypto wallet in the space via
a P3P transaction.*

When do you need a portfolio manager?

Outsourcing your portfolio management is an option if you are a busy person but want to gain exposure to stock markets and crypto markets. A financial professional who is adept and well-experienced in handling money-related matters helps you jumpstart your investing journey without hassle.

You may wonder about the difference between a portfolio manager and an investment manager, which is another common title of a professional handling financial matters for individuals or companies.

- Investment managers/advisors have broader roles which include investment management, estate management, debt management, tax management, budgeting, retirement planning, and more.

- Portfolio managers are mainly focused on providing sound recommendations, support, documentation, and portfolio management. They understand the financial needs of their clients and create investment solutions to maximize profits while minimizing the risks.

A portfolio manager will do the following for you:

- ✓ Helps you select the right assets to customize your portfolio and suggests where to invest or avoid

- ✓ Tailor-made the portfolio to match your age, risk tolerance, income, expectations, and investment horizon

- ✓ Designs customized investment solutions for you by analyzing your background, capacity to invest, and earnings

- ✓ Makes you aware of the available investment tools and the benefits of every investment plan

- ✓ Helps you realize the advantages of investing in particular asset classes and alternative assets

- ✓ Provides professional and unbiased advice on market trends and asset allocation to help you decide

- ✓ Maintains and monitors your portfolio

- ✓ Submits reports on individual investment assets

- ✓ Takes daily trading decisions to meet your financial goals

- ✓ Works to rebalance the account to ensure that it aligns with your risk appetite and preferences

Portfolio managers earn through commissions or fee-only cost, which is typically between 3 to 4%. They do not charge a per hour rate, retainer fee, asset-based fee, or fixed compensation.

How to find the right portfolio manager?

When choosing the right personal portfolio manager, you need to exercise maximum caution by doing the following:

➤ Choose someone with deep knowledge about the existing investment plans, financial markets, policies, and risks.

➤ Check the trustworthiness of the portfolio manager and with a good background. It is necessary to make a character check to find out his reputation in the industry. You do not want your hard-earned cash to be at the mercy of a dishonest, unprofessional, and shady person.

➤ Beware of a person who tries to impress you with professional jargon and complex terminologies about investing. A good portfolio manager should not confuse the clients, but help them become knowledgeable about the rewards and risks of investing.

Managing your personal portfolio

If you don't like someone to handle your personal investment portfolio, you can always choose to do it yourself. However, you need to brush up on your knowledge and skills to ensure that you are doing everything right.

Step 1

The first thing to do is learn how to **create your personal portfolio**. It should reflect your investment goals, investment strategies and approaches, risk tolerance, and capital requirements. Every investor has a unique personal portfolio to match his future income needs.

• Evaluate your financial situation, resources, age, and time you can spend growing your investments.

- Determine your future income needs and objectives.
- Consider the level of your risk tolerance and stress meter. Investing is highly speculative and if your tolerance bar is low, you might end up not sleeping over losses when the worst scenario comes along.
- Pick asset classes that are not high-risk if you are a newbie and diversify your portfolio.
- Understand the risk/return tradeoff principle, which means the greater the risks of securities, the higher the returns. But never invest blindly or just because of the potential returns. You should weigh your options and start small if you decide to invest in volatile assets.

Step 2

Next to portfolio creation and asset allocation is to **determine the capital** you need for the asset classes you have picked up. This will fulfill the strategies you set for asset allocation. Make time to study the potential, risks, reward, and nature of every asset you want to invest in.

- **Stocks**

  When stock picking, consider the vital factors to satisfy your objectives and make you comfortable with your choice. They are the stock type, market capitalization, and sector. Make a shortlist of your preferred stocks and analyze each one before going forward. Stocks are high-risk investments and work-intensive, which means you need to be updated with the current market trends and regularly monitor the changes in the valuation/price of your holdings.

  Subclasses:

- o *Large-cap stocks* are shares offered by companies with more than $10 billion market capitalization.
- o *Mid-cap stocks* are shares from companies with a market capitalization that range between $2 billion to $10 billion.
- o *Small-cap stocks* are shares issued by companies that have less than $2 billion market capitalization.

- **Bonds**

  When selecting bonds, consider the type of bond, the interest-rate environment, maturity, coupon, as well as credit rating.

- **Mutual funds**

  They are baskets of asset classes that are professionally picked and handled by fund managers.
- **ETFs (Exchange-traded funds)**

  In essence, ETFs are also mutual funds but they are traded like stocks. Both represent a group of stocks or index funds by market cap sector, location, and types. However, ETFs are not actively managed by fund managers, instead track a basket of stocks or a particular index.

- **Equities**

Equities in investing are company stocks or shares. When you buy a share of stocks, you are technically getting a stake on the ownership interest or a fractional portion. You buy equities with the expectation that you will be earning capital gains when the value of the investment increase. Examples of equities are common stocks, preferred stocks, and treasury stocks.

- **Derivatives**

The derivatives are complex securities whose value is determined or dependent on their underlying assets or benchmarks. They are actually a form of advanced investing with agreed-upon contracts between the provider and the investor. The common examples of derivatives in investing are futures contracts, options, forward contracts, warrants, and swaps.

- **Alternative investments**

They are the asset classes that are not included in the traditional list of investment vehicles. They include cryptocurrency, real estate, precious stones, gold/silver, venture capital/private equity, oil, managed futures, hedge funds, antiques, commodities, wine, and artwork. Gold is the most preferred tangible inflation hedge because of its long-term store of value and liquidity.

Alternative investments are usually favored by investors because they are excellent tools for personal or institutional portfolio diversification. Investing in hard assets (real estate property, gold, oil) is considered an effective hedge against inflation. They have a low correlation with bond and stock markets, typically moving on the opposite or counter position. This is many private endowments, pension funds, and other institutional funds allocate a portion of their portfolios to alternative investments. Currently, a lot of large investors are accumulating cryptocurrencies, in particular, Bitcoin to diversify their investment pool.

These types of investments are subject to the review and approval of the Securities and Exchange Commission (SEC). They also fall under the purview of the Consumer Protection Act and the Dodd-Frank Wall Street Reform. There are account providers that only offer this option to accredited investors. These investors have over $1 million net worth excluding their primary residential property or with at least $200,000 annual income.

Step 3

After establishing your personal portfolio, the next step is to periodically analyze, evaluate, and rebalance it. These tasks are crucial because the prices in the market are constantly moving, making a direct or indirect impact that changes your initial pool of assets.

Other elements that can alter the weightings of asset allocations over time are your risk tolerance, current financial situation, and future income needs.

- In terms of risk tolerance, perhaps you're more ready to invest in high-risk assets that offer greater rewards or your tolerance has dropped significantly and want to let go of some equities.

- Your financial situation also makes a difference. If you can afford to add more capital, start exploring other asset classes or alternative investments like Bitcoin. If you are still weighing the pros and cons of crypto investing, buying bitcoin futures ETFs is a good start.

Assessing the balance of your portfolio is important to know if the strategies are working favorably or you can still achieve your goals within the time frame you set. To determine the actual allocation of your investment vehicles, categorize them quantitatively and find out the value's proportion to the whole.

Step 4

The final task is rebalancing or adjusting the weightings of assets in your personal portfolio from time to time. It is done by selling and adding assets after evaluating which are in overweighted or underweighted positions.

- For instance, you have a 40% holding of small-cap equities but your asset allocation should only be 25%. You need to sell the exceeding volume and use the fund to buy other asset classes, probably a bitcoin futures contract or physical bitcoins and other alternative investments.

- Also, if you see that your growth stocks investment has appreciated over the past year beyond your expectations, you can stop adding a new asset class in this category. Selling your equity positions just to rebalance your financial portfolio would incur significant capital gain tax. The best decision is to balance it by adding other asset classes. However, if you think that your overweighted growth stocks would fall soon, selling them would mitigate a great loss.

Trivia

Satoshi Nakamoto wrote 31,000 lines of codes to create the Bitcoin software. It was more than the 19,000 coding lines

How often do you need to rebalance your personal portfolio?

The frequency of rebalancing your investment portfolio will depend on the type of accounts you have, tax considerations, transaction costs, and personal preferences. An annual portfolio rebalancing is sufficient when there is no extraordinary growth appreciation anywhere in your portfolio assets.

The following general guidelines come in handy when you need to rebalance your portfolio:

> ➢ **Keep a record.**

   Recording the cost of every security you bought and the total cost of your portfolio assets is important. The numbers will give you historical data that you can use to compare to future values of your portfolio, making it easy to see where to adjust.

> ➢ **Compare the value**

   Anytime in the future, when you need to compare the values of the asset classes and the portfolio, you just need to review the record. To do the comparison, divide the current value of the individual asset class by the current total portfolio value. Find significant changes that may necessitate adjusting the assets allocation. But if you see that the figures are good and there is no urgent need for short-term liquidation of securities, then keep the original structure.

> ➢ **Adjustment**

> If the weightings of some of your asset classes expose your personal portfolio to risk, make an adjustment. Simply get the current total value of the portfolio then multiply it individually on the original weightings assigned for each asset class. The results are the figures that you should invest in each class to revert back to the original allocation of assets.

How to measure your ROI?

The return of investment (ROI) measures the performance of any investment portfolio (personal, business, institutional).

The formula never changes: **ROI – (Gains-Cost)/Cost**

But ROI varies depending on the condition of the market and the type of securities/assets that investors hold.

When to sell or buy asset classes?

Timing is everything. Know when to sell your securities or buy new asset classes to balance your portfolio. Do not invest blindly, but always with a clear purpose. Never allow your emotions to influence your investing decisions. Reassess your purpose regularly to suit the market conditions and risks.

Key takeaways

- Building a profitable and winning portfolio requires learning the essential elements. Learn the art & science of investing.

- Be clear when establishing your investment goals.

- Diversification is not just owning different asset classes, but also spreading your securities holdings from each asset class to avoid exposure to great risks and volatility.

- Asset allocation is the basic investing principle in portfolio management because it helps investors to leverage the assets to gain maximum profits while minimizing various risks.

- Go for long-term investment if you want to earn compound interest, grow your investment, and avoid numerous transaction fees.

- Don't panic. Use the best strategy to mitigate losses. Remember that every asset has a good and bad time that may affect the weightings of your portfolio.

- Patience is a virtue when it comes to investing.

Point to Ponder

Never put all your investment eggs in one particular asset just because it is the current hottest investment vehicle and everyone is buying it.

Chapter 7

What Should Comprise Your Crypto Portfolio?

> *"With DeFi, we are building the finance system of tomorrow."*
> — Olawale Daniel-

Cryptocurrency is the new breed of asset class with a characteristic of higher risk and higher returns. The strong interest and global adoption of Bitcoin and other alternative coins make it possible for crypto to merit inclusion in the portfolio of investors and even in the traditional stock market.

While investing is subjective and the portfolio depends on the financial need as well as risk appetite, striking a balance is crucial to protect the assets. Whether your goal is to purely invest in Bitcoin and other cryptocurrencies or want to include bitcoin-linked exchange-traded funds, creating a well-diversified portfolio is crucial to successful investing.

What makes a good crypto portfolio?

- ➢ A 2% bitcoin allocation to the overall personal portfolio is a safe start for beginners. Advanced investors that are more risk-tolerant and daring can allocate more than this figure.

- ➢ Bitcoin remains the leading crypto with more than a 40% share of cryptocurrency market capitalization. It means, the price movement of Bitcoin influences the other cryptocurrencies.

- ➢ If you're into crypto investing, the best way to begin is having 60% of Bitcoin in your portfolio, then Ethereum. A portfolio of 75% Bitcoin and 25% Ethereum is an ideal composition for risk-adjusted returns.

Pro tip: *Most alternative coins (altcoins) do not survive the 4-year cycle or halving of Bitcoin. During this cycle is the bear-and-bull market periods, which are characterized by massive growth (bull) and accumulation (bear) of bitcoins. As Bitcoin keeps its ground during these cycles, other coins lose their market value and get busted in a flash.*

The evolution of crypto

Cryptocurrency evolves from Bitcoin (pure crypto) to Ethereum (decentralized platform with a proprietary currency), and DeFi (decentralized finance that uses smart contracts).

- ▪ Bitcoin in your personal portfolio

  Regarded as the 'king' of cryptocurrency, Bitcoin is the most popular and widely-used virtual currency. People want to own this coin because it has a solid user/holder base. No wonder, investors call it 'digital gold' because it can be used for many digital transactions anywhere in the world. Bitcoin investors believe in its enormous ability to continue growing value because of the fixed supply which is capped below 21 million coins. It makes Bitcoin a highly-prized asset and worthy to be part of the investment portfolio.

If you have a diversified investment portfolio and allocated a portion of it in Bitcoin, you understand its high risk-reward characteristic. You may consider your crypto capital as a fund that you can afford to lose and the other asset classes are the ones to give you good ROIs. Counter-balancing is important in investing, hence the need for asset diversification. Keeping high-risk asset classes to a minimum and having fixed deposits and securities would protect your portfolio when volatility strikes.

- Ethereum in your portfolio

Ethereum's native token Ether has also proven its value for long-term investment. Like Bitcoin, it has gained popularity because of the network effect where new investors want what old investors have. Aside from this, Ethereum has successfully established itself as a global computing platform with an ecosystem of decentralized applications or "dapps". It has supported other cryptocurrencies, letting them grow in terms of users and value.

As a platform, it uses 'smart contracts' and collects Ether in exchange for contract execution. As Ethereum becomes increasingly popular across the globe, Ether also gains more value and utility, resulting in its long-term and sustainable value. Investors are now looking closely at the ability of Ether to provide direct profit.

- DeFi in your portfolio

  The term "DeFi" or decentralized finance is one of the frequently-mentioned words in the financial markets. Since Bitcoin and other cryptocurrencies operate on a peer-to-peer basis, it is not surprising that DeFi becomes the next big thing in the investment world because of this feature.

What exactly is DeFi?

In the digital world, DeFi offers the convenience of doing transactions without the intervention of a third party. It delivers quicker transactions, eliminates the high cost of fees to the intermediaries, and allows investors complete control over their assets.

In a way, DeFi is similar to Bitcoin and other cryptocurrencies because of its decentralized nature. It achieves distributed consensus with the help of smart contracts on the blockchain. These smart contracts perform certain actions when the required conditions are met.

What makes DeFi different from other cryptocurrencies?

DeFi represents the third wave of cryptocurrency. It pivoted the future of the financial and economic world, just like the explosion of stock companies during the 16th and 17th centuries.

In essence, decentralized finance (DeFi)) delivers efficiency. One of the cores of economics is the ability of a product to efficiently convert work into output or stuff. The blockchain's new structure of issued crypto with smart contracts spurs this efficiency.

In addition to the efficient way to do the established things, DeFi also offers exciting new ways to complete tasks. At present, the next generation of financial institutions is being invented to provide an infrastructure system that is free from the common issues that plague financial services such as layers of cost, waste, redundancy, and more. Expect that DeFi will spawn new strands of functionality to any kind of business.

Why should you use DeFi?

1. It is the future of finance.

In a nutshell, blockchain technology has disrupted the system of traditional finance and DeFi is now disrupting blockchain in a good way by harnessing the power and efficiency of digital contracts. DeFi platforms have become a place to trade, save, lend, borrow, and earn interest without the hassle of bureaucracy. The high level of accessibility via the DeFi platform gives equal opportunity for people who cannot open bank accounts or get loans from financial institutions.

2. It redefines cryptocurrency.

DeFi tokens are utilized as a medium of transactions at a lower cost. The automation process that it offers becomes the foundation to easy access to crypto worldwide as well as transparency. The decentralized nature eliminates the barrier of entry that most countries put up against cryptocurrency. DeFi removes the limiting country-specific requirements for investors.

3. It is diversified.

With DeFi, you go beyond the traditional method of exchanging and storing tokens. It gives essence to true decentralization, removing the need for any authority to accept, restrict, approve, and monitor financial transactions.

4. It ditches the paperwork.

Blockchain processed the transactions that use smart contracts, eliminating the hassle and trail of paperwork. There is also no waiting period, unlike the conventional process that involves bank clearing of financial transactions.

5. It quickens the pace of transactions.

Without the waiting time for clearing or approval of authorized people to complete the transactions, DeFi has the advantage of a providing quick and smooth experience for investors.

6. It gets rid of middlemen.

With automated smart contracts on the blockchain, there is no need for mediators like lawyers to make an agreement between the involved parties.

7. It equalizes financial opportunities.

The DeFi platforms offer financial opportunities that are normally offered by banks, hedge funds, and major financial institutions. With Defi, individual investors can access them without the usual strict requirements.

8. It is immutable.

The blockchain's records are tamper-proof, making them safe from unscrupulous people. Once the transactions are completed, there is no way to modify or delete them from the ledger system.

What are the downsides of DeFi?

1. Complexity

Compared to centralized finance where the institutions basically do everything, DeFi requires more engagement from the investors. This complexity makes the conservative and passive investors

2. Scalability and liquidity

While the locked-in liquidity value of DeFi as of October 2021 is around $12.5 billion, this value is relatively little compared to the traditional system. DeFi has the perfect structure for a small number of users. The problem of liquidity happens when huge withdrawals are made.

3. Insurance

Most of the DeFi projects are not covered by insurance, which can pose a great risk for investors who preferred security to safeguard their investment.

Quick Facts

DeFi is designed to eliminate two basic risks: operational mistakes and fraud.

Several ways to make money with DeFi

Decentralized finance helps investors maximize the potential of their assets and earn passive income. The growing ecosystem of DeFi makes it more attractive to investors and businesses who want to leverage its functionality.
Here are some straightforward approaches:

- **Lending**

   Most of the DeFi platforms specialize in lending. Holders of tokens can stake them for lending to earn APY (annual percentage yield). It works by lending your virtual assets and locking them into smart contracts. The interest accrued will be distributed to the lenders by the smart contracts in proportion to the locked-in asset value.

The funds are accessed by borrowers in the form of loan that requires them to lock up collateral. When they fail to pay the interests on the set date, the smart contract will automatically enforce repayment from the collateral.

- **Staking**

  Staking refers to the process of utilizing smart contracts to lock in the digital assets for an extended period. The idea is similar to the regular savings bank account where the staker's balance accrues interest. Once you deposited your share in the smart contract, you can periodically claim your rewards.

  As an incentive, investors earn a proportionate share from the generated revenue of the DeFi platform. The incentives are in the form of tokens (similar to your token or another type of token in the blockchain). Some platforms require a minimum stake amount and an extended period of investment.

- **Becoming a liquidity provider**

  In this method, you can contribute liquidity to DeFi platforms' liquidity pools that offer token pairs. If your portfolio has multiple cryptocurrencies, you can invest a certain amount in the trading pairs.

For example -

You want to invest $2,000 worth of assets, so you contribute $1,000 worth of bitcoin and $1,000 worth of Ethereum. Once you lock them into the pool, you will earn LP (liquidity provider) tokens. They represent the shares you have in the total liquidity pool. When you redeem the LP tokens, you will receive your invested money plus the generated revenues that they earn from the crypto pair.

The more they are traded, the more tokens you will earn. But if the value of one of the tokens in the pool fluctuates significantly, you will lose money via IL or impermanent loss.

- **Yield Farming**

  Yield farming or liquidity mining involves locking your digital assets to LP (liquidity pool) in exchange for the native token rewards. Most often these tokens hold the right to vote (governance tokens) and participate in the reforms of the protocol or platform. In case you want to redeem your LP tokens, you will get back your stake plus the accrued share of income.

- **Borrowing and lending**

  In this approach, you are going to borrow a coin or token from the DeFi platform and use them to earn rewards by investing it back on the same platform or another platform.

Example:

- o You swap $2,000 worth of BTC for wBTC.
- o Next, you deposit it to earn a 0.5% APY.
- o Since you have a Bitcoin deposit, you can apply for a collateralized loan (for another coin or token) for up to 75% of the total value which is $1,500.

In this example, you unlocked the 75% value of your Bitcoin and earn passive income while benefitting from the original asset's capital growth.

- **Leveraging Non-fungible tokens (NFTs)**

Non-fungible token (NFT) is a new concept in decentralized finance that refers to the digital asset whose value is locked into a physical or digital asset like real estate property, works of arts, videos, or music.

NFTs in DeFi serve as proof of digital art ownership. They can be used as collateral for loans. NFTs also offer investors fractional ownership of the items sold by creators. In a way, NFTs represent the modern-day collectibles.

- ➤ NFTs went mainstream when a collage of images from Beeple fetched $69.3 million at Christie's auction house. The digital artist's collection was the first-ever traded NTF work of art.

- ➤ Other NTFs versions of collectible assets that went viral were LeBron James video clip of his slam dunk (more than $200,000), Nyan Cat GIF ($600,000), and the first tweet of Jack Dorsey ($2.9 million).

- **Participating in No-Loss Games & Lotteries**

  DeFi features a No-loss lottery where players use stablecoins to buy tickets. All the participating tickets are put in a pool where one winner is randomly selected. The winner gets all the accrued profits of the games. Those who lose can buy more tickets to have chances of winning or get back their capital back.

Top 10 DeFi altcoins that are revolutionizing the world

With the increased adoption of decentralized finance (DeFi) and the preference of users to use smart contracts in the blockchain, DeFi altcoins and tokens have become more popular. They do not only offer speculative value but they earn real revenues and offer great utility in the crypto industry.

AAVE

Date of Release: November 2017

Market Cap: $3.6 billion

Market Price: $266.76 *(COINBASE)*

subject to change

AAVE is the "governance token" that powers Aave, the decentralized money market protocol that allows investors to deposit or borrow cryptocurrency. It is the native utility token of the protocol that gives a right to the holders to participate in the future of protocol governance. AAVE is generally safe since it is created on the Ethereum blockchain. It has raised more than $16 billion in Initial Coin Offering (ICO) and was on the 2020 Top 100 cryptocurrencies.

What are the uses of AAVE tokens?

- ✓ It can be used to earn rewards through staking.

- ✓ It can be posted as loan collateral.

- ✓ It offers advantages to users like free use of certain Aave services or discounts on fees.

- ✓ It is given to lenders who deposited their crypto in the lending pool as compensation.

- ✓ It can be liquidated when the system needs more capital.

Project: Aave DeFi Network

Aave is a P2P lending system that is Ethereum-based and utilizes smart contracts that automate loan transactions. It is regarded as the first-ever DeFi application that is developed. It is existed and thrived before decentralized finance becomes a mainstream concept.

At present, Aave exists in the algorithmic money market. It enables users to profit from their crypto by lending and receiving loans through pools. To protect the assets of the investors, Aave requires over-collateralization or locking-in collateral that is worth more than the amount of loan.

Lenders are given aTokens or symbolic tokens to recognize their participation when they deposited their cryptocurrency in the lending pools. If you deposit an Ether (ETH) for instance, you will receive an aETH. Once you withdraw your ETH from the pool, the aETH will be converted to ETH.

The recent introduction of Aave's flash loan is a game-changer in the DeFi industry as it allows borrowers to secure quick loans without posting collateral and pay it before the mining of the next block of Ethereum. It also launched the Aave Pro for institutionalized or organized investors.

Where to buy AAVE?

AAVE tokens can be purchased and traded on Binance, Uphold, Huobi Global, and other cryptocurrency exchanges.

How to store your AAVE tokens?

Storing AAVE is relatively simple. You just need to secure an ERC-20 compatible wallet like MyCrypto or My EtherWallet (MEW). If you want more secured storage, hardware wallets like Ledger Nano X and Ledger Nano S support this token.

Is AAVE good crypto for long-term investment?

In the DeFi industry, AAVE is one of the most promising long-term investment assets because its market value is increasing by the day.

- ➢ It is the world's 45th largest digital asset.

- ➢ Since June 2021, AAVE recorded at least $150 million daily trading volume.

- ➢ According to the expert analysts of the Economy Forecast Agency, AAVE's market price will reach $528 by the end of 2022 and $1,254 by the end of 2023.

- ➢ There is a high expectation that if AAVE commands a $1,000 price, it would be in the list of large-cap assets in due time. Large-cap assets are worth over $10 billion.

At the moment, AAVE is growing as one of the largest altcoins in terms of market capitalization. AAVE offers lucrative benefits for individual and institutional investors along with attractive interest rates. It is one of the top 30 digital assets in the world as it benefits from the success of the project behind it. With innovative and unique features that offer great returns on investment, a safe network environment, and strong fundamental/technical aspects, investing in Aave is a great option. Its protocol Aave is considered by crypto enthusiasts and traders as the world's cryptocurrency bank.

How to start investing in AAVE?

Step 1: Register in an exchange platform where you can buy, trade, or invest in AAVE.

Step 2: Wait for the verification of your account. You may be required to upload a valid identification card as part of the Knowing Your Customer (KYC) process.

Step 3: Deposit your funds. AAVE can be purchased with fiat currency or cryptocurrency.

Step 4: Explore the AAVE page of the exchange and start buying AAVEs. Buying transaction is easy and fast. Within minutes, you can view your AAVE coins in your account.

Who should include AAVE in their investment portfolios?

- **Value investors** – While value investing is usually linked with stocks, the growing popularity and value of cryptocurrencies and tokens make them strong tradable assets. The high potential of AAVE to command its trading price and other functions make it a good addition to your personal portfolio.
- **Growth investors** – AAVE is a relatively new trading asset that can help growth investors on their goal to increase capital over time. With its increasing market

price, AAVE is a dynamic asset for long-term investing and promises 5 to 10 times of trading price.

- **Crypto traders** – With high market potential and solid project backup, AAVE is a strong DeFi coin that offers multiple percentage swings that bring significant ROIs for cryptocurrency traders in the long and short-term horizons.

- **Day traders** – AAVE's volatility benefits active traders who execute multiple intraday strategies to earn profits from the traded asset. It is ideal for various trading strategies like Range Trading, Scalping, High-frequency trading, and News-based trading.

- **DeFi/Blockchain enthusiasts** –_These investors understand how Aave protocols work and the great potential of AAVE as crypto. They know that including AAVE in their personal portfolios would be profitable in a long-term timeframe.

ADA

Date of Release: September 2017

Market Cap: $52 billion

Market Price: $ 1.56 *(COINBASE)*

subject to change

ADA is Cardano's native cryptocurrency. This decentralized, open-source crypto began in 2015 but started trading in 2017.

Uses of ADA tokens:

- It is used by Cardano as a currency to run smart contracts.
- It is used to store value.
- It is used to send and receive.
- It can be used as payment for transaction fees on the network.
- It is used for staking or participating in the network's consensus process. It gives you passive income as you earn network fees for validating network transactions.

Project: Cardano

Cardano is both a smart contract and crypto platform that aims to be the next-generation evolution of Ethereum. It has enough flexibility, scalability, and sustainability to allow assets exchange as well as the creation of a wide range of DeFI apps, games, new tokens, and more. The first official usage of Cardano happened in December 2017 where Greek student diplomas were stored and verified on its blockchain.

Cardano's blockchain has two layers:

1. **Cardano Settlement Layer (CSL)** – It stores the accounts and balances ledgers. Transactions in the network are validated in this layer by the Ouroboros consensus mechanism.
2. **Cardano Computing Layer (CCL)** – It is where the apps' computations are executed through smart contracts.

Its primary objective is to become the crypto's most environmentally-friendly blockchain platform. It is often referred to as the "Green Blockchain." It uses Ouroboros, a unique POS (proof-of-stake) consensus mechanism instead of the energy-intensive POW (proof-of-work) that Bitcoin and Ethereum are utilizing.

How to buy ADA?

Step 1: Create an account on a cryptocurrency exchange that allows LINK trading with other virtual currencies like Bitcoin or fiat currencies like US dollars.

Step 2: Deposit funds in the account via bank transfer, cryptocurrency from a crypto wallet, or pay using a debit/credit card.

Step 3: Look for the "Buy Crypto" function to buy LINK tokens.

Step4: Complete your LINK purchase and connect your crypto wallet where you can transfer your tokens.

The official desktop wallet for Cardano is Daedalus, which is an open-source crypto wallet for ADA. It is compatible with Mac and Windows. Other great software options are Exodus and Atomic wallets.

The best hardware wallets in conjunction with Adalite (the open-source, client-side wallet) are Ledger Nano X, Ledger Nano S, and TREZOR Model T.

Is ADA a good long-term investment?

While Cardano crypto is still at its early stage of development, its growing popularity and widespread adoption of the crypto community make it a very good investment asset. Experts in the industry believe that ADA will remain on the top list of cryptocurrencies in the future, becoming a fierce rival of Ether, EOS, and more.

This digital asset offers plenty of long-term strategies and use-cases that suggest its longevity in the market. The platform is data-driven, peer-reviewed, and transparent. With a systematic approach, the volatility is minimized. The future projects of Cardano include a peer-to-peer crypto trading platform, a digital art marketplace, and a platform that trades real-world assets and stocks in its blockchain.

Cardano may appear as a high-risk investment now but its several innovative projects and strength despite being relatively new in the industry would pay big dividends in the future. The long-term growth plan of Cardano is an indication of its sustainable value that will benefit investors.

Long-term investors of ADA enjoyed huge profits during the first half of 2021 when its value increases to over 610%. It means that a $1,000 investment would be worth $7,100.

Forecasts

- ➢ Wallet Investor predicts that ADA's average price would climb to $4.44 by 2022 and up to $4.98 in 2025.
- ➢ PricePrediction's estimate for ADA would be $2.66 in 2022, $7.68 in 2025, and $54.29 by 2030.

COMP

Date of Release: September 2018

Market Cap: $1.7 billion

Market Price: $275.85 *(COINBASE)*

subject to change

COMP is the native token of the Compound DeFi protocol. Launched in June 2020, it serves as the network's primary governance token. Anyone who holds this investment instrument can vote on crucial decisions of the protocol such as borrowing power, introduction of new collateral types, or interest rate models.

Why invest in COMP?

✓ It represents the holder's right to vote on important issues that will impact the protocol's environment. One COMP means one vote. Users with 1% of the total supply of COMP can submit proposals about the protocol's plans and vote for the proposals of other investors.

✓ It allows COMP holders to earn passive income.

✓ It is perfect for HODLers and investors who prefer long-term investing.

✓ Its protocol allows smart contract audits by third parties like Open Zeppelin and Trail of Bits to ensure the highest level of integrity and security.

✓ It is backed up by strong and solid teams, all working to innovate and improve the protocol's ecosystem.

✓ It is easily accessible, leveraging its value growth and liquidity role in the network.

✓ It is a very solid and legitimate crypto coin that can be found in the list of major exchange platforms including Coinbase, Binance, BitPanda, Gate.io, Uphold, and Kraken.

✓ It can be stored in all major hardware wallets like Ledger Nano.

✓ Its supply is capped at 10 million, making it a much-sought altcoin with potential value appreciation. At present, COMP has more than 6 million circulating tokens in the market.

- ✓ Its price history since its launching in September 2020 has shown progressive growth with over 145% year-to-date returns.

Project: Compound

Compound is another DeFi lending protocol that offers APY rewards to depositors of cryptocurrency assets. Investors can use their deposits as collateral to borrow another kind of cryptocurrency. This flexibility makes Compound a much-sought DeFi project in the industry. Just like Aave, it runs on the blockchain system of Ethereum.

This network started the current craze of decentralized finance and was also the first one to launch a yield farming strategy to the crypto market in 2020. The farming pools locked the crypto of investors and provide corresponding rewards in a shorter period. Rewards come in the form of tokens that can be converted into supported crypto assets in the system. All investors who contributed funds receive cTokens that can be used for staking, trading, and transferring their crypto.

Compound has revolutionized the crypto market by offering an open lending environment to users who want to invest or get a short-term loan. The decentralized nature of the system eliminates credit checks and facilitates easy funding, provided there is collateral.

This protocol also utilizes Bitcoin in the DeFi markets through WBTC (Wrapped Bitcoin), which is the locked Bitcoin ERC-20 representation. WBTC allows HODLers of bitcoins easy access to the decentralized finance sector. Recently, this new token was voted to function as collateral in the protocol. Bitcoin holders are now given another way to unlock their coins' value.

How to buy COMP?

Step 1: Open your online account with an exchange or crypto broker.

Step 2: Purchase a crypto wallet where you can transfer or store your COMP coins.

Step 3: Place your order to buy COMP. Depending on the exchange or broker, you can pay through bank transfer, PayPal or other payment services, or credit card.

Step 4: Wait for your order's fulfillment.

If your goal is to hold them in the long-term period, transfer your COMP tokens immediately in cold storage or hardware wallet to ensure protection against cyber theft.

Why should you include COMP in your portfolio?

In a nutshell, allocating a 1% portion of your investment portfolio to COMP gives you the opportunity to enjoy the coin's speculative value growth and take part in its future direction in the crypto market.

Adding COMP to your personal portfolio of investment is a smart decision as it gives you voting rights to participate in its future as well as earn passive income as long as you keep it in the DeFI network. Currently, COMP is the world's 69th largest digital asset.

Another way to earn ROIs from your COMP investment is to leverage its high volatility level by capitalizing on the crypto market's short-term price movements. Buying and selling your assets would give you profits.

Crypto experts believe that COMP is a smart investing vehicle with room for growth. With the substantial increase of the Compound's Total Value Locked feature (or the number of assets being staked in the protocol) which is currently at $9.5 billion, there is a high expectation that its price would increase exponentially.

Forecasts

> ➢ Digital Coin Price predicts that by the end of 2021, the market price of COMP would reach $512 per token. By 2022, it would be $663 and in 2025, the price of COMP would be $982.

> ➢ CoinPedia has a fearless forecast of $1,800 to $2,200 by the end of 2022.

> ➢ Coin Price Forecast has a more conservative forecast of $412 (2022) and $814 (2025).

UNI

Date of Release: November 2018

Market Cap: $13 billion

Market Price: $21.30 *(COINBASE)*

subject to change

UNI is the native governance token of Uniswap. It was introduced to the market in September 2020 at $2.94 and has skyrocketed to $39.52 in April 2021 (a 703% surge within four months).

What are the functions of UNI?

- It gives holders the right to vote on major changes and new improvements in the platform like fee structure modification and distribution method of minted tokens.

- It is used to sustain the liquidity of the network.

- It is used as payment for fees in the platform.

Project: Uniswap

Uniswap is a prominent DeFi network that runs on the Ethereum blockchain. It is known for being AMM (automated market maker) which solves the usual liquidity issues that Decentralized exchanges (DEXs) typically experience. Uniswap can process more than $10 billion worth of transactions in a week, gaining 50% of the DeFi market as it functions as a market maker.

Its proprietary AMM system provides pooled liquidity through token swapping. It offers full control over private keys, low transaction fees, user-friendly operations, and integration of external wallets.

With unique and innovative features, Uniswap turned out to be one of the millionaire makers in the crypto industry.

Currently, UNI is the 12th most valuable cryptocurrency. Its DeFi ecosystem is growing steadily as well as the adoption of investors and traders.

In terms of past price performance, UNI has displayed an 8,200%+ROI which increased the investors' confidence and trust.

How to buy UNI?

Step 1: Sign up in your chosen Uniswap cryptocurrency exchange or broker. An exchange will enable you to swap UNI with Bitcoin, Ethereum, or any crypto of your choice.

Step 2: Deposit funds in your online account.

Step 3: Look for Uniswap from the available cryptocurrencies on the platform.

Step 4: Enter the amount of UNI you like to purchase and click Buy Order.

Step 5: Confirm your order and pay using the options in the exchange.

Is UNI ideal for long-term investment?

UNI is regarded as a future-focused altcoin. It has a clear roadmap and solid whitepaper that details where it hopes to be and achieve in the long run. The primary goals of this DeFi project are to empower the developers as well as the liquidity providers (or investors).

Proof that is a good long-term investment is the fact that the project is currently headed by an Ethereum developer and backed up by Vitalik Buterin.

The market price of UNI is driven not by celebrity endorsements or social media pronouncements, but by practical elements like its significance in the decentralized finance (DeFi) ecosystem, decentralized exchange, revolutionary upgrades, and increasing mass adoption for the governance token.

Forecasts

> ➤ According to Wallet Investor, UNI is a great choice for long-term investment and has predicted that its market price would hit $101.42 in the next 12 months and in 5 years, a piece of UNI would be worth $380.13.

> ➢ DigitalCoin's forecast for UNI would be $49.89 by the end of 2021 and up to $98.0 in 2025.

> ➢ Longforecast believes that UNI's price by the end of the year is $45.39 and $51.65 in 2023.

Maker (MKR)

Date of Release: December 2017

Market Cap: $3 billion

Market Price: $ 3,021.76 *(COINBASE)*

subject to change

Maker is the governance token of MakerDAO, the decentralized platform that is powered by the Ethereum blockchain. It has shown an impressive price jump from $597.37 in January 2021 to a high of $4,943.66 in April. One of the reasons that triggered the price increase was the news that MakerDAO has minted $38,000 DAI coins as funding for a mortgage loan. This means that it is bringing the real estate sector to the decentralized finance ecosystem.

What are the functions of Maker?

- It gives holders voting rights to the protocol's key reforms.

- It supports the creation of DAI stablecoin on the Ethereum blockchain.

- It is used by the Maker ecosystem to govern and manage the stablecoin DAI.

- It functions as support crypto to ensure that DAI is pegged to the price of the dollar.

- It unlocks the potential of DeFi for everyone in the global marketplace.

- It has a unique feature known as a deflationary protocol that helps in maintaining the value over time.

Project: MakerDAO

MakerDAO is governed by the autonomous organization or community, making it truly a decentralized network. This DeFi lending platform operates on "overcollaterization" to eliminate the concerns about the wild price fluctuations.

By locking in the collateral into smart contracts, users can get newly-minted DAI tokens or borrow cryptocurrencies. It uses advanced smart contracts called Collateralized Debt Position (CPD). This unique contract is initiated whenever the user sends tokens to the platform to get hold of DAI tokens.

Another proof that MakerDAO is secure and stable is the presence of Ether as an additional backup to withstand the crazy fluctuations. At present, about 2.52% of Ether is locked into the network.

MakerDAO also holds the record of being the first DeFI protocol that was able to achieve a TVL (total value locked) of $1 billion in 2020.

How to buy MKR?

Step 1: Open an online account in the exchange or broker with available MKRs.

Step 2: Purchase a crypto wallet. You can also store your MKR coins in a hardware wallet to protect them from possible hacking.

Step 3: Look for Uniswap from the available cryptocurrencies on the platform.

Step 4: Make your purchase order.

Step 5: Wait for your purchased MKR to appear in your account.

Is MKR a good long-term investment?

MKR is both good for short-term and long-term investments. If you decide to be an active trader, you need to capitalize on short-term movements of crypto prices throughout the day. For this, you need to convert them into stablecoin to start trading. Once you decide to stop day trading because the crypto prices are falling, sell your coins and keep your profit.

If you prefer long-term investing, make sure to store your MKRs in cold storage with a private set of keys.

Forecasts

The prospect that Maker token will explode in terms of market cap, mass adoption, and popularity is attributed to the platform's reinforcement of gaming networks and acting as a credit scoring and lending platform for merchants.

> ➢ Trading Beats forecast for Maker's price in 2022 is $3,459 and a maximum price of $3,635 by 2023.

> ➢ Waller Investor predicts that the long-term increase of MKR value in 2026 would be as high as $18,490.60. A 5-year investment would give back a return of approximately 473.89%.

Solana (SOL)

Date of Release: February 2018

Market Cap: $66 billion

SOL is the native coin of Solana, a DeFi network that operates as a cryptocurrency and a platform exchange. This token has its own growth pattern that is not associated with Bitcoin's price movements. It is listed as one of the 2021 top ten largest cryptocurrencies, surprising the crypto industry when its price went up 13,300% from January to November 2021

Uses of SOL

- It functions as a payment for transaction fees.

- It is used for staking.

- It serves as the protocol's governance token.

Project: Solana

Solana is primarily designed to rival and outpace Ethereum in speed and efficiency. With a growing network, thriving DeFi and NFT platforms, as well as teams of more than 400 developers, Solana is indeed a powerful Ethereum killer.

Its ability to process 50,000 transactions every second has defeated Ethereum's 15 transactions per second.

➢ Ethereum uses a Proof-of-Work mechanism to validate its transaction. POW operates by mining or staking.
➢ Solana combines Proof-of-Stake and the revolutionary Proof-of-History consensus mechanism to unlock the high transaction speed. POH time-stamped the transactions on the blockchain or decentralized network,

eliminating the need for all computers to relay messages or agree to complete the transaction.

How to buy SOL?

Step 1: Open an account in the crypto exchange that supports Solana.

Step 2: Deposit money or cryptocurrency in your account.

Step 3: Look for the "Buy Crypto" function to purchase the number of SOL tokens you want.

Step 4: Pay using your preferred payment method.

Step 5: Wait for your SOL to appear in your account.

Is SOL a good long-term investment?

Crypto analysts are very confident that SOL will continue performing well in the market because of the popularity of its blockchain technology. Currently, there are more than 500 dApps (decentralized applications) built into the system by independent developers. It includes NTF trade, dating services, DeFi services, lending and borrowing services, lotteries, Play-to-earn (P2E) games, and more.

All the applications require SOL to complete the transactions, which is the reason why its value soared incredibly. For investors who want to add an exciting and promising altcoin to their personal portfolio, the Solana token is a wise choice.

Despite the high volatility of SOL which can be attributed to being relatively new and is still a work in progress, crypto experts believe that it is worth holding in a long-term period. Based on the technical and fundamental analysis of its price in the next few years, SOL would continue enjoying its uptrends. By holding your altcoins in a 5-year timeframe, your investment would multiply many times when the projected price of over $1,000 per token happened.

Forecasts

> ➤ Coin Price Forecast predicts that before the end of 2021, SOL's price would reach $774, more than $3,412 in 2023, and by December 2025, it would hit above $12,000.
> ➤ Digital Coin Price believes that Solana would reach a high of $376.22 in 2022, above $450 in 2023, and up to $658 by 2025.
> ➤ Coinpedia forecasts that SOL would be above $300 by the end of 2021, over $500 by December 2022, and up to $1,000 in 2025.

LINK

Date of Release: November 2017

Market Cap: $12 billion

Market Price: $ 26.16 *(COINBASE)*

subject to change

LINK is the native token and backbone of Chainlink, a decentralized oracle network running in the Ethereum blockchain. It started trading in September 2020 and was originally created to help finance the project's growth.

Uses of LINK tokens:

- It is used by users to pay for the network's services.
- It resolves liquidity issues of the decentralized exchange (DEX).

- It enables the trading of DeFi tokens.
- It is given as an incentive to the nodes (global computer network) that are verifying transactions and working to deliver accurate data. Those who want to be a node and offer data to Chainlink must first stake LINK into asmart contract. This is to ensure that they will provide false data or misbehave.

Project: Chainlink

Chainlink's decentralized oracles connect different data sources and off-block feeds to the smart contracts. It has two components that interact with each other- blockchain and off-chain. The blockchain sets the oracle needed by the smart contracts based on the requested parameters while the off-chain is the oracle nodes in the Ethereum network that collect the information that users want. The pooled data is then processed by the Chainlink software.

Technically, Chainlink supplies value to other projects in the blockchain space by offering real-world data. It connects a smart contract to any of the following:

- Another smart contract
- Bank payment systems
- Various API's
- External sources

Oracle transmits and reviews real-time data to the network's ecosystem, verifying that the smart contracts' conditions are fulfilled correctly. It acts as the middleware between parties during the transfer of data and is particularly useful in DeFi because the network needs reliable and accurate data from several sources to eliminate errors.

How to buy LINK?

Step 1: Create an account on a cryptocurrency exchange that allows LINK trading with other virtual currencies like Bitcoin or fiat currencies like US dollars.

Step 2: Deposit funds in the account via bank transfer, cryptocurrency from a crypto wallet, or pay using a debit/credit card.

Step 3: Look for the "Buy Crypto" function to buy LINK tokens.

Step4: Complete your LINK purchase and connect your crypto wallet where you can transfer your tokens.

Is LINK a good long-term investment?

LINK ranked 16th by market capitalization in October 2021. When it was first traded, the price of LINK was $0.126297 and after a week became $0.50. It reached an all-time high of $52.20 in May and then fell down. Currently, its trading value is around$26.

Based on the popularity that this token and the success that Chainlink's team has gained, the prospects of exponential growth are tremendous.

> ➢ Linkchain's recent partnership with the biggest names in the decentralized finance sector and integration with IBM and Microsoft made LINK more valuable and attractive to investors.
> ➢ Linkchain has assisted Goggle, Binance, AAVE, Gartner, and other big names in the industry.

Forecasts

- Trading Beast predicts that the price of LINK will be stable until the end of the year and will trade between $21.52 and $29.35 in 2022.
- Wallet Investor believes that LINK is a great long-term investment and its price will reach $45 by 2022 and $100 by 2025.

- The fearless forecast comes for Coinlikers, saying that based on the continued growth of Chainlink, LINK's price will be at $210 in 5 years. This means a tenfold increase annually, making it one of the DeFi altcoins to invest in.

ATOM

Date of Release: March 2019

Market Cap: $6.2 billion

Market Price: $ 27.85 *(COINBASE)*

subject to change

ATOM is the native cryptocurrency of Cosmos.

Uses of ATOM:

- Users stake ATOM to earn rewards.
- It is used to make the "Global Hub" secure.

Project: Cosmos

Cosmos is designed to become the "internet of blockchains" or the "blockchain of all blockchains." It allows developers to create their dedicated blockchains (or zones) and provides them with prebuilt modules that are customizable to suit certain use cases.

Compared to other DeFi projects, it has wider use cases. It resolves three particular issues that typically limit the crypto institution.

- **Usability** – The easy modular framework of the Cosmos platform allows developers to implement the blockchain system on their specific projects.

- **Scalability** – Cosmos uses the native Tendermint BFT (byzantine fault-tolerant) consensus mechanism for this purpose.
- **Compatibility** – The Inter-Blockchain Communication (IBC) protocol allows all independent blockchains to connect.

How to buy ATOM?

Step 1: Open an account.

Step 2: Buy a hardware wallet to store your ATOM securely.

Step 3: Make your purchase through exchange platforms that support Cosmos ATOM.

Step 4: Transfer your Cosmos to your wallet.

Is ATOM a good long-term investment?

Investing in ATOM is a wise financial decision not only because of its relatively low market price but also the positive growth that it has shown. Experts in the industry are confident that it is the right asset for investors who are eyeing long-term gains. Also, right now is the perfect opportunity to invest in ATOM as it continues bringing high yields to the holders.

It has now over 256 services and applications existing on the platform which translates to about $131 billion in assets under management. This makes the Cosmos ecosystem healthy and more exciting.

Forecasts

- ➢ Coin Arbitrage Bot believes that Cosmos crypto would be trading at $25.70 by 2022, $41.58 by the end of 2023, and $67.28 by 2024.

- ➤ Wallet Investor fearlessly predicts that the ATOM's average trading price in 2026 would range between $111.86 and $172.17.
- ➤ Coin Price Forecast forecasts that ATOM's market price would soar to $1,387.19 by 2030.

DOT

Date of Release: May 2020

Market Cap: $35 billion

Market Price: $ 35.34 *(COINBASE)*

subject to change

DOT is the Polkadot network's native currency that was rolled during the phased process. About 58% of the original supply was given to the investors during the token sales, 30% was allocated for the Web 3 Foundation's development and development, and the remaining 12% are for the future fundraising activities of the network.

Uses of DOT:

- It allows holders to participate in the platform's governance by voting on key matters like network upgrades, network fees, and adding parachains or new chains.
- It is used for adding new chains (multiple, customized chains) to the network. The tokens are bonded or locked for a specified period.
- It is used by users for staking.

Project: Polkadot

Polkadot is the brainchild of Ethereum's co-founder Gavin Wood. This ambitious project aims to transform the structure of the blockchain network. It was launched in 2016 and developed by Web3 Foundation. Polkadot operates like Ethereum, with a blockchain platform that runs decentralized applications at very high speed. But rather than a single blockchain, its operating system accommodates a network of diverse blockchains to form a single ecosystem that interacts with each other. The more users who create parallel chains, the faster the Polkadot's network becomes. This DeFi project can process up to 1000 transactions per second and does not require forks to initiate updates and system improvement.

Its architecture has four elements:

1. **Relay chain or the main chain**- It is the heart of the system, providing interoperability and consensus to existing blockchains.
2. **Parachains or parallelizable chains** – These are blockchains that connect to the system and operate on their own. Each one has its own functionality and token.
3. **Parathreads** – They are blockchains that are like parachains but are more cost-efficient because of the pay-as-you-go payment scheme.
4. **Bridges** – They create connections, allowing the users to transfer data or tokens between blockchains.

How to buy DOT?

Step 1: Purchase a Polkadot-compatible wallet then locate your DOT address.

Step 2: Register to online crypto exchanges like Binance or CEX.io.

Step 3: Deposit funds in form of cryptocurrency, fiat, or bank card.

Step 4: Buy the amount of DOT you need.

Step 5: Wait for the tokens to reflect in your wallet.

Is DOT a good long-term investment?

Polkadot is one of the largest cryptocurrencies by market capitalization and has proven to be a worthy rival of the Ethereum network. The market cap influences the dominance and popularity of cryptocurrency. A high market cap (over $10 billion) is relative to "safe to invest in" and reduces its volatility.

In terms of returns on investment, this over a year-old token has given the early investors 1000% of their invested money. Crypto experts believe that DOT is a great option for long-term investment. It has already shown its ability to resolve the interoperability issue. It is also backed by the industry's most experienced people which include developers who come from Parity Technologies, researchers from ETH Zurich and Inria Paris, and capital partner Polychain Capital.

Price forecasts

> ➢ Wallet Investor forecasts that the price of DOT will increase to $74.0 by 2022 and $94.73 by the end of 2025.
> ➢ Long Forecast believes that this token will be $19.03 in 2022 and the longer-term forecast will be around $19.50.
> ➢ Digital Coin predicts that the average price of DOT in 2022 would be $93.93 and up to $159.59 in 2025.

YFI

Date of Release: July 2020

Market Cap: $ 1.1 billion

Market Price: $29,085.68

subject to change

YFI powers Yearn. finance. This governance, Ethereum-based token is distributed to the users of the network but can be sold or bought like other types of crypto. It is recognized as one of the precious crypto coins in the market that offer high annual percentage yield (APY) to users.

Uses of YFI:

- It gives holders the right to vote on the changes to the operational model or structure of the protocol.
- It is used by users as yDAI, yUSDT, and yUSDC to executive transactions.
- It also helps the users to earn trading fees and lending fees.

Project: Yearn

Yearn. finance or yEarn is a service aggregator that focuses on borrowing, lending, and yield farming. It simplifies the task of depositing funds to various decentralized finance (DeFi) projects by offering a streamlined portal. The interface uses an advanced "yield farming" tool that automatically moves liquidity to the DeFi projects through smart contracts. This process enables investors to achieve maximum returns. In addition, the unique automation toolset helps investors to make decisions about where to invest their money by using a streamlined DeFi approach.

How to buy YFI?

Step 1: Find an exchange that supports YFI.

Step 2: Once you decide which exchange you want, make an account and wait for its verification.

Step 3: Deposit funds that you will use to buy YFI.

Step 4: Make a purchase.

Is YFI a good long-term investment?

YFI is indeed a good investment asset considering that it operates on the Ethereum blockchain, allowing users to maximize passive income by holding crypto assets. Industry experts are calling it a DeFi giant because it has attracted developers and investors who want to take to leverage its usability and profitability.

Price forecasts

- ➢ Wallet Investor predicts a long-term increase of $225, 342 by the end of 2026. It means that a 5-year investment would bring a return of about +621.18%.
- ➢ Long Forecast believes that there will be a bull ride in 2024 and YFI may be trading between $47,959 and $55,179. It may climb as high as $315,257 in 2025 if the uptrends will continue.
- ➢ GOV Capital believes that the future price of YFI would climb to $90,379 by the end of 2022.

Key takeaways

- Ideally, a good crypto portfolio has Bitcoin and Ethereum on it.

- A diversified crypto portfolio with Bitcoin, altcoin (top crypto other than bitcoin), and DeFi tokens optimize your profits.

- Decentralized finance (DeFi) is revolutionizing the world with its infrastructure that can host individual investors and provide quick, automated services via smart contracts.

- DeFi altcoins are backed up with revolutionary projects that are pushing initiatives and advancing the way to deliver financial equality.

Point to Ponder

Successful investors do not rely on luck.
They observe, speculate, and leverage
the tipping point of market trends.

Chapter 8

Everything You Need to Ask About Bitcoin & Resources for Bitcoin Investors

"Bitcoin is absolutely the Wild West of finance...It is the frontier. Huge amounts of wealth will be created and destroyed as this new landscape is mapped out."– *Erik Voorhees*-

Frequently Asked Questions

Why so Bitcoin possess value?

Bitcoin's value comes from being a form of money that people trust and accept as payment, an investment asset, or trading vehicle. It possesses the characteristics of money like portability, durability, scarcity, fungibility, recognizability, and divisibility.

What can Bitcoin do?

Bitcoin has successfully altered the financial landscape.

- It is a digital currency.
- It is known as a global reputation and identification application.
- It initiates contracts, trusts, and wills.
- It offers decentralized domain names.
- It has a voting mechanism.
- It is used for crowdfunding.
- It attracts future markets.
- It is a micro-tipper.
- It has the ability to do what the basic financial system can do.

Why should you trust Bitcoin?

While trust in Bitcoin is subjective based on the human faith in numbers, algorithms, and encryption, this crypto offers 3 technological freedom principles that speak of integrity:

- Open source code
- Decentralization
- Peer-to-peer technology

Is it easy to buy Bitcoin?

Bitcoin is everywhere, meaning it can be purchased from various sources like exchanges or brokerage services. Check out the list of Bitcoin sellers and pay for it using fiat currency, PayPal, debit or credit card, or bank transfer.

How to sell Bitcoin?

Bitcoin can be sold using different methods- online, on exchange platforms, or through peer-to-peer transactions. The process is similar to the buying process, but this time you are setting the price for your bitcoins.

Is Bitcoin truly anonymous?

Transactions in Bitcoin use public addresses, a long string of about 30 characters that are usually difficult to remember. While this address is publicly-viewable, it does not have any identifying information or name of the user. This is why Bitcoin is called an "anonymous currency," but publishing this address and re-using it many times anywhere can be associated with your real identity because of the pattern. Hence, it is recommended to use a new address for every transaction you make. For this purpose, use a modern software wallet that is designed to let you generate a new address for every transaction you make.

For this reason, industry experts said that calling Bitcoin "pseudonymous" is more accurate rather than anonymous. This means that someone who is adept at uncovering real identities can potentially uncover the person behind the public address.

Who is in charge of Bitcoin?

None. Bitcoin is a software protocol just like the email's SMTP and the internet's HTTP. No person, group of people, or authorities can exert influence on how Bitcoin functions. In essence, the users are the ones in charge of their bitcoins.

Do I need to buy a Bitcoin wallet?

Think of your Bitcoin wallet as a physical wallet to keep your cash. It secures your money, giving you peace of mind because you have it in your possession. There are many choices in the market now, but the best option, if you want to prevent online hacking or theft, is to hold your coins in a specialized hardware wallet that lets you keep the keys offline.

What Bitcoin is good for?

As *payment or medium of excha*nge, Bitcoin is better than gold. This is because bitcoin is transportable, divisible, and a fixed unit of account. Its massive potential as a *store of value* makes institutional and individual investors convert portions of their portfolios to Bitcoins for diversification and hedge purposes. Bitcoin has already unlocked the *financial sovereignty* of investors by giving them the ability to make transactions without the need for permission from outside authorities.

What can you buy with Bitcoin?

Bitcoin can be used to buy about anything now from goods like foods, electronics, clothing to real estate, cars, and investment assets.

Why does Bitcoin price move a lot?

The price of Bitcoin is subject to the supply and demand of the market forces, which are in turn influenced by the trends/news in the financial world and whims of speculators. This is the rationale behind the sudden movements of its price, causing sharp upward or downward motion.

How to track the price of Bitcoin?

If you want real-time price movements of Bitcoin, track them in the data charts of Bitcoin.com. Use the Instant Price Converter to convert the price of Bitcoin to your local currency.

Is it profitable to mine Bitcoin?

The answer can be yes or no. Gone are those days that mining Bitcoin is possible using GPU cards or desktop computers. It now takes specially-designed computers or ASICs (application-specific integrated circuits) to unlock proof-of-work algorithm. Take note that this kind of equipment consumes a large amount of energy that can diminish your profits.

How do Bitcoin transactions work?

Bitcoin transactions involve an input (sending address), the amount, and the output (receiving address). Using the corresponding private keys, the transactions will be sent and verified by the miners within the blockchain.

How long does it take for Bitcoin transactions to be confirmed?

The typical time is roughly 10 minutes but because of popularity growth, the confirmation time can be one hour or more. When after 72 hours, the transaction fails to get confirmation, the fund is returned to the sender's wallet.

Is Bitcoin legal?

Regulations vary in different nations and some even banned its use. While it is not regulated, the use of Bitcoin is not illegal in some jurisdictions but users need to comply with certain conditions.

Is Bitcoin for criminals?

Bitcoin is money and like any representation of money (cash, checks, credit cards) can be used for legal or illegal purposes. The anonymity and decentralization features of Bitcoin (also of other cryptos) make it an attractive tool for criminal syndicates who are into peddling drugs and illegal goods, cyber theft, and kidnapping for ransom.

It is speculated that about 1% to 3% of transactions in the blockchain are used for illicit transactions. There are also reports that it is used for money laundering. But this narrative does not mean that it is for criminal activities. The majority of crypto-related crimes are scams. This means that crypto like Bitcoin is not a haven of illegal financial dealings of criminals, but a medium to enable trackable, secure transactions.

Will Bitcoin crash?

Bitcoin is notoriously volatile, which means its price collapse is always a possible scenario. Its history has large highs and falls, so prepared for the loss and enjoy the profits during a bull period. What's great about Bitcoin, it rises phenomenally and crashes down badly then recovers strong.

Is Bitcoin mining a waste of materials?

Bitcoin mining is essential to sustain the transaction ledger or blockchain. It requires a large amount of electricity and leaves e-waste. According to reports, the yearly carbon footprint of bitcoin mining is as big as the metro area of London or Romania. Its e-waste production accounts for more than 24 kilotons, the same amount of electronic waste in the Netherlands. Miners are using specific hardware that usually becomes unusable after 18 months are thrown away. If not properly disposed of, the heavy metals and toxic chemicals can leak into the water supply and soil.

Is Bitcoin taxable?

Since Bitcoin does not possess a legal tender status, its tax liability will depend on the jurisdiction. It can be in the form of sales tax, capital gain tax, income tax, and other tax liability.

Can Bitcoin become worthless?

It is possible that Bitcoin will lose its worth due to competing currencies, technical failures, political issues, and so on. All forms of currency are not immune to hard times that can make them worthless. But as of now, there is enough room for Bitcoin to grow and no one can predict its future.

Is Bitcoin a bubble?

A bubble is the artificial over-valuation leading to sudden downward correction. Bitcoin's quick rise is not considered a bubble. The reasons for Bitcoin price changes are mostly due to the users' sentiments that are influenced by the following:

- Loss of confidence in Bitcoin
- Increased press releases that stimulate speculative notions about the crypto coin
- Fear of uncertainty
- Irrational greed and exuberance
- Huge difference between price and value of the coin that is determined by Bitcoin's fundamentals

Is Bitcoin a Ponzi scheme?

No. A Ponzi scheme is an intentional fraudulent investment that is designed to get the invested fund of participants, affecting the last line of investors. Bitcoin is a software project where nobody can make fraudulent representations about its transactions and investment returns.

Will the finite amount of Bitcoin become a limitation?

While Bitcoin has a cap of 21 million only, there will be no limitations in the transactions because bitcoins can be denominated into sub-units. One bitcoin equates to 1,000,000 bits.

What will happen to Bitcoin if there is a better cryptocurrency?

To date, Bitcoin remains the leading cryptocurrency in the market. It continues to dominate the scene. When its price moves, the other cryptocurrencies usually follow. Also, it has inspired the creation of alternative crypto or altcoins.

Is Bitcoin secure?

The protocol and cryptography of Bitcoin have a solid record of security. The rules of its technology are still the same after more than a decade of operations. This is a clear indication that it is well-designed with strong security measures in the structure. The security issues in the software are promptly fixed and give Bitcoin more maturity. In addition, the common vulnerability and security problems lie in the errors of users like losing their wallet's private keys.

Resources for a smart Bitcoin investing

1. Bitcoin.com

https://www.bitcoin.com/get-started/

2. Investopedia.com

https://www.investopedia.com/bitcoin-4689766

https://www.investopedia.com/articles/forex/081815/benefits-risks-trading-forex-bitcoin.asp

https://www.investopedia.com/articles/investing/082914/basics-buying-and-investing-bitcoin.asp

https://www.investopedia.com/articles/investing/012215/how-invest-bitcoin-exchange-futures.asp

3. Robo-Advisor Pros

https://www.roboadvisorpros.com/best-portfolio-management-software-for-investors/

4. Bitcoin.org

https://bitcoin.org/en/

5. Trading Education.com

https://trading-education.com/

6. Management Study Guide.com

https://www.managementstudyguide.com/security-analysis-and-portfolio-management.htm

7. The Motley Fool

https://www.fool.com/quote/crypto/btc/

https://www.fool.com/investing/stock-market/market-sectors/financials/cryptocurrency-stocks/

https://www.fool.com/investing/how-to-invest/etfs/

Conclusion

"You can't stop things like Bitcoin. It will be everywhere and the world will have to readjust." – *John MCaffe*

Thank you for reading my book **Bitcoin & Cryptocurrency Investing: Top 10 DeFi Altcoins to Change the World and Your Finances, Blockchain, Cold Storage, NFT & Mining Explained, Smart Contracts & Decentralized Finance for Swing Trading.**

If you are here, then you have digested every single piece of information from the 8 chapters. If you find them useful, let them be your guiding wisdom in your exciting, exhilarating, and challenging journey in crypto investing.

Today, Bitcoin is the most powerful digital asset in terms of market capitalization, value, popularity, unit of account, and store of value. Perhaps, even its creator Satoshi Nakamoto is surprised by what Bitcoin has achieved so far. Or maybe, he knew this all along because just like his mysterious persona that many wants to uncover, unlocking Bitcoin's capabilities is like opening a Pandora box.

The technology behind Bitcoin has also opened a plethora of opportunities for the Fintech industry, sparking a revolution of digital projects that unite virtual technology with the traditional forms of investing. Major financial institutions including banks are considering Bitcoin, blockchain, and other forms of crypto to scale up their services as well as safeguard their hedge funds.

You and I have a lot to gain from what is happening in the cryptocurrency world. Bitcoin is truly an incredible trailblazer asset. It has made its mark in the economy and becomes an instrument to certain global issues. Bitcoin is an enabler of functions, an instrument for monetary transfer, and a powerful asset of investment.

Chapter 1 Hail to the King of Crypto: Bitcoin provided a lot of information and insights about this cryptocurrency. You've learned how blockchain works to empower Bitcoin and how it inspired other developers to create their own virtual currency. The world of crypto has become an exciting battle of crypto coins and tokens that now account for hundreds of varieties, all aiming to become the next Bitcoin.

You've met the world's Bitcoin millionaires and billionaires in *Chapter 2 The Digital Gold Rush.* These people believed and trusted the potentials of Bitcoin. They leveraged its volatility, braving the risks, and are now enjoying the fruits of their investment.

Bitcoin has transformed the investment sector's landscape as institutional investors joined the retail investors on the bandwagon of the virtual currency world. This solidified the position of Bitcoin in the financial realm, increasing its speculative value.

Your answer to my question in *Chapter 3 Is Crypto Investing for You?* is obvious now that you are here on the final pages. You are becoming more curious about what more I can share. And I say that you are ready for Bitcoin investing. However, it is important to learn more, read more, delve more to become a credible and successful player in crypto investment. The more informed and skilled you become, the higher your chances of enjoying the rewards and eliminating the risks.

In *Chapter 4 Bitcoin and Stock Market*, you've learned that Bitcoin-linked futures have succeeded to join the stock markets. Moreover, the growing list of payment services and technology companies that are using blockchain and cryptocurrencies to maximize their profits is providing more opportunities for retail and traditionalist investors to invest in Bitcoin, albeit indirectly.

Use the information you gained from *Chapter 5 Guide to Bitcoin Investing: Let's Gear You Up* to help you avoid the traps and pitfalls in crypto investing. Like any kind of investing, there are risks and rewards to consider. By knowing how to reduce the risks like portfolio diversification, starting small at the beginning of your journey to the investment world, and matching your risk tolerance with the investment option, you are good to go.

A good personal portfolio is always a diversified one. It is unwise to put all your money in a single investment asset. In *Chapter 6 Personal Portfolio Management*, you've learned how to manage your own portfolio or hire a competent portfolio manager to do it for you.

In *Chapter 7 What Should Comprise Your Crypto Portfolio?* you've identified the best cryptocurrencies to include in your investment coffer. Now that DeFi is revolutionizing the financial world, picking up any of the popular DeFi cryptos in the list I've suggested is the key to optimizing its benefits.

Are there lots of questions in your mind? It's fine because *Chapter 8 Everything You Need to Ask About Bitcoin & Resources for Bitcoin Investors* answers your questions about Bitcoin. The list of resources would also lead you to more answers and strategies in investing.

At this point, you are equipped with the knowledge about investing in Bitcoin. This is the initial step that every investor should take and master. Preparation is the key to winning and eliminating the traps. When you are mentally prepared, you are more observant and vigilant. You know how to avoid or reduce the risks that can eat up your investments. You know what and when to buy or sell your holdings and anticipate the best returns.

Balancing your portfolio is a good way to start. Bitcoin is always the winning asset, so it should be your primary asset plus Ethereum, and the DeFi altcoins that are now showing growth potentials. They are the safest in terms of survival and liquidity.

A lot of altcoins didn't survive the Bitcoin halvings, so you have to be smart and trust only the cryptocurrencies that can hold their ground through these cycles. Never invest in random cryptocurrencies or participate in ICOs no matter how tempting the returns they offer without studying the risks and rewards, the people behind the projects, and other important factors. Remember that when your money is involved, you want returns of investment not saying goodbye to it. Choose your assets wisely and apply the learnings you get from this book.

The past and present performance of Bitcoin has shown us that it is a powerful force in the digital world, so everyone is expecting how it will transform the landscape of the economy in the future. Will it remain the best and major crypto player in the next decade or will be it ousted by Ethereum or other altcoins? That's for us to find out.

Finally, I wish you success in your journey to Bitcoin and crypto investing. Analysts and experts in the industry are predicting that in the next 5 years, the overall market of long-term investors would grow 10x, hence the best time to position yourself and begin investing is right NOW.

Thank You

You could have picked from dozens of other books in crypto space, but you took a chance and chose this one.

So, THANK YOU for getting my book and for making it all the way to the end.

Before you go, I wanted to ask you for one small favour.

Could you please consider posting a review on Amazon or Audible?

Posting a review is the best and easiest way to support the work I do.

If you signed up for my email list, expect soon a some really good golden nuggets for crypto space...

Such as:

New hot coins launched or about to be launched so you can be there first one to get it

Where to find the best TINY market caps coins and make 100x returns and so much more!!

If you haven't sign up yet, simply click the link in attached PDF and also get my gift to you.

Your feedback will help me to keep writing the kind of books that will help you get the results you want!